The First Line
A Manager's Handbook

(2nd Edition)

Rob Burlace

The Book Guild Ltd

First published in Great Britain in 2017 by
The Book Guild Ltd
9 Priory Business Park
Wistow Road, Kibworth
Leicestershire, LE8 0RX
Freephone: 0800 999 2982
www.bookguild.co.uk
Email: info@bookguild.co.uk
Twitter: @bookguild

Typeset in Minion Pro

Printed and bound in the UK by TJ International, Padstow, Cornwall

ISBN 978 1911320 623

British Library Cataloguing in Publication Data.
A catalogue record for this book is available from the British Library.

Without the financial help of the following contributors, my book would not have become a reality. I will be forever grateful to:

John Beukes
Chris Billington
Mary Burlace
Phillip Burlace
David Harvey
Clive Owen

Thank you!

Contents

Foreword   ix

1. Introduction   xiii

Section 1   1

2. Background   3
3. Why be a 'First-Line' Manager – the desire for power   10
4. Why be a 'First-Line' Manager – power into practice   16
5. Why be a 'First-Line' Manager – expectations   25
6. What being a First-Line Manager involves   29
7. Meeting the challenge   47
8. What kind of manager do you want to be?   55
9. What are you good at?   65
10. Becoming a manager   71
Intermission   79

Section 2   85

11. Introduction   87
12. The ADDRESS model   88
13. Know your STUFF!   107
14. TOP-DRAWER solutions   125
15. CRAFT-T planning   137
16. Exercising CONTROL   153
17. Have a REASON for every encounter   156
18. A CHEAT'S Guide to feedback   175

Section 3   185

19. Introduction   187
20. Establish yourself in the role   188
21. Working with your team   199
22. Communicate, communicate, and communicate!   211
23. Watch, listen, feel   240
24. Manage every encounter – let's be grown-ups   249
25. Manage your team's performance   283
26. Friend or friendly   294
27. How's your trust meter?   303
28. It's OK to be selfish   309
29. Persevere   320
30. Get a punch bag!   327

Conclusion   340
Bibliography   343
Index   345

Figures:

Figure 1: The Development Planning Cycle   72
Figure 2: The ADDRESS Model   89
Figure 3: A Debriefing Cycle   99
Figure 4: Source of Situations   105
Figure 5: Solution Scoring Format   134
Figure 6: Sample Gantt chart   144
Figure 7: A Feedback Cycle   183
Figure 8: Chinese Symbol for 'Listen(ing)'   243
Figure 9: The Trust Meter   306
Figure 10: An Experiential Learning Cycle   323

Tables:

Table 1: Reasons for Bad Time Management   39-40
Table 2: Promotion Circumstances & Required Tasks   193
Table 3: Team Roles   201

Case Studies:

Case Study 1: The Boss has noticed!   32

Case Study 2: Available for comment   100

Case Study 3: Party Boy   109

Case Study 4: Who to choose   143

Case Study 5: Early Drift   194

Case Study 6: Time for a Change   233

Case Study 7: Out of Stock   242

Case Study 8: The Job's not over 'til the paperwork's done!   271

Case Study 9: Dealing with Discipline   298

Case Study 10: I Need a Break   314

Foreword

Have you ever noticed people always seem to be chasing what's next, whether it's the smartphone upgrade, the bigger house, or the next promotion! They do so without actually savouring where they are in the present, celebrating the achievement and taking time to perfect what they do now.

As a result they are never satisfied and are rarely happy, unless of course they're the type that revels in 'the chase'. Many do this because they're told they have to, as that's the only measure of success. They embark on the chase irrespective of the fact they currently lack the knowledge, understanding, skills and abilities, or behaviours (KUSAB) necessary, or are unlikely ever to do so.

Maybe they're chasing a dream. Nothing wrong with that! So long as they remember dreams, aspirations, hopes, whatever you want to call them – are not real. They are born out of desire, which can often be so strong it suppresses reality.

To fulfil one's potential; one must convert dreams into a realistic, achievable plan and work at it.

How many of today's 'celebrities' enjoy more than a relatively fleeting spell in the spotlight? Why do they fall from fashion as quickly as they broke into it? Why is it that so many who might now be called 'old timers' have endured and held their place in the spotlight for decades? Why is music created centuries ago – and its composers – still celebrated today?

I believe it's because they have substance; because very often they have had to work exceedingly hard to get what they have; and because they took time to perfect their art at every level before trying to hit the next one.

Have you taken time to completely examine why you want to take the step into a management role? Have you fully considered what the role will give you and what you can give to it? For many the role is fulfilling, rewarding and esteem-building. For others it can be quite the opposite. In many workplaces today, and in society generally, the measure of success is the degree to which you are able to climb the management ladder. Pressure is put on those who otherwise really enjoy what they do – and are good at it – to leave that all behind. If the role is not right for you, there can follow years of regret and mental hardship. You will underperform and neither you, nor your organisation, nor those working for you will benefit. If management is not for you, there are other ways in which you can have a rewarding and fulfilling life.

If you are contemplating the move, or even if you have been in a management role for a while, time spent now in honestly and accurately assessing your potential will enable you to decide whether to make the move, or reverse it. There is no shame in the latter and in the long run everyone involved will be better for your honesty and bravery.

If your assessment concludes that it is a good thing to be doing, others will benefit from you setting off with and maintaining a set of effective and consistently applied techniques and practices. Doing so also increases the likelihood of it being a personally rewarding role.

Don't embark on the chase, embark on a journey and savour it. Enjoy the scenery and the people you meet on the way. Stop off in a few places to charge the batteries and prepare yourself for the next stage. Can everyone climb Everest? Potentially yes! But even the most proficient and experienced of climbers need help to do so; but you can't stay on the summit forever; and as the way down is often more tricky to negotiate than the ascent, care is needed that the right degree of safety is in place.

This book encourages you to examine your potential, to make the best decision and to move forward. For the latter, it illustrates and promotes models to support you in applying good-practice to the role and some guiding principles.

It is not a Gospel, nor a 'Do this and you'll be perfect' book. No book will make you perfect; will get you rich quick; or (unfortunately) teach you anything; especially if you are using it in the hope it will save you time and effort in the process of betterment. How many people you know got rich quick after reading a 'get rich quick' book? How many have religiously followed the way of the 'ten steps to success' or the '100 rules' only to feel the disappointment of not achieving all that was promised and inferred?

You must have a keenness and yearning to develop. If you really do want to learn, if you really are ready and willing to apply yourself to the tasks and work that's necessary, there is a good chance that you can use the contents that follow to help achieve your goals. It will only ever be a 'teaching' book if *you* choose to learn. It will only have succeeded if it moves you, through the choices *you* make, to develop to the extent *you* wish.

Set your own goals. Don't let this, or any other book set them for you. Use the book as a tool and in the same way that you might use a map and choose the right transport for any journey from 'A' to 'B'.

1. Introduction

My definition of the First-Line manager is:

"An individual, responsible to their employing organisation and its more senior managers, for: the control, direction, discipline, monitoring, performance and welfare of subordinate operational employees. They are there to ensure – through operational goal setting and control – achievement of the organisation's aims and objectives. Often requiring knowledge and understanding of their subordinates' roles and functions and the ability to fulfil them, they are invariably required to gather, record, and report upon performance data. They are expected to deal effectively with variations, thereby ensuring organisational viability through the maintenance of productivity and standards."

Understand this and you will understand the basis and reason for all that follows.

For me, this level of management is the most crucial in any organisation. Getting it right brings potentially enormous personal benefits, both financially and psychologically. It makes you a better 'prospect', opening up opportunities of greater earnings and further advancement. Money aside, the feeling of leaving a task finished and knowing that you got the best result possible is hard to match. You enjoy the challenge.

For organisations the benefits to their 'bottom line' are not just financial. In difficult times if they can recruit, develop and retain good managers at this level, the potential operational cost savings are enormous. To fulfil expectations, the First-Line manager requires sound levels of knowledge, understanding, skills, abilities and behaviours (KUSAB)[1].

1   You will be seeing a lot of this acronym as you progress through the book

Most people grow professionally by learning from experiences and challenges. Many of those challenges can be perceived as 'negative'. Alternatively, there might be too many challenges to be faced all at once. Recognising these seemingly simple concepts prompted me to offer those facing these challenges some more support, more guidance and more resources.

If you operate at higher levels of management, you can still apply the ideas in Sections 2 and 3, or use them to coach and support those junior managers you are responsible for. They can provide a basis against which you could assess the performance of those managers.

When I took my first steps into the role of a manager, there was very little help around; I was ignorant as to how any help could be accessed. It was very much 'learn-by-experience'. One just had to trust to luck that a few of the experiences would be good ones. Invariably it was the 'foul-ups' that taught me the most. How often with hindsight, I wished there'd been something – or someone – around who could give me a better steer.

There are several drivers for this book:

1. I have yet to find a study that (a) strips back to the basics and gets anyone to question why they should ever want to be a manager in the first place; and thereafter (b) gets you to test yourself as to whether the role is indeed right for you.
2. Theory-heavy academic works appeal to a limited number of learners and often require lab conditions for them to be applied or function properly.
3. I think the role should be fun and rewarding – otherwise why do it?
4. Existing and prospective managers need as wide a range of options as possible that can readily be applied to their personal environment, regardless of what that might be. There are others out there; the ones I offer simply add to the choice.
5. 'Self-help' books make one feel compelled to take on the 'challenge' of 'managership'. There's inference that if you do not, you have failed in some way. I do not believe this to be the case – reward can be found in other places too. You can be made to feel somehow inferior if you do not make the best of it, or move on still further, rather than accept it's not right for you and help you to develop an exit strategy.

6. As a trainer I'd like to use my experiences positively and provide a resource for others involved in training delivery to develop others.

My aims are to help you avoid the difficulties, worries and costs associated with not getting it right; to encourage enjoyment of the role; to help you with process; and to foster a sense of realism and relevance.

I have included case study scenarios based on incidents that I encountered whilst I was a First-Line manager. I came through most of them relatively unscathed, though they have had considerable influence on my subsequent attitude, behaviours and direction.

You will be encouraged to focus on *you* and the pressures and potential consequences of *your* role (current or intended). It's often easy to make excuses for walking away from the challenge and not doing something. However, you should finish the book more knowledgeable, with more options; more secure in your capability; and more confident to take on the challenges. It's up to *you* to learn!

There's a good quote from American MC Talib Kweli Greene[2], "I'm not looking to set a standard… but, I believe I have offered a challenge to others with my work."

There are not just 'ten steps' – or ten minutes – between you and success. It's like saying you can get 'washboard abs' in four weeks! I remain to be convinced that the number of steps, or attributes required of any manager can be accurately or conveniently quantified.

That is not to belittle others' contributions. Indeed I will be referencing a few that I have found to actually be of some help. The point is, that with the right will, skills and behaviours can be developed, and knowledge and understanding can be acquired. However, without the appropriate attitude and grounding, all of the work involved in achieving KUSAB can prove to be a waste of time and effort and be seriously de-motivating.

You are either contemplating becoming, or have recently become a First-Line manager. Maybe you have been in the role for some time so are reappraising. You might be considering the future and further promotion. Consider this:

"Most people can look back over the years and identify a time and place at which their lives changed significantly. Whether by accident

2   Talib Kweli Greene – American Hip-Hop artist & social activist

xv

or design, these are the moments when, because of a readiness within us and a collaboration with events occurring around us, we are forced to seriously reappraise ourselves and the conditions under which we live and to make certain choices that will affect the rest of our lives."[3]

3   (Flack 1979)

SECTION 1
To be, or not to be

Without the genuine, well-founded desire to be a manager, and the capacity to accomplish all that is required, no amount of training, nor reading of books will make one.

2. Background

'To be or not to be', that is indeed the question! The aims of this section are threefold: first, to prompt you to consider why you want the role. Second, whether the role is right for you – and you for it! Third, I want you to understand the benefits of setting realistic goals – aiming to be the best you can be in the role – nothing more, nothing less. You should understand the implications of weak or inappropriate activity at this level and the benefits to you of honing your KUSAB – regardless of your motivation now, or your future aspirations.

There are some undoubted benefits or 'pros' to acquiring a First-Line manager role. These are frequently cited as the motivators for pursuing it. More often than not, the role brings greater remuneration and benefits; it makes your CV more attractive for the future; gives greater authority, the power to influence and – maybe – change; and (not least) a sense of achievement.

On the 'down (or cons) side': you become a focal point in bad times as well as good; the number of people to whom you can pass responsibility diminishes; you may (some would say should) lose friendships and relationships based on the workplace; and you become responsible for others' failings and dealing with them. I challenge you to find an advertisement for any manager position that mentions any of these cons.

Most organisations say they have a well-structured, effective system for identifying, placing and supporting First-Line managers. Still more would assert that they *do* have some form of process through which prospective post-holders must pass. If that is the case, why do we witness so many management failings? I refer to failings that fester and grow to Employment Tribunal or lawsuit status. As effective as such programmes may be, they work on the assumption it has some inherent infallibility that guarantees the right people, with the right motivation have been selected for the manager role.

If you can develop appropriate skills and techniques and (most importantly) the right attitude, you should be able to demonstrate that you are indeed the best candidate to take or keep the role. OK, the organisation may have initiated the process and have chosen you. However, it is *you* who most often puts yourself forward and *you* who always has the choice whether to participate in the process. So you share responsibility.

You cannot change your organisation's culture or practises overnight. It's unlikely you'll be able to change the personalities in your 'team', or (in the short term) their regular behaviours. If you want to give being a good manager a fair run the responsibility lies with you to try and do the best you can with what you've got.

If your mind were to need focussing on why it's important to have the best First-Line managers in place, let's briefly examine an area over which they have serious influence and impact. Think about 'industrial relations' specifically the issue of workplace grievances.

In England and Wales in 2011/12 over 321,000 jurisdictional complaints were received by the Employment Tribunals system (actually reflecting a downward trend). These include claims for unfair dismissal, discriminatory practice, etc. They disposed of 230,000. The remainder were outstanding. Whilst 33% were resolved via an arbitration service and 40% were withdrawn or struck out, just 12% were successful.[1]

Only '12% of cases being successful' does not sound a lot, does it? Some use the low incidence as evidence that businesses are largely 'getting it right'. However, the average payout for successful claims for unfair dismissal was £9,100. The maximum awarded was over £173,400 (approx. €12.5k or $13.6K, to €240K or $260k). Discrimination cases were much more costly. Maximum payout for race discrimination was nearly 4.5 million pounds (€6.2 million or $6.3 million).

Statistics never provide a complete picture. They do not tell us the number of grievances handled by businesses as part of their internal grievance procedures. We don't know about issues that never get reported, but which impact on individuals' productivity, or remaining with the organisation.

Even where managers resolve issues relatively quickly and effectively,

---

1   Employment Tribunals and EAT Statistics, 2011-12, 1 April 2011 to 31 March 2012 (Ministry of Justice, 2012, London) © Crown copyright

you must consider the time cost and the loss of ordinary 'production'. There's investigation time, possible disciplinary hearings, possibly appeals. If that doesn't work it can lead to an Employment Tribunal. It might involve: witnesses, more managers, HR professionals, your organisation's legal services department (if those exist), and lawyers and so it goes on. Your business would have to make sales of £62,000 to fund the average payout for a sex discrimination case (if you operate at 30% net profit). The 'hidden' costs would drive that much higher.

How many businesses can afford to lose these sorts of sums? How many organisations would look favourably upon a manager who caused or could have prevented it?

Some argue these costs to businesses are actually preventing them from employing more staff. In my view, they perversely go on to say this is good reason to limit access to the tribunal system and thereby to any redress in genuine cases. I think this is lazy and misses the point. Consider too the impact of such cases on participants' mental and physical wellbeing; their loyalty and commitment to the organisation; and the organisation's long-term reputation and viability.

How about trying to remove the causes and symptoms of the need for tribunals in the first place by having professional, effective managers?

I have witnessed managers at all levels that avoid confronting and challenging inappropriate or incorrect performance by their subordinates for a host of different reasons. Often the reasons (or excuses) are spurious and based on the manager's desire for a quiet life. Maybe the manager is still 'finding their feet'; maybe they don't know their options; or maybe they don't know enough. Whatever the reasoning, the failure by a manager to acknowledge the existence of a situation that requires their attention, very often causes it to fester and grow into a far greater challenge for them, their own manager and their organisation.

Managers simply cannot ignore what's going on around them. They always have the choice as to whether to do something and as to what that something might be.

I'm not so naive as to suggest that there will never be issues or situations for managers to address. We should be preparing for and equipping ourselves to deal with the bad. However, the intention is that the more we do that, the less of the bad develops. This frees us to enjoy what's good about the role. Making the bad easy to deal with brings about its own satisfactions, benefits and rewards and often affords us the time to concentrate on the good.

There's an old adage that some are born great, and some have greatness thrust upon them. Some seem to have an inbred capacity to flourish; others need it to be nurtured, even teased out; still more find themselves in a position that wasn't quite what they thought it would be, struggle to cope and will probably never progress beyond the First-Line.

It is a role in which you should not be able to hide. You must be conscious of and face up to, the fact that the decisions you make and activities you engage in *will* have long-term implications and repercussions for individuals, relationships and organisations. The hope is that these will be positive, but hopes can be dashed. All too often situations can have a negative impact on everyone involved.

First-Line management is a role that puts you squarely between operational colleagues and 'the bosses'. Paradoxically, the First-Line manager is very often not seen by the workforce as one of the 'bosses'. But they are often seen as the bosses' (sometimes reluctant) 'mouthpiece and/ or the workers friend'. The First-Line manager can be the sponge for others' issues and problems; the filling in a communications sandwich of operators and middle/senior managers; or a key component in making organisations work. In my experience you must be the ears and sometimes, the mouthpiece of your subordinates and concurrently, the eyes and mouthpiece of the organisation – a difficult 'ask'. Those of you already in the role may have experienced this already. I would be surprised if either you, those of you considering the role, or who are new to it, will never do so.

A few individuals become managers and then realise that it may not be right for them. Some organisations have helped them to that conclusion. Even fewer have returned to the position below and remained within the same organisation. Organisations like to think their selection processes eliminate that possibility. Whether or not they do, few organisations or hiring managers like to think they got it wrong and go on to correct the error.

Taking the step into management should never be taken lightly, or for the wrong reasons. Yet, it is not for me to say a particular reason or motivation is better than any of the others. For example, for some it is the only step upwards you want/wanted to take – it suits you. For others it's a stepping-stone. Don't get me wrong. We would be at a standstill if no one had drive or ambition, but I submit these traits are best tempered with realism, potential, skill and acumen. Eric Hoffer tells us "A preoccupation with the future not only prevents us from seeing the present as it is but often prompts us to rearrange the past."[2]

Whilst Longfellow thought "Most people would succeed in small things if they were not troubled with great ambitions."[3] Put these two ideas together and it is arguable that having ambition and an eye on the future is not inherently bad, but that this should not be at the expense of ensuring we make the best of the present.

The book will have done its job if you work through it and either: a) conclude you are actually better at, and would be happier *not* being a manager (either at all, or with your current organisation); or b) that your approach is appropriate and, more importantly, that you can live up to it. If you feel in any way uncomfortable with the approach you are taking, I would urge you to consider an alternative as soon as possible.

It is essential that you are happy and comfortable doing what you do. The money you may get for stepping up (remembering that some actually lose in cash terms initially) may nowhere near compensate for all that comes with it. The American philosopher and author Henry David Thoreau wrote, "Many men go fishing all of their lives without knowing that it is not fish they are after."[4] Keep that in mind, whatever you seek to do from now on.

Whether it's personal development, or addressing a specific situation, from now on you should be thinking 'precisely what is it am I seeking to achieve?' This is about you making a conscious effort to visualise the type of manager you want to be – and what you want in life.

Everything flows from your response(s) to that question. Take a look round at those whom you deem to be successful (managers or not) and you will see that firstly they have identified a challenge; secondly they've accepted it; thirdly they are very clear and focussed on what it is they want to achieve. Usually it's the 'getting there' that people might need some help with.

Successful people choose not to ignore what's going on around them, even though they may then choose not to do anything about it. There is a trait acquired though the application of a combination of skills that is

2   (Hoffer 2006)
3   (Longfellow 1857)
4   (Thoreau 1854)

often attributed to being 'proactive'. It involves you having the ability to recognise what's going on around you; gather or assimilate and analyse information; determine whether it requires your attention or contribution; and then to have the knowledge, understanding, skills and abilities – and the will – to take control and do something about it. It requires you to know and understand your environment, what and who affects it. Putting these elements together so that you are able to react to and deal with situations as they arise is the key requirement of any manager. In short you need to be in control.

The First-Line manager role brings challenges of varying importance and complexity. Every situation you detect, perceive or are given is an opportunity to demonstrate your qualities as a person and as a manager. It is important to examine your foundations; and assess how ready you are for the role. Is the role suitable for you? Indeed, are you suitable for the role? "Here's a sobering thought… " Says American EMMY award-winning writer and producer Jane Wagner "… What if, at this very moment, I am living to my full potential?"

To answer that proposition, Section 1 prompts you to address these fundamental questions:

1. Why are you/do you want to be/do you wish to continue being a First-Line manager?
2. Have you considered what being a First-Line manager really involves?
3. What is your feeling about and approach to challenge?
4. What kind of manager do you want to be?
5. What do you have in your arsenal or toolbox?

If you are evidently at your full potential, your time might be better spent enjoying that fact rather than striving for something that is ultimately unachievable. I'm being careful here because I certainly do not want to stifle your ambition. All too often talent remains hidden and untested. The phrases 'you don't know until you try' and 'don't knock it 'til you try it' certainly have some resonance. The point is that you should become accomplished in the practise of self-assessment. Be realistic about your current capabilities and those that can be developed in the right environment and with the right resources and support.

Make notes on your existing capabilities and identify within the areas covered here, any aspects that you would benefit from developing. You are encouraged to develop a personal plan for achieving your aims and objectives; to maintain a record of your progress; and to take control of your development rather than trust that others will do it for you.

Exercise:

On a scale of 1 to 10 (1 being the lowest), rate these statements as they relate to you:

I am committed to being the best manager I can be

I am capable of being the best manager I can be

I have a full complement of tools and techniques and models at my disposal

I always apply the best tools and techniques to a given situation

If I asked others to rate me as a manager right now, my average rating would be...

Add your ratings together, then multiply by 2 to get a score.

Write that score on a blank sheet; sign and date it; fold it and place it an envelope. Seal and label the envelope and mark it with your name, the date and a 'tag' such as 'where I was'. Then lodge it in a safe place.

3. Why be a 'First-Line' Manager – the desire for power

You have the opportunity to understand the principal driver(s) for you wanting the role of First-Line manager and test whether your motivation is appropriate. The greater the clarity in your own mind, the easier it will be to communicate this to others by your words and actions.

The question is "Why do you want to be a First-Line manger?" The short and simple answer is that you want the role because of your desire for power and profit. Sorry! Have I shocked you? Did you think you were in it for more altruistic reasons? Maybe you are, but the bottom line is that all of us have sought or obtained promotion for profit! Maybe I should explain.

The desire for power

Power per se is not a bad thing. The term comes from the Latin '*posse*': to do, to be able, to change, to influence, or effect. A chap called Al Gini says it is not power that's the problem; it's how it is exercised. He says, *"To have power is to possess the capacity to control or direct change. All forms of leadership must make use of power. The central issue of power in leadership is not will it be used? But rather will it be used wisely and well."*[5]

This is a clear statement that there can be good and proper exercise of power and the opposite, bad and improper use. There can be little doubt that in order to get what you want done you need some form of authority or power.

With the role comes enhanced responsibility and in the non-tyrannical

5   (Gini 2004)

sense, another source of power. For many, their motivation for taking on a manager role is the desire to be able to control their own lives more and/or to influence. The first step in understanding the exercise of power and your authority to exercise it is to understand where it comes from and how you acquire it.

Poet Charles Bukowski said *"there is only one difference between dictatorship and democracy. In democracy, you vote and then take orders; in dictatorship you don't waste time voting."* It is unlikely your team voted you in. There won't be an election to get rid of you. There's usually a process involved, but the organisation decides (through those senior to you) whether or not you get the job. So democracy it is not!

The sources of your power

Theories abound as to the sources of individuals' power as does their categorisation and number. Most agree that your power to control or influence comes from one or a variety of the following sources[6]:

1 **The position you hold** – sometimes called 'legitimate power' – but it can be illegitimate if your position is obtained through fear or fraud, oppression or unwarranted force. To be legitimate, your position is secured through a democratic process – election; or you were appointed to it via some other recognised means – selection. To build and maintain the compliance of those over whom you hold 'position power', there needs to be elements of trust on the part of those you manage. They need to accept that you did indeed secure the position legitimately. Otherwise, you end up with malicious or half-hearted compliance or even resistance.

There is often a corresponding, upwardly dependent trust by you of those who chose you. You need faith that they did so for the right reasons, with objectives that match yours. No one likes thinking we've been given a job expecting us to fail like a scapegoat.

2. **The expertise you possess** – sometimes called 'expert power'. Here you have knowledge, understanding, skills or abilities that others do not

---

6   See *Bases of Social Power,* John R.P. French and Bertram Raven, (1959) & Bertram Raven (1965)

have, but need. Alternatively you may be more proficient at something than they. If you are an acknowledged expert in your field, people will seek you out to complete things for them. It matters not that they might be your subordinates, your peers or your managers. Problems can occur when someone with position power is assumed to have knowledge power too – purely because of that position. The two do not necessarily correlate.

It could be harmful if you have the required expertise, but for whatever reason decide not to share or use it for the benefit of your colleagues or organisation.

3. **Coercive power** – This is your capacity to get others to do what you want. This could be through their fear of the consequences of non-compliance. Use of words such as 'coercion' and 'fear' render it difficult to put a positive spin on this source of power. It is akin to bullying and harassment. It actually betrays weakness on the part of the user: weak knowledge of more suitable methods; fear of challenge; and difficulty in justifying their position.

4. **Referent power** – is gained because others like, respect and/or trust you. It is something your subordinates have as much – if not more – control over as you.

This is probably the strongest and most secure long-term power source, probably because it is more in the gift of others than any other. Paradoxically there is a negative to it, one that can destroy the trust and ultimately the source of the power. That is in using this kind of power to get someone to do something they otherwise wouldn't freely or willingly.

5. **The power to reward** – If others know or think they will be rewarded for doing what you want or need, it affords you another source of power. It stems from the fact that the person wielding it has previously suggested/demonstrated in the past that if others do (or refrain from doing something), they will be rewarded somehow now.

The simplest version of this is the contract that exists between you and your employer: if you turn up for work you will get paid. This simple philosophy has become somewhat muddied over the years because just 'turning up' is not sufficient. Turning up and 'doing what is expected' of you is more appropriate. A problem occurs when management has legitimately, but perhaps clumsily tried to enforce the contract. It has led to confrontation and a breakdown in industrial relations, but more of that later.

Another positive use of this power occurs when it is clearly understood that if someone performs over and above what is expected, perhaps due to increased or changed demand, they will be compensated accordingly. Reward power is the carrot to coercion's stick. This source of power will quickly dry up if promises of reward do not materialise.

6. **The information you possess** – or information power. In a similar way to how others will seek out those with particular expertise, they will also seek out those deemed to have greater knowledge and who can use it to influence decisions and actions. Note that the information needs to be relevant and up to date. To some extent they have control of the information, how it is accessed, the amount that can be released, or the time at which it can be accessed. Organisations can save time, effort and resources by going direct to someone who already possesses the knowledge they need. But of course they will still need to pay and the cost will depend on how complex the information, how rare it is, and how much they need it.

A negative use of knowledge power occurs when it bleeds into coercive power (see below). If the knowledge you possess could be deemed harmful to another or malicious, it could be used as some sort of undue leverage e.g. "I know Mary's been signing in for you, cover for me or I'll let the boss know."

What happens with power

All sources of power have positive and negative sides. Those over whom you can exercise power always have a choice as to whether they accept it (with varying severity of consequence). They may go along with you whilst it suits them, or until such time as they can take no more and/or they feel brave enough to do something about it.

Think of the demise of dictatorships across North Africa: Tunisia,

Egypt, and Libya. This happened from the bottom up! It proves that whilst existing at opposite ends of a spectrum, like democracy, autocracies only exist for as long as those regarded as being at the bottom of the pile allow them to. Those who rise up usually do so when they can no longer tolerate the abuse of power – however obtained and from wherever derived, because for them the consequences of continuing to comply are deemed worse than withdrawing 'permission'. They are prepared to face the consequences in search of the exercise of their own position power.

Your team has position power. Until you 'find your feet' they might well also have knowledge power. In extreme cases, it has been known for teams to gang together in a show of non-compliance demonstrating coercive power. So if the desire to exercise greater autonomy or power is, or was your main reason for securing the post – beware! You're not the only one! Your team can bring you down. They may not of course mean it. Left to their own devices, without objectives, guidance and information, they – like sheep – will eventually wander off in the wrong direction. If you go beyond boundaries of acceptability (written or unwritten), their permission for you to exercise power can, and probably will be revoked.

I'm not suggesting that you should avoid contact; be permanently suspicious; or treat everyone as an enemy (existing or potential). That's an excellent recipe for paranoia! It is highly likely to be noticed by colleagues and result in the very things you're trying to avoid. It's also unlikely to create the best working environment in the world and apart from that: it isn't much fun!

Neither should you seek to 'buy' the support of your team by acquiescing to their every whim and demand; refraining from confronting situations, or taking difficult decisions for the sake of a 'happy ship'. It's the equivalent of them making all the decisions; *their* power is being maintained – if not increased – and you might as well not be there.

I highlight these points to help avoid such circumstances, minimise the risk, and enhance your capabilities. It is to caution on the exercise of your newfound power. The 'people' may not have put you there, but if you don't treat them right, they might eventually be the engineers of your downfall. If, for instance, you don't let teams have their say (when it's appropriate) about their feelings or their knowledge of potential solutions, it's like maintaining a pressure cooker with the heat constantly on. Eventually it will blow up in your face. So how about asking for views occasionally? Think a little more about your actions. Above all be fair, considered, equitable and consistent.

Most sources of power are not inherently bad and you definitely need some sort of power in order to achieve the 'profit' you seek. Consider why you want the power in the first place and then, whether seeking and acquiring promotion will deliver what you expect. We are talking about the profits you wish or intend to make financially and the intended psychological profit: in your feelings of wellbeing; your esteem or achieving your ambition and being the best you can be.

Financial profit – and loss – is easily recognisable courtesy of your bank balance. Beyond the purely financial benefits (profit) that a management position may bring, we cannot and should not ignore the potential for psychological or emotional profits. If you're seeking more than you have now in terms of your self-esteem etc., and get it, have you not made a profit?

More often than not, if you are improving and developing, there are spin-off benefits to those around you and for your organisations. Shared profits are good profits, whereas if we alone make a profit it may be harder to accept by others. Can you recall someone who appears to be only interested in their own personal gain'?

Having made a case for the proposition that you are in it for power and profit; it's time to examine how that manifests itself through your reasoning for seeking or being in the role of First-Line manager.

4. Why be a 'First-Line' Manager – power into practice

Once you understand where your power comes from, you should understand how it might be translated into your practice in the role of manager. You may find more than one source applied to you. Similarly you may have more than one reason for wanting the role – translating that power into practice. Of course it's NOT just about the exercise of power. However, few people take time to identify exactly why they want the role. In consequence their objectives are hazy and difficult to measure. You should be able to clearly explain your reason(s) for being a First-Line manager to anyone. If they are to help you, they need to be clear what you are aiming for. You also need to understand what else may be driving you or impacting on your direction and choices.

Constantly focus on answering the question why you want the role. Focus – if you weren't already – on the implications of your chosen approach and determine whether it is right for you. You might need to change your mind. That doesn't matter so long as you take the opportunity to consider the potential benefits of changing course. Your reason/driver for taking on the role must figure high in your list of personal life goals. Otherwise why bother?

Determine what success will look like for you. When *will* you be happy and content? How will you measure that? Remember the shortest and quickest route may not be the safest or most effective. Similarly, you can travel as many miles over a similar route as the next person, but may not reach the right or the same destination.

Reason 1: Good operator turned manager

Probably deriving power from a combination of position, expert and knowledge, someone, somewhere decided the good operator should try their hand at management. Do you want the role solely because you are a good performer at the lower level? You will need a new set of knowledge and skills and may even be starting over. It's possible that you would lose money initially. So you must really want it! A candidate good at their current role at their current grade is not automatically suitable to be a manager. Promotion is often made as a way of rewarding past good work – not appropriate!

Having a strong operational background within the task functions you supervise is an undoubted benefit. It may shorten the time taken to get a grasp of situations. It may give your subordinates greater confidence in your ability and also that you understand them. You might be better equipped to translate communications from above into a language your team will understand and accept. The fact that you are helping others and perhaps building their skills and knowledge may provide the required psychological profits to you.

Reason 2: "It's the only way I can make more money"

Some larger organisations have salary banding that allows individuals to accrue salary without promotion (paradoxically meaning they can be earning more than their managers). In many others promotion is indeed the only way you can move up the salary ladder.

If this is your motivation, you clearly desire financial profit. It ignores the fact that money is not the only source of profit. If you're only in it for the cash, your source of power is in danger of coming only from the position itself. When that starts to falter, you head for coercion. Your organisation's culture, policy and structure might permit this approach, but that doesn't make it appropriate.

Is everything that comes with the role worth the money? You will only know the answer to that once you have been in the role for some time. It's very easy to be focussed on financial benefits and so lose sight of what you really want. If money *is* all you're after and in your organisation promotion is indeed the only route to it, could you do your current job for someone else, somewhere else for more?

Most of us need money to provide shelter, feed, clothe and entertain ourselves. It takes an unusually strong person to be poor and say that money doesn't matter. Woody Allen jokes "Money is better than poverty, if only for financial reasons." Even Ghandi assured us that money is itself not evil. However, if you like money, promotion is not the only way to get it.

Reason 3: "I want to get on in life"

You are looking for some psychological profit; some 'self-esteem'; to reach the pinnacle of Maslow's[7] hierarchy of need – some self- actualisation; and for a feeling of achievement. This reason implicitly acknowledges that to secure this 'profit', you need to acquire some power. This is not necessarily position power, though it will help. It is highly likely that you would want to exercise some existing, or soon-to-be-found legitimate and expert power; with a bit of reward power thrown in for good measure. Of course individuals who want to get on in life might do so for purely selfish reasons. That opens up potential for negativity, but let's stick with the positives.

You may believe acquiring promotion equates to and/or is a means to 'getting on in life'. However, work takes up about 25% of the time that we are judged to be able to do it – the time between leaving education and when we are required to retire. I have always believed that if you're healthy, happy at home, and happy with your work life, you're not doing too badly. We can usually cope with one of the three not being great at any one time, but if two or more start to go awry we find it difficult.

The question has to be whether it's appropriate for you to have the desire to get on in life as the principal reason for you wanting to be a manager. You have 75% space for achievement elsewhere. This is a sound reason for wanting the role. However, be realistic as to the contribution it can make to your overall life profit.

Reason 4: "I want to get on in the organisation"

This is distinct from reason 3 in so far as being a star in one organisation does not necessarily mean you would thrive in another. Organisations have different goals, processes, policies, structures and cultures. So making a sideways move between organisations because you cannot profit where you are, means you are to a large extent trusting to luck.

Will the new organisation allow you to flourish, or will it impose its own

7   (Maslow 1943)

set of restrictions? This reason tilts more towards the emotional profits than the pure financial. So it can be more palatable – provided it is handled the right way and is not seen as a selfish endeavour.

Ambition should be balanced by accurate assessment and shared opinion of capability, achievability and realism. Blind ambition can easily lead to loss of profit. Sir Winston Churchill said: "It is a mistake to try to look too far ahead. The chain of destiny can only be grasped one link at a time." The problem with using/misusing the role of manager with one's eye on 'greater things' is that it can cause loss of focus on the 'now'.

Consider also what 'getting on' in the organisation really means. As poet Robert Frost put it, "By working faithfully eight hours a day you may eventually get to be boss and work twelve hours a day."[8] This is fine if you thrive on those kinds of hours and don't want a life outside of work. What if you have a young family or lots of outside interests?

Reason 4 requires you to assess a) whether you have an existing power source that can get you ahead and earn your profits within the organisation without promotion; and b) what kind of profit you are seeking psychologically and how you will measure that. When will you be satisfied? Be realistic about your goals and ambition.

Reason 5: "I want the authority"

You want the authority and the power – why? What do you want to do with it? I'm contrasting the type of power referred to in Reason 9 below, which is largely positive, with the seeking of power for power's sake. This is a quest for position power and hints strongly that to keep it, you will throw in a dose of coercion. It has negative connotations. Apart from the old and well-worn phrase 'Be careful what you wish for', there are the words of Abigail Adams, the wife of the second President of the US, "Arbitrary power is like most other things which are very hard, very liable to be broken."

Reason 6: "It's about time I was recognised for all the good work I've been doing!"

This reason doesn't stand up on its own. Very few organisations would consider accepting it today. They look for potential against competencies

8   Unsourced

19

and the job spec, not what you've done in the past unless it evidences that potential. You may well bring substantial expert and knowledge power to the table, but that too is past behaviour. It does not mean you will be a good manager.

You're actually saying "I should be rewarded for what (in my opinion) is my past good service and/or loyalty". It's suggesting that you are leaning towards the need to make profit in terms of your self-esteem. It's not self-actualisation, as you're not really seeking to be the best you can. You feel that promotion will do that for you. As Mark Twain allegedly put it, "Don't go round saying the world owes you a living. The world owes you nothing. It was here first."[9] (Substitute 'your organisation' for 'your world'.)

History is littered with examples of promotion being granted as a reward. It can be an organisational or senior managers' rationalisation for moving someone upwards and/or keeping them quiet. That can never be in itself a sound reason for promotion.

Reason 7: "I think I have the ability to pick up the skills; I think I'd enjoy it"

On the face of it, this is a harmless reason for wanting to be a manager. It implies that you've assessed your current skill levels and you believe you'd make some emotional profit from the role. Unfortunately it's also a little bland and half-hearted! You're likely to secure a power base with the consent of your subordinates and also some referent power. But unless you're in control, that's more likely to happen by accident than design.

You're currently 'not there' when it comes to having a good balance of the requisite knowledge, skills and behaviours. Do you know how far away you are and what that would take? What do you possess now, or will likely need to possess in the future that you need to perform the role effectively? What kind of profit are you hoping to achieve and how much? How are you going to measure whether the move has been worth it?

This reason needs a lot more substance. More research is required for you to make an accurate assessment as to whether you could make the transition without hurting yourself, your colleagues, or the organisation. It's always a risk that someone promoted will not live up to the promise shown by past activity or performance in an assessment centre. The idea is

9   Some attribute this to Mark Twain, others to humourist Robert J Burdette

to minimise that risk. Very few organisations are ready, willing or able to gamble on you with poor odds.

Reason 8: "I believe others will benefit from my experience"

Provided you have some sound, relevant experiences, readily applicable to your future situation and you've learned appropriate lessons from them, this is a good reason for taking on the role. As Sister Mary Rose McGeady puts it, "There is no greater joy, nor greater reward than to make a fundamental difference in someone's life."

You're saying "I'm going to profit" with a sense of wellbeing, achievement and self-actualisation by fulfilling your ambition of being a role model and support to your colleagues. You're implying you need a mixture of position, knowledge, expert and referent powers that will make others sit up and listen.

Maybe there's a touch of arrogance in assuming you have what others want or need. It depends on the quality of your experiences, what you've learned from them, how you use them, and how you communicate that. For instance, constantly referring to a previous role in a previous organisation to express how things should be done now will eventually cause the audience to 'switch off' and to ridicule. You'll lose your power base(s) quite quickly and therefore would be less likely to hit your profit targets. Ensure the experience, and application of it, is relevant to the current task and the people involved, and is up to date.

Properly introduced, applied and managed, this is one of the best reasons for seeking the role. Remember though, that few want to have wisdom thrust upon them. Few react well to a 'know-it-all'. Apply your knowledge and experience by invitation, in response to the "I/we've got a problem"-type question, or "What would you do if...?" This further illustrates the referent nature of your power and the permission others give you to exercise it.

Reason 9: "I know I can make more of a contribution and make things 'happen' if I'm more than just a worker"

Here you are much clearer that you need the power and authority to bring your ideas to fruition. You're looking towards the future, rather than making expectations based on the past. You are implying a need for the psychological boost from the recognition that making things happen should bring. This can be a very strong driver for seeking promotion.

You think you know what is required – and how others above you perform. You are thinking, "I could do that", or "I could make a better job of it!" These comments are made less and less, the more you get to know your role. That said, you should also be able to recognise traits and behaviours in others that you would *never* employ were you in the role.

You're an ideas person, possibly finding it difficult to convince those above you of the brilliance and benefits of them. You consider an upward move will in some way make that easier. Bear in mind that as well as convincing those above, you must now convince those below too. It is the latter who most likely have to implement your schemes. Promotion may not necessarily be the best way for you to ensure you get the opportunities you want or need in order to feel valued.

Consider the environment and culture in which you operate. What is your organisation's attitude towards innovation and change – and those who seek to introduce it? Do they relish and support fresh ideas and internally driven challenges? Or would they rather you just 'got on with it' and left the thinking to someone more senior/qualified? Do they welcome being tested by new faces or slap them down as impudent upstarts? If you are an innovator, a problem-solver, or an inventor, it is easy to become stifled in an organisation that doesn't support that.

Reason 10: "I want greater control of my own life and destiny"

This is aligned to the desire to have fewer people able to tell you what to do. However, at the first level of management, there will still be people who can tell you what to do. No matter how high you ascend there always will be! Equally, your subordinates have as great a capacity to control or influence your life as your seniors do. What happens if they decide not to do something you ask, or do it incorrectly. Their error reflects on you just as much as them.

You are looking to have control over your financial and psychological profit making; of achieving your goals; of your esteem and self-actualisation. As you will still have others who have some form of power and control over you, you are seeking to maintain a greater say in whether and how you are going to respond to situations.

As far back as the mid-twentieth century, psychologist Albert Ellis said, "The best years of your life are the ones in which you decide your problems are your own. You do not blame them on your mother, the ecology, or the President. You realise that you control your own destiny." In other words it's not necessarily your role or position that gives you control of your destiny, but acceptance that it is your responsibility.

Decision Time

The time has come for *you* to identify the reason why you want to take the first step into management. What's driving you? One or more of the preceding descriptions may have resonated with you immediately. Alternatively, it could be that having read the descriptors you might now have some doubts. Perhaps what you consider to be your primary reason didn't get a mention above. You might disagree with the explanation of the benefits and drawbacks, you might think of others. All of this is totally fine.

The essential need is for you to identify what is right for you; that you are clear on the benefits and drawbacks of your choice. Pay heed to your capabilities and capacity to live up to the reason driving you into the role within your organisation. Be clear and structured in what you do to reach your goal.

Exercise:

Write **in your own words** why you want to be a First-Line manager.

Next: Make your own list of benefits and drawbacks of that/those reason(s). This can include, exclude or add items to the illustrations above.

Finally: Relating it to the organisation in which you are/will be performing the role, highlight the benefits you believe will be easy to secure and which of the drawbacks are likely to manifest themselves.

It is one thing to identify which of the reasons are driving your quest for promotion, or to remain in the role. It is another to balance that with the kind of motivation that your organisation is most likely to want to see.

For instance, some organisations, especially the younger ones, generally want individuals in the role who are very keen to develop and progress, and who can pass on their infectious enthusiasm to others within the organisation. Other organisations – especially those with very defined and rigid hierarchies – might well expect those at the first level to put aside, or delay thoughts of further promotion in favour of maintaining control and getting on with what they should be doing in maintaining output.

Exercise:

Relating it to the organisation in which you are, or will be performing as a First-Line manager, detail as far as possible your perception of the expectation of the organisation in respect of manager progression. Is it 'ad-hoc', 'dead man's shoes'? Is there succession planning? Are you encouraged to progress as far as you can? I want you now to consider how your particular motivation manifests itself and is communicated to those above and below you. For instance, we could all cite an example of individuals whose implicit, or even explicit attitude is that of "I don't care. I won't be here that long before my next move up!"

End of Chapter Exercise:

What – if any – feedback have you received that is evidence of you demonstrating and evidencing your reason(s) for wanting the role?

To what extent has this been positive or negative? Has it been direct or indirect feedback?

What – if anything – have you done with that feedback?

5. Why be a 'First-Line' Manager – expectations

No matter what their purpose, all organisations have expectations of their managers. Members of their teams and other operational staff (subordinates) have always had expectations. In the eyes of the latter, their manager is someone to whom they can go to for support, guidance, advice, or understanding. Many subordinates perceive the First-Line manager's job to be not far removed from their own. Whilst they probably appreciate the manager has additional responsibilities, they do not often understand, or are unable/unwilling to acknowledge the distinction that exists. It is not uncommon for the First-Line manager to be perceived as 'one of us' because very often there is also an expectation from all directions that they know (can even perform) their subordinates' job.

If you vocalise a sentiment, or display attitudes and behaviours that suggest you are using the position for self-serving or ulterior motives, there is considerable risk that you are likely to get a negative reaction from subordinates and seniors alike. Your performance in the role can then be more difficult and less effective. It has been known for subordinates sufficiently aggrieved by this approach, to take active steps to sabotage those seen to have ideas above their station.

Furthermore, those above you have expectations. You were put in the role for a reason – whatever it was. If you are thinking of other things; working to your own agenda more than theirs; and are not paying sufficient attention to the job in hand; you might find life becomes difficult.

There is a difference between you knowing that you wish and intend to move 'onwards and upwards'; and letting others know it. I'm not advocating lying, or being economical with the truth. It may be totally appropriate for you to disclose your ambition, especially to those who might coach, mentor or support you on your journey. However, it is very much the *way* you communicate your purpose that counts.

Whilst at this level a lot is based on what you are doing, and are seen to be doing now. The old adage "be careful who you upset (or step on) on the way up, as you may well meet them on the way down" may be a cliché, but how true! Once again we are looking for balance. Consider these points:

- Your organisation may have a reasoned structured route to the top requiring you to complete this preliminary step – if only for appearances' sake.
- Your organisation may have a different view of your abilities and your potential for advancement. They might think you're fantastic at what you do, and how nice you are, but that you can't/ won't go any further.
- Your organisation might think that you are great and that you would be great as a more senior manager, but *you* don't want to do that, have no intention of doing that, and don't even want to give it a try.
- Alternatively: Everyone including you, thought it would be a good idea at the time but on reflection and after lots of effort, it becomes evident that you have reached the most appropriate or ultimate level of your managerial effectiveness.

Distinguish and define the gap that lies between your reason(s) for wanting to be a First-Line manager and your capacity to perform the role to the extent and standard expected by your organisation. You will have the chance to devise strategies to bridge any gaps as you progress through this book.

Expectation of Leadership

This is not a book discussing the efficacy of particular theories, rather an attempt to give some practical help in the role. I do however want to briefly consider the question of leadership.

You won't find many people walking round your organisation with the job title 'Leader'. Some may be called this-or-that 'Lead', but that's different. Being the 'lead' on something does not automatically confer upon you the skills, abilities and behaviours of a leader. It would be nice to think though that everyone given such a role did in fact carry some of those traits.

The 'Leader' is recognised through displayed actions and someone to whom we respond more willingly. Even though we have a choice, we feel almost compelled to follow them if only because we can't find an argument not to. They can be someone whose work, personality or conviction we trust and admire. They don't have to hold a management position, but most organisations will expect managers at all levels to utilise leadership traits (at incremental levels of proficiency).

There will definitely be quite a few whose title includes the word 'Manager'. We still have a choice as to whether to do as they say, but the compulsion to do so can be derived more from the repercussions of non-compliance. Being given the title of 'Manager' does not bring about some immediate and automatic 'New You'; fully armed and ready to go either. 'Old you' will still be there and much of that might be right and suitable. It was 'Old You' who secured you the position. But it is probable that you will have to perfect some embryonic skills and acquire some new ones. It is also probable that your own and others' expectations and perception of you will develop as you go along.

Are leaders born or made? I find myself observing individuals and recognising attributes that make them (in my opinion) a good manager, a good leader, or both. On balance I go with the notion that it is more effective and better for all concerned if the manager can utilise and display leadership qualities, but it's not always essential. This is especially true at the First-Line manager level.

You should have more decision-making power and autonomy than before and be able to display more initiative. However, much of your work remains directed by others more senior or with control over you. Indeed you may have additional constraints placed upon you, such as how to handle policy disputes, grievances or operational problems that a 'leader' is not bound by. Many in the role find their lives also constrained by the attitudes and behaviours of those they manage.

US author and leadership scholar Warren G. Bennis says, *"The manager has his eye on the bottom line; the leader has his eye on the horizon."*[10] So whatever your motivations, at the First-Line level you must focus on managing the production process of your organisation, be that a service or a tangible product. For the time being the focus should be on utilising and displaying leadership qualities in order to achieve the expectations of the manager role.

10   (Bennis 1989)

Summary

We have asserted that you are seeking some form of (hopefully benevolent) power to realise your desired profits. These may be purely financial or include some psychological or emotional profits too. You have examined the sources of that power. You have also had the opportunity to accurately identify and confirm the most appropriate reason for you wanting the role. Later you will have the opportunity to design an action plan to steer you appropriately in the direction of your power and profit. So please complete the following short exercise.

In the next chapter I want you to consider – if you haven't fully done so already – just what the role entails. What are the expectations of someone in the role of First-Line manager that are different from those above or below? In the meantime, we leave this chapter with two messages, separated by two millennia. The first from Greek philosopher Epicurus who lived between 341 BC – 270 BC:

"Do not spoil what you have by desiring what you have not; remember that what you now have was once among the things you only hoped for."

The second from comedian George Burns:

"I honestly think it is better to be a failure at something you love than to be a success at something you hate."

End of Chapter Exercise:

It will help if you get hold of a bound notepad for this and subsequent activity.

Create a section in the pad headed 'Areas for Development'

Under that heading make a note now if you wish to work on building or adjusting your power base and why.

There's no need to do anything else at this stage.

6. What being a First-Line Manager involves

Chasing the role, focussing on the goal of greater financial reward and power, could lead you to skip over or even ignore this vital question. Have you considered what being a First-Line Manager involves over and above the exercise of power? If you don't know the answer how can you realistically assess whether you can or will be able to do the job?

If you are considering taking on the First-Line manager role, or are very new to it I want to raise your awareness of the various and sometimes competing, requirements of the role. This chapter may come too late if you're already established in the role. So feel free to skip to the next.

Try to establish the areas in which you might wish to concentrate for your personal development. Your ideas can be expanded on in the next chapter. For now you should be able to explain the key requirements of any First-Line manager. You should be able to accurately read your working environment

There's a great quote from the Canadian academic and author Henry Minztberg that says, *"If you ask managers what they do, they will most likely tell you that they plan, organise, coordinate and control. Then watch what they do. Don't be surprised if you can't relate what you see to those four words."*[11]

I have had little luck finding an off-the-shelf list of what is involved, which specifically targeted the first level of management. Perhaps there's a reason for that. Is it necessary to have a separate list when many of the traits and expectations in terms of KUSAB are common across all levels of management? You will find common themes included in programmes delivered by establishments offering 'management training'. Unfortunately these can be quite prescriptive, theory-laden, and contain the 'usual

11   (Mintzberg 1989)

suspects': Problem-Solving, Decision-Making, Communication, Planning, Time Management, Team-Building etc., etc.

I'm not trying to 're-invent the wheel', nor to dismiss any of the themes listed above. They are the building blocks you need. External commercial training providers exist to make a profit, by selling their programmes and implicitly maintaining the impression that: a) so much can be learned in a classroom; and b) being a manager only requires knowledge and practice of theories.

Go beyond that theory. Get a handle on some of the things that can't easily be slotted into an established academic box. It's not a separate or novel list that's required, but one that clarifies how those competencies are applied and displayed at the level you operate in. Look on what follows as being in addition to, not instead of.

The first time I thought I wanted promotion I was wrapped up in my motivation and was determined to succeed. My consideration of what was involved was not – with hindsight – a very analytical, scientific, or structured affair. Certainly, my eventual elevation did benefit from a substantial period of performing the role on an acting basis. However, I realise now that my awareness of the requirements and responsibilities only developed as I encountered more and more situations – or stumbled into them!

There was no control over the types of situation I might be facing from day to day. There were extremes: from a subordinate not filling in some paperwork, or reporting on a minor incident – hardly life-threatening – to managing situations in which colleagues might have been at least seriously injured whilst at work. I hasten to add this was when I was a police officer, not an office manager! The point is that there was little opportunity to go in a planned sequence from dealing with the simple to the complex; little chance to make some easy simple, non-threatening mistakes early on; and numerous occasions that were not 'covered by the book'.

When I moved from policing into a profit-driven environment. I went in naive and blind to some of the 'tricks' that could be pulled. I was far too trusting and realised not everyone shared the same ideals of honesty, responsibility, goals, or commitment as me. In my defence, the induction process I went through proved far from adequate. However, I now realise the responsibility was mine. Thankfully I survived and managed to turn the situation round. But being told within a few months of making a dramatic career change, that there was a danger of my services being dispensed with, did little for my self-esteem, nor my sense of security.

Be more scientific and enquiring. Accept less the headlines and read more the 'small print'. The move into management is a significant one. It is not one I would recommend if you were (substantially) unaware of what you're letting yourself in for.

Remember the words of Frederick F. Flack quoted in Chapter 2 about looking back at a significant life-changing moment. Taking those moments seriously can save a lot of hurtful soul-searching at a later date. We tend to use hindsight after a disaster. Why not use foresight to avoid one?

What is involved?

It's like being the filling in a sandwich: you are between two substantial forces (the bread). From above your managers representing the organisation, requiring you to control and enforce policy, procedure, standards and targets. From below, your team expect you to be an ear when they have a problem and a 'voice' for upward communication.

Some relish this 'linchpin' role and have no difficulty managing the contradictions and any divided loyalty. Some on the other hand do: knowing that they should be loyal to the organisation that promoted them and do what is necessary, but torn by their affiliation and empathy with the level that they were up until recently operating in.

The question is not just 'what does being a manager involve?' That means different things to different people and can depend on who teaches you; from whom you learned; or even what books you read. The question has to be 'what does being a manager in the organisation and environment that you will be operating in involve?' Not so much what you do as how you do it; how much of it you do; and with what degree of autonomy, confidence and support.

Take the following example:

CASE STUDY: The Boss has noticed!

It had been three months since Denise got her promotion from quality controller to manager of the quality control team after the previous incumbent retired. It was a role she'd always wanted. She was known to be good at the job and everyone always came to her for advice anyway.

Denise had apparently made the transition quite well. There didn't seem to be the grumbles about management that there used to be. Staff seemed happier.

After a month or so, the sales director started fielding calls from the sales team reps, who in turn had been receiving complaints around product quality.

A meeting was called with the site director, sales manager and Denise. There it was agreed that the quality control team would be reminded of the need to ensure all products were properly tested and nothing sub-standard would leave the site. It was also agreed that there would be a review of production processes.

Another month down the line and complaints were still being received. Customers were openly considering looking elsewhere. An independent audit of the production process showed that products were coming out with acceptable usual tolerances, no more faults than catered for, but that items with faults were not being picked out during quality checking.

The director had walked through the unit that morning and noticed the volume of chat and the numbers on 'a cigarette break'. He was fairly sure that a couple of workers were also late.

At a subsequent meeting in private with the director, Denise confirmed that she had 'advised' her team, but agreed that this had been more of an informal mention during one of her regular team meetings. Denise was left in no uncertain terms as to her responsibilities and the implications for her and the team if the situation did not improve within a week.

Case Study 1: The Boss has noticed!

Exercise:

Why do you think the situation has developed in the manner that it has?

If you were a manager colleague of Denise and she came to you for advice, what do you think you would be suggesting?

My thoughts: Denise's motivation for wanting the role may not have been totally appropriate. She appears to have wanted the position (and the rewards that came with it), but not to lose the friendship of her colleagues. It seems she is reluctant to seen by them to be a controlling or enforcing manager. She had not made the transition as well as appearances suggested. The organisation must bare some responsibility for the situation. It promoted her. It may not have overseen the transition as well as could be expected. However, there are some pretty fundamental things going wrong here:

- Denise's power appears to stem from the fact that her team like her – referent power. They don't seem to show her very much respect. Otherwise they wouldn't be taking advantage. In reality it comes from her position, though she seems unwilling to exercise it for fear of losing her friendships.
- Denise has been making a financial profit thanks to the increase in salary and physiologically as she has chosen not to address the issues. She has been having a nice friendly time of things. Securing the position has done wonders for her esteem. Unfortunately her concept of the requirement does not appear to be matching those of the organisation.
- Denise is ignorant of, or unwilling to address the need to control her team and to appropriately enforce the house rules and processes.
- She does not appear to have reconciled her responsibility to those paying her salary with her own personal motivation and way of working.
- She apparently does not want to get into potential conflict situations.
- It's a possibility that she has not had sufficient support to make the transition and to have any structured development to make her aware of these issues and work towards addressing them – until now!

What if Denise came to you for help? Hopefully you would not slap her (verbally) about the face a couple of times and tell her to 'sort herself out'! However, there are some fundamental things you might advise that she must do:

1. She must (in baseball parlance) 'step up to the plate', meet with her team, and tell them:

a. Standards have slipped below the point of acceptability
b. They are all responsible for complying with accepted requirements and
c. The implications of not doing so

She could use what remains of her referent power, rather than coercion. The latter would establish the wrong demarcation between her and her team. This is something *she* should have noticed. So using the boss as a whip might seem like a good idea. However, it actually weakens her position in all sorts of ways. It reinforces that *she* hasn't been watching. It confirms that *she* had to be told what to do. It invites challenges such as 'well if the boss saw it, why didn't he/she do something about it?'

2. She must start to shift her position from being 'one of the guys'. They deserve and need to be clear as to what she will accept as their manager. She needs to re-draw the relationship. I choose the words 'start to' because a dramatic 'that was me then, this is me now' approach could be too much of a shock to the team resulting in loss of her referent power.

3. It's possible that completing stage 1 above will have the desired effect on most – if not all the team. If not, she must start to address individuals' performance. This must be on a one-to-one basis, taking each case on merit. Blanket 'telling-off' sessions, or notices are unlikely to succeed. Neither does it have to be an iron-fist with her standing next to the entrance every day, clipboard and discipline forms in hand.

This is quite a 'sea-change' for Denise – and for her team, that by now has become accustomed to doing its own thing. How these things should be covered off must be very much down to her personal style. Feel free to jump forward to Chapter 18 on Feedback if you want to reach a conclusion on the activity, but remember to come back!

I am not ignoring the long-term activity Denise might have to undertake in this and other areas of her performance. Substantial significant changes in attitude and behaviour take a lot longer than acquiring a bit of theory knowledge. The (very rich) industrialist and philanthropist Warren Buffet is quoted as saying "It takes twenty years to build a reputation and five minutes to ruin it. If you think about that, you'll do things differently." [12]

12 (Buffet n.d.)

It seems Denise has quickly obtained a reputation for being a *laissez-faire* kind of manager. She has to prevent that developing further. It's going to take a long time for her team to be convinced that she means business. She may have to work more on her character – what she really is, what personal profits she really wants or needs to make – rather than her reputation and what others think of her.

You might think of something else for Denise to do that has worked for you in the past, or which on reflection, you think would work better in your environment. All good! Because you should start reviewing situations accurately, identify (true) causes and consider all possible solutions before coming to a final one. There will be times when there will be clashes between what your subordinates expect, what your managers require and what you are ready, willing or able to deliver.

What else are you expected to do that are the broad responsibilities of any manager (as opposed to what's written in a specific job description)? At the outset I defined a First-Line manager and made the point that many requirements are not really distinct from the requirements and expectations on any level of manager. The difference is the amount of time that a First-Line manager has to resolve the situations they encounter, the proximity they feel to situations, and the level of accountability.

The definition can be expanded to include this fuller, though still not exhaustive, list of role requirements: coaching/training; communication, including public speaking; conflict management; controlling; decision-making; disciplining; investigating; planning; problem-solving; recruiting; reporting; team-building and time management.

All of these functions are carried out at the operational level to a different degree to the strategic overview and foresight required of a managing director or CEO, or the tactical skills required of a regional or department head. But they are no less important. Getting these functions right at the First-Line level can be critical to an organisation's continued existence.

The time frame in which a First-Line manager operates is generally more immediate and short-term, though the implications and ramifications of their activity can indeed have long-term effects. Generally, a First-Line manager deals with small teams at a local level. Both require a different application of the relevant skills.

In the following exercise you can identify which functions you currently undertake, the proportion of your time that is devoted to them, and an assessment of your abilities. It's a snapshot intended to highlight some of the skill areas you need to develop

Exercise:

Complete the grid by allocating yourself a rating from 1 to 10 with '1' meaning 'Forget it, give up now!' and '10' meaning 'I'm perfect and need do no more!'

Function	Currently Performed by you? (Y/N)	Proportion of working day performed? (%)	How do you rate yourself? (1 to 10)
Assessing (others or situations)			
Analysing			
Business delivery (e.g. escalations)			
Coaching			
Communicating			
Conflict Management			
Controlling			
Decision-Making			
Investigating/Enquiring/Research			
Observing			
Organising others			
Planning			
Problem-solving			
Public Speaking			
Recruiting			
Reporting (Preparing & Delivering)			
Self-Assessing/Reflecting/Learning			
Subordinates' tasks			
Team Building			
Time Managing (Yours & Others)			
Training			

Of all the responses you had to provide, I would guess that the amount of time spent on each activity was the most difficult. They are often tasks that we reel off unconsciously. They are viewed as 'soft skills'. Many are completed all at the same time and it can be difficult to differentiate between them – problem-solving and decision-making being two good examples.

If you scored an activity particularly low, remember that a skill that goes unused is a bit like that piece of fitness equipment that you bought as a good idea at the time. It will be stuck at the back of the garage, moved occasionally when you're having a clean out, maybe even used briefly as part of a guilt trip. You'll remember how it should be used, but it will be a struggle and you won't get the full benefit.

It's not for me to say whether the amount of time you spend on a particular aspect of the role is too little or too much. I neither know you, your preferences or style, your job, nor the environment in which you're operating. However, extremes in any area suggest something of an imbalance and warrant some further examination as to whether those extremes are appropriate. I wouldn't expect there to be too many extremes in anyone's results after they have worked through a programme of manager development.

It might also prove interesting to give a blank copy of the list to some of your trusted colleagues and get their perception. If their responses are broadly in line with yours it provides good evidence that you are self-aware and are portraying a genuine 'you'.

If there are some fairly extreme variations such as you thinking you're an '8' in something – say communication – and your colleagues reckon you're a '3', maybe you should do some further investigating as to why they believe that.

Finally as an option, you could observe colleagues with the same role and job description as your own and whom you perceive to be proficient; see if you can identify the functions and how much time they allocate to each.

This part of the exercise is also interesting to do at the start and again at the end of a scheduled period of development so that you get evidence as to whether you have been successful – pat yourself on the back – you're perfect! Or whether you still need to do a bit more.

Exercise:

Revisit your function assessment and, focussing on the 'Time spent' column and mark each element as to whether in your opinion you spend on it too much time, too little time, or about the correct amount of time.

You could use different coloured highlighting or use TM for too much, TL for too little and CA for correct amount.

This has to be based on your knowledge of what is expected of you as a First-Line manager by the organisation you're doing it for; and your subjective assessment as to whether you're achieving. There may be some functions that are neither explicit, nor implicit in your job description, but that you spend time on. If that's the case one is tempted to ask why you're doing them. If you shouldn't or are not expected to be doing them and you are, you're automatically spending too much time on them.

If you're comfortable that you *are* required to complete these functions it would be unfair to leave you dangling and not examine some of the reasons why there might be an imbalance. If you're also satisfied that particular items receive about the correct proportion of your time, you can put those to one side for the time being. What we need to do is afford you the opportunity to accurately assess why you give too little or too much time to the remainder.

Exercise:

Referring to your functions list and for each of the items you have highlighted as receiving too much or too little of your time; identify the reason(s) that in your opinion have led to that being the case. Try and keep it to single word responses or 'bullet points'

When we examine the reasoning behind our choices, it is possible to group them in such a way that they are metaphorically the two sides of a particular coin. In the table that follows I have identified some of my ideas. Please note that these are examples rather than definitive answers. The centre column headings can manifest themselves in a variety of ways and there is some overlap between them. For instance, if you were to lack a particular skill or the knowledge required for a function, you might avoid it. Similarly, if you know you have a particular 'gift' or skill, you might spend more of your time on that function to the detriment of others.

Too Little Time Spent		Too Much Time Spent
Bare minimum of time on a function – usually for one of the reasons listed below	**Avoidance**	More time on one function so you can claim to be too busy to deal with another you wish to avoid
Avoid a function for fear of getting it wrong – even though you've had the training or have done it before without failure	**Fear of Failure**	You check over and again! Efforts to dot every 'I' and cross every 'T'. Worry you have missed something and don't want to be shown up
Busy with tasks that really should be completed by others.You may allocate tasks but not explain fully what is required or then distance yourself without offering enough support and supervision.	**Inadequate/ Inappropriate allocation of tasks**	Maybe a new or weak team, because of resistance, or a lack of skill, you may allocate tasks spending too much time explaining, or overseeing to the point where the team says, "Why don't you do it yourself?"
You might want to spend more time in a particular function, but your organisation requires you to spend more time or puts greater emphasis on others.	**Organisational Constraints**	You might want to spend less time doing something – gathering data and reporting – but your organisation demands that you spend more time and effort doing it.
See problem – jump to solution too quickly, not considering enough the required outcomes – No **CRAFT-T** plan. Not enough thought to long-term consequences or resources. You lack skills in gathering and analysing data	**Planning**	You lack skills in gathering and analysing data and trusting yourself and/ or others information. Maybe over planning in to address every eventuality.

Not enough time spent analysing what is urgent & important – you might not know how to: less important matters (possibly easier) get dealt with first.	**Prioritising**	You believe you have insufficient information to make a decision or you might 'over-analyse' as to which are the urgent and important tasks.
You lack or have never had the opportunity to learn a particular skill or knowledge set. So as you know you must do it, you do what little you can. But this is not enough for the task.	**Skill**	You have a talent for a particular task or function. So you concentrate on doing that, rather than being a 'Jack-of-all-trades'. You do this to the detriment of other functions required
The volume of activity you are required to complete because of the organisation's business (as opposed to processes & policies) means you have less time for each individual instance. So you cut corners with the ones you do get involved in.	**Volume**	The volume of work in each function you are expected to complete is high, but because you might lack a particular skill set, you spend too long in a particular one resulting in backlogs or neglected other functions.
Maybe you lack a skill set, or you disagree with a policy or procedure, or feel 'hard-done-by' because there's too much to do. So you lack the will to put much effort or time in.	**Will**	You really like a particular function and have the skill to do it; or maybe it's a new opportunity you've been given and is a chance to shine. So you are more than willing to put a lot of effort in to the detriment of other tasks

Table 1: **Reasons for Bad Time Management**

I realise that I am blurring the lines a little between what is involved in being a First-Line manager and the skills required, but that's for a reason. Whilst the two are inextricably tied, it is one thing to say what's involved, something else to provide evidence that you can actually do it. There's a process and journey that has to be followed for knowledge to be translated into activity. Like any journey, there's a lot that can happen on the way to affect the speed, the quality and even the route.

Your Environment

I'm introducing this now because it is important to be realistic. You might have completed all the exercises so far and come out with some confidence. You might do likewise with the exercises in the following chapters. You might be very clear in what you think the role 'should' involve. However, there is another question to be answered: Is the environment in which you are expected to fulfil the role conducive to that ideal?

Many new managers return from their management course bristling with ideas, full of enthusiasm, and fired up to succeed, only to be told by their immediate manager – or indeed the team – to "forget all that theory nonsense, it doesn't work here!" Alternatively, they start the role in a new organisation, or new department and are uncertain about whether (a) it is capable of supporting that new enthusiasm, or (b) it actually wants to.

This is rarely down to the status of the business, or what it does. Rather, it is about the age, perception and position of the business in its market; the attitudes and cultures it promotes; its objectives; and the management methods it applies. You have little control over the first element and ideally the other elements match your aspirations and intentions in the role.

All organisations go through phases, often called a life cycle. Like us humans, there's birth (start-up); youth (growth or development); adulthood (maturity and consolidation); senility (decline), and death (the same wherever you are). Whatever stage they are in, organisations will always display some traits common to that stage.

At birth organisations are likely to be very proactive: defining aims and objectives; setting targets for success; telling the world they're here; launching a new concept, product or service; securing innovative methods of getting their product to the customer; establishing working practices and cultures; recruiting staff and managers; possibly securing investors. It's an exciting time and potentially very rewarding for the First-Line manager to be in at the start. But what if the founders have definite and fixed ways from the outset? What opportunities are there for you to bring your own unique style into the mix and how will they be received? Of course you could well have been brought in for that very purpose.

In the growth stage the organisation will continue to be proactive, but is also likely to start dealing with what it perceives to be the reaction of its real or potential customers, or others with influence. It might fine tune products or services. It might tweak the structure. If the outputs are well received it could well need new outlets to reach a larger market. That could well provide you with the opportunity you've been looking for – a bit of internal promotion. Or you might be happy just to have been part of the first wave and content with your lot.

Original products or services can be expanded upon, updated, improved. However, growth cannot be assumed, nor can it be automatic and is dependent on a lot of factors, not least of which is whether the original concept was right and was well received by the target market in the required volume. If they got it wrong you could find yourself working much harder than you thought; trying to get the team to cope with greater demand than was anticipated (a victim of their own success); or if they overestimated, it could be that your post quickly withers away.

If the organisation is growing and does so to acceptable levels and/ or the leaders become complacent, it is always possible that they will not bother to develop new ideas; improve or update their range; or react to new entrants who are doing the same thing, but better. So their customers will look elsewhere and the organisation will go into decline. This could well start to ring alarm bells as to the security of your post. You might find that your anticipated or desired opportunities to be innovative or challenging are limited. That your job of motivating your team becomes ever harder. If nothing is done the organisation will go directly, albeit at different speeds, to death. However, in many cases organisations are prompted into action once they realise they are in the decline phase.

Decisions are taken to renew, refresh or re-invent the organisation and how it is set up to deliver. This is often accompanied by a corresponding updating of the organisation's outputs to bring them in line with what the customer needs, and preferably at least on a par with the competition. We see it all the time with de-mergers of businesses that have become too big or that have 'lost touch'.

You may have been involved in situations where organisations have re-structured or reorganised; introduced new technology, processes or systems. Unfortunately these are rarely accompanied by changes at the level that led the organisation into decline in the first place, or by appropriate culture changes. This rather limits the benefits and only causes a short and temporary upwards blip into growth before the rot sets back in. It's a bit like constantly patching up an old banger until eventually you have to acknowledge that no matter how much you love her, she has to be replaced. Of course I'm referring to a car or piece of machinery here!

Such renewal or reinvention can provide opportunities for you as a First-Line manager: you might be able to help shape the new organisation; you might be able to move upwards or use your latent skills to new or better effect; of course you may have to prepare yourself for a reduction in the levels or numbers of managers that always seem to accompany these events; you might even be able to use the opportunity to 'escape' from an organisation in which you have been unhappy – especially if you believe with good reason that the proposed changes will still not remedy the main causes of your unhappiness.

If the organisation won't or can't stop the decline for whatever reason it will eventually cease operating. Occasionally this is due to environmental or political factors. Invariably it is due to the way the organisation has been led (or not) and the decisions that have been taken (or not). This may not be the end for you with that organisation of course. It's possible that a competitor might step in and take over – hungry for your organisation's assets. This could start the whole life cycle off again and bring about a whole host of opportunities for you to achieve what you want.

Once you have an understanding of where your organisation is in its life cycle, you can move on to take a look at how it's doing in that stage and how what it's doing matches your aspirations.

In the same way that forward-thinking organisations can assess where they are in the world using analysis, you too can – if you are concerned enough – analyse the organisation's suitability for you and what you want to achieve in the role. Here are some questions you might like to consider:

1. Does the organisation have any political perspective? For instance, a leaning towards a particular political doctrine? Is it a business that is in, or out of favour with local or national government? Is it highly regulated

by law? Can it only operate in certain locations because of what it does? If it's a public sector organisation are its practices affected by whoever is in ultimate control? Are any of these things likely to change in the short or long-term?

2. Is your organisation vulnerable to significant changes in the local, national or global economy? For instance, does it produce goods that only sell well when people have spare cash? Does it provide a service that is called upon significantly when people are in need? If it exports heavily, what effect do interest or exchange rates have on outputs?
You might say, "What has what's going on in the world got to do with me?" Well remember that when 'belts are tightened' it's most often the management levels that are pruned first. Can you live with being in post for only a short time before getting made redundant? Another question you can ask here is, can they afford you, or is the salary appropriate to the responsibility? Is it enough for you to live on?

3. On the inside does the organisation live up to your social expectations? Is it socially responsible in terms of the effect of its outputs on the environment, its neighbours? Does it take safety and the wellbeing of its employees seriously? On the outside, is it an organisation that caters to a particular demographic or size of population? In which case, what will be the effect of any significant changes in that demographic on the organisation's ability to employ you?
Similarly, do the organisation's social credentials live up to your expectations? If not, to what extent will you be happy in the role – enforcing something you're not happy with – or would you not enforce them and risk your position?

4. How is technology impacting upon, or being used in your organisation? For instance, is technology likely to be introduced that will (a) lead to you having to lay off or communicate redundancies to a team; or (b) impact on your capacity to interact with your team such as reducing the need for them to come into a central location for meetings?
Are you the type that revels and embraces the wonders of technology; or does it fill you with dread? Even though you have proven interpersonal skills, what is your feeling about being forced to use particular systems

or methodologies? It might be something as simple as a new computer operating system that you would have to get used to in addition to taking on the new role.

5. Is the organisation reasonably *laissez-faire*, or does it operate under strict structures and rules? Can you live with either? Could impending changes in the law put your organisation out of business – not because it's doing something wrong, but because it cannot afford to continue operating according to the new regulation and so goes out of business?

6. What is the organisation's philosophy towards First-Line managers, towards their upward challenges and towards keen, enthusiastic newcomers? Welcome or not?

In difficult times when you may just be concerned with holding on to your job, or are keener to secure the promotion than worry about such things, it may be a challenge to question the organisation like this. It might well be that you don't like the answers it generates. In this case you then have the dilemma as to what is most important: your long-term happiness, or your immediate needs. I would certainly not blame you choosing the latter as there are very few of us who can sacrifice needs for an ideology. I would balance this however, with encouragement to take stock every now and again – ask the same questions in 6–12 months' time to establish whether circumstances have changed sufficiently to enable you to return to your original (higher) ideals.

You may want some questions of your own answered. Consider asking them all before accepting the post, rather than when the fur starts flying.

Summary

You have had the opportunity to clarify what is required of a First-Line manager. In particular, fulfilling the role in your organisation or intended organisation. You have been prompted to step back and take a look at that organisation and to assess whether it meets your needs. You have also had the opportunity to identify some of the functions or tasks– as opposed to skills (which we will examine later) that you might like to focus on in your short to medium-term development.

Consider this: What you do, and the amount of time you spend doing it, is directly related to your ability and desire to do it.

There is also a balance to be had between thinking about doing something and actually doing it. You should be excited at the prospect of being the best manager you can be, in the best organisation you could work for. It's often when that euphoria has worn off that reality sets in.

Think ahead, be realistic and rationalise the extent to which you will be allowed by circumstance and the organisation to achieve what you want. In some ways you will be marrying your organisation. Keep in mind the words of Canadian playwright and lecturer, Raymond Hull, "All marriages are happy. It's the living together afterward that causes all the trouble." [13]

To conclude this chapter, please complete the following exercise:

Exercise:

Using your notepad and the section 'Areas for Development'

Make a note now if you wish to work on: building your skills in particular, specific manager functions or balancing the proportion of your time spent on each function in line with your personal and the organisation's needs

There's no need to do anything else at this stage

13   (Hull n.d.)

7. Meeting the challenge

It's time to establish precisely how you intend to meet the challenge of turning your motivation into reality. It's not a 'grand plan', more about your style and approach to the role. Consider how you will address the various challenges of being a First-Line manager. How will you explain your approach to challenge? I will provide some example possible reactions, you should decide which of them are applicable to you.

US baseball umpire Ed Vargo said, "We're supposed to be perfect on our first day on the job and then show constant improvement." You might be unlucky and start the role in an organisation where everyone subscribes to Ed's view. Even if you're fully charged, confident and ready to go, there will probably be something you – or they – have forgotten. There'll be at least one thing that trips you up early on.

That's not necessarily a bad thing if it's handled properly. However, it's neither appropriate nor fair for everyone to expect you to be perfect from the 'off'. Some of your subordinates and some of your managers might 'cut you some slack' during your honeymoon period. Your subordinates might have higher expectations than your boss and vice versa. It's about how you face the challenges that their expectations create.

How challenges are met

Challenge is 'a task or situation that tests someone's abilities'[14]. How you meet them will be determined by your appreciation and understanding of the situation; your knowledge of methods to deal with it – or of methods to find a new way; and your capacity and skills in applying a solution. All these requirements will be affected by your attitude to challenge.

14   *Oxford English Dictionary*

Few of us are apprehensive of, or will refuse to do things we know are not threatening, or which we know to be easy. Martin Luther King Jnr. Said, "The ultimate measure of a man is not where he stands in moments of comfort and convenience, but where he stands at times of challenge and controversy."[15] I'm sure he would have been happy to include women too, but the principle holds true.

I want you to consider your approach. To do so, I have borrowed from the Thomas-Kilmann Conflict Management Inventory[16]. Their work on conflict management styles provides the basis for this chapter. I am paraphrasing Thomas and Kilmann (yes, it's two people) by substituting 'conflict' with 'challenge'. As we're considering 'situations' rather than 'problems', I want you to appreciate that not all challenges necessarily involve conflict, neither does your activity when you choose to confront situations. Not all conflict is bad. It's how you handle it.

Reaction to Challenge

Thomas and Kilmann identify five conflict styles: Accommodating, Avoiding, Collaborating, Competing and Compromising. Some people relish a challenge as an opportunity to do or prove something. Some don't relish conflict, but are comfortable and competent in dealing with it. What about you? How do you react to a challenge or potential conflict?

Maybe you and others see you as the bridge-builder, everyone's friend. You keep the peace and make sure everyone gets on – even if they ultimately fail the task. You do nothing to 'upset the applecart', nor turn your team and colleagues against you. Maybe you don't like clearing the air and discussing a challenge or conflict for fear of damaging relationships.

Perhaps you're the sort of person who withdraws into yourself so as to avoid conflicts or challenging situations? Do you stay away from issues or people whom you perceive will be the cause of such? Have you ever sacrificed what you want for a quiet time, or for the sake of keeping the peace? Have you ever not gone for something as there was no hope of winning?

Maybe you're the one who, because your goals are so important to you, is willing to forego the niceties of relationships. You 'go for the high ground', trying to overpower your opposition and forcing them to accept your

15   (King Jnr 1963)

16   (Kenneth W Thomas 1974)

48

solution. Maybe you'll stop at nothing. You're *the* winner – the one and only! Have you ever thought you'd 'lost' (according to your standards) and so felt weak and inferior? Have you ever caught yourself coercing, threatening, or bribing to get your way?

Alternatively, do you perform a balancing act – matching achievement of your own goals and objectives whilst preserving positive relationships? Can you compromise without being seen as weak; and manage the process of dealing with challenges and conflicts so that both sides gain something? Maybe you promote the 'vanilla' solution and are seen as the one to keep both sides happy whilst still getting the job done. You might even be prepared to give up part of what you want if it's definitely for the greater good.

Finally, you might be the sort who values your own goals and relationships on an equal footing. To you, challenges are problems to be solved – opportunities. You look for solutions that end in 'win-win'. Maybe you look on such situations as a way of actually strengthening and improving relationships. If properly managed, they're a way of clearing the air and reducing problems in them. Do you find yourself with a niggling feeling when you know that a solution doesn't achieve everyone's objectives, restless until you've found it? And what about bad atmospheres in the office when two factions can't agree on the right solution?

Exercise:

Think of a recent occasion involving a challenge to you, your plan or proposal in which you were confronted by complications brought about by others' needs. Were you successful?

In terms of approach to challenge: what approach did you employ and why?

What other approach(es) might have achieved a better outcome and which would you never consider in such circumstances?

A whole industry has developed around the 'science' of management style and, in particular, identifying one's approach to challenge using psychology-based tests. However, unless you really want to complete them, or need the reinforcement that the resulting feedback might provide, why not trust to your own self-assessment? Most of us are sufficiently self-aware that we can recognise in ourselves a pattern of behaviour that we can accept and live with (requiring others to do likewise). We can do something about it if we recognise potentially better alternatives. However, if you're very new to the concepts or process, there is nothing wrong with seeking some reassurance or reinforcement that these tests can provide.

To assess yourself on the 'Thomas-Kilmann inventory', type that into your search engine on the web. Bear in mind that such evaluations are only as good as the information you feed in to them. They only ever provide a snapshot of 'you' at the time you complete them. It would be unwise to act on their results in isolation. Use them as a foundation for investigating further.

Practical Challenge

Putting theory aside, what does your choice to apply a particular approach to challenge mean in practical terms? A lot can depend on the situation. Just as you can apply a different management style to a situation, you can overlay your approach to challenge too.

In some situations it could be appropriate to be prescriptive and/or assertive, taking others' needs into account less than usual. For instance, when quick, decisive action is vital; when it's an important issue and you anticipate the action will be unpopular; when you know you're right and following policy; or maybe when you realise others are taking advantage of your normally easy-going and accommodating nature.

Alternatively, suppose the situation is one in which you have to get the job done, but it's not worth the effort, or potential disruption to be overly assertive; maybe your goals are as important as the other side's, or you need to compromise for the time-being, because a short-term or 'quick-fix' is needed; or maybe you've tried other styles and they just haven't worked. So you choose to hold back from being overly confrontational.

In some cases it could be appropriate to withdraw from the fray and 'live to fight another day'. Maybe it's a trivial matter that you would deal with if you had the time, but you don't. You could realise from the outset that you have little chance of success. The potential damage of what would be for you a successful confrontation outweighs the benefit of doing so.

Passing an issue to someone else – not so emotionally involved, or who is better equipped with knowledge or skill than you – is sometimes a reasonable and responsible thing to do. Backing off a little, or taking yourself out of a situation, could defuse it if there's a personality clash involved. It could be an occasion when it's more important to listen and therefore, to take a stance on the side lines, rather than get embroiled in the mêlée. Finally, it would be OK to withdraw from a particular challenge if you recognised that it was a presenting problem, rather than the core issue and you then addressed the latter.

If you're not normally known for your collaborative skills, you may best be served by developing and using them in circumstances such as those in which you intend to learn something; when you need to get your team engaged in a challenge or situation. Do this by incorporating their concerns and inputs into your solution. Maybe you don't have all the knowledge or resources you need. So you must recognise that others' goals are equally as important as yours and that the situation needs both to be resolved. This may well involve greater negotiation.

In some circumstances the need to build or maintain a relationship might be more important than getting the job done there and then – if at all. If the situation is not particularly urgent then maybe it can be used to build up the networks that you need. Sometimes you might recognise that your objective is not as important as others'. You may share the same objective, but it means more to them than you. You choose to remain involved in the situation. So you're not avoiding or withdrawing. However, care is needed not to do anything that might damage the relationship(s). Alternatively, this style might be adopted if you wanted to give someone else the opportunity to learn from an experience. So you let them take more control. As a tactic for withdrawal, you could also adopt this style if you realise you are being beaten by a better player and you want to minimise the potential damage.

If you rely heavily on a single style, those with whom you're interacting might view a sudden, dramatic shift to one that's very different, with considerable suspicion. So as well as recommending that you are not too extreme with any one style (unless you can handle the response and repercussions), the advice would be to exercise subtle and slight variations as each situation warrants.

No single style is right or wrong 100% of the time, though some can be more appropriate than others in certain types of situation. It's very unlikely that you'll get the chance, or be allowed to deal only with challenges that are appropriate for your particular and predominant style. So if the challenges vary in nature, so should your style. If we're going to use analogies – be a chameleon.

Fear of the Future – Walking the Tightrope

Another thing to consider now is the 'fear of repercussions', what I refer to as a 'fear of the future', and the self-imposed limitations that that fear leads to. This implies that we know the potential risks and the consequences. The alternative – fear of the unknown – is equally limiting.

When we have experienced things ourselves, or seen them happen to others, it's possible to project an outcome onto a similar situation; for instance, most know that fire is dangerous and that it can cause serious damage. So when presented with a fire we tend to know the potential outcomes. Some will be fearful, doing whatever they can to get away from the fire. Others may still be fearful (maybe not to the same degree), but somehow they can control their fear enabling them to confront the fire and if not put it out, minimise the damage.

The first level of management can be likened to walking a tightrope. If the rope is just a few inches off the ground most people will give it a try. They know the consequences of coming off, and that they are unlikely to be too severe. Some may achieve a degree of mastery at that height and seek to raise the rope ever higher. They still know they can fall off. They retain the proficiency of walking the rope. The difference is they deal with the additional psychological pressures that recognising the more severe effects of a fall might bring.

Our attitude to those consequences and the limitations that we ourselves then apply, determine just how high we are prepared to take the rope and go on to make the walk. It's the courage thing! *"Courage is resistance to fear, mastery of fear—not absence of fear."*[17]

How different would it be if we knew for certain that no matter how high the rope, if we were to come off, there would be a great big airbag to catch us to prevent any injury? Unfortunately few of us are afforded that luxury. So you need to consider not only how high you can comfortably take the rope, but also how you are going to deal with the risks of falling

17   (Twain 1894)

off. It's better now to acquire the necessary skills, the appropriate attitude to the risks, and acceptance of all the potential outcomes, rather than having a plan to deal with what happens when we fall off. It's right what they say: prevention is better than cure.

There's a passage in the Bible – Ecclesiastes in the Old Testament[18] – that explains there's a season or time for everything, a time for every purpose. A pop band, the Byrds, penned, "Turn, Turn, Turn" based on the passage. When I hear it I am reminded how readily it illustrates the concept of 'situational management'. It sums up what our approach to challenges could be.

Rather than applying one style or approach every time, we should be analysing the challenge more accurately. What is the situation, and who's involved? What are the time frame, and the objectives? When we have accurate information we can begin picking the most appropriate response. I say that, because the best response may not necessarily be the most appropriate – or possible – at the time. Many factors can preclude it – something we explore later. To heavily paraphrase:

For every challenge there's a style and approach. There's a time to be: creative; a time to use what exists; a time to be a 'starter' and one to join in. There are times to step in and stop, or step in and help. Some occasions you need to dismantle, others to build. Sometimes you have to be serious and others to be fun. It's OK to be sad when something's gone wrong, and to celebrate when it's all gone right.

Some challenges result in parting company; others require you to recruit. There's a time to be distant and a time to draw near. Sometimes it's a time to win, others a time to lose. There's a time to keep and a time to ditch, a time to stay silent and one time to confront. 'Where there's a will there's a way!'

Whatever your preference, or predominant methodology, you may have found that using your tried-and-tested style in a new situation didn't work. This reinforces the need to consider looking for alternative styles and approaches.

18   Ecclesiastes 3-8

Your approach

Exercise:

Having read more about it, note down which one, of the five styles, you think you use most. How do you think they are displayed? What if any reactions have you noticed from those with whom you use it?

Which of the other style (s) do you use from time to time? Which of the other styles might you now attempt and why – what do you think would be the benefits?

If you react to all challenges – regardless of their nature – with the same style it will limit your options. Accepting that a particular style serves us well in some situations more than others opens up alternatives. If you have identified a particular style in yourself that you're using too much, or not enough, or one that's not appropriate to your role and position, make a note now. You will use this information when we're looking at your development plan later.

In Section 2 we will apply your use of particular approaches to challenges when we examine how to **ADDRESS** situations and test any plan you intend to apply. In the meantime please complete the following.

Exercise:

Use your notepad and create a section 'Areas for Development'. Make a note now if you wish to work on:
    a)   Your principal approach to challenge and/or
    b)   Developing your knowledge, understanding and application of other styles in order to have options available to you in differing situations

There's no need to do anything else at this stage.

To paraphrase Martin Luther King, Jr., "The ultimate measure of a manager is not where they stand in moments of comfort and convenience, but where they stand at times of challenge and controversy."

8. What kind of manager do you want to be?

You have some decisions to make: one on the 'style' of manager you wish to be; the other (for now) is about how you wish to be perceived – if indeed you care about that. Both will impact on how you perform in the role, how effective you are and, indeed, what you get out of it. Many taking on the role rarely take the time to establish their style – trusting to luck that something appropriate will develop. So here you have the opportunity to make those decisions based on an understanding of the possibilities available to you and the potential implications of your choice.

I want you to understand what is meant by 'management style' and the various styles available to you. If you wish to consider how others might perceive you and the impact thereof, you can do that too.

I have very vivid memories of one manager who I vowed I would *never* emulate. Unwittingly I became a disciple of Carl Jung who said, "Everything that irritates us about others can lead us to an understanding of ourselves."[19] When it came to being the manager I wanted to be, there wasn't one practitioner in particular whom I felt I could fully emulate. Instead I 'cherry-picked' the attributes and styles I felt comfortable and competent in delivering.

Often it was trial and error. We are all very different; no two situations are ever exactly the same, and the host of parameters and variables mean that what worked for them, sometimes came up short for me when I tried it. That's why I have something of an issue with 'quick-fix' books. As Helen Keller said, "Character cannot be developed in ease and quiet. Only through experience of trial and suffering can the soul be strengthened, ambition inspired, and success achieved." [20]

19   (Jung 1963)

20   (Keller 1938)

It follows that "a *manager* cannot be developed in ease and quiet. Only through experience of trial and suffering can they be strengthened, ambition inspired, and success achieved." That's not to say it should be a painful experience. Rather we must deal openly and honestly with what may be the difficult process of realising and recognising where our current and future abilities lie.

It would be folly to think that you can maintain a single approach to all situations. To be effective you must consider, amongst other things: the nature of the situation; who is involved and their personalities, intentions and objectives; the urgency and importance of the matter; your own abilities, will, objectives and current capacity.

Here we can identify the skeleton framework of the manager you want to be. We'll look to add some muscle and skin later on. It is the core values to which you will return when times are hard, or when you wish to evaluate your performance. It's when you ask yourself, "When I did that, how did it match my values and purpose of being a manager?"

No one is saying that what you've done up to now is wrong. No one is assuming that your concept and perception of what you are or should be, is misplaced. No one is saying you must change! However, if we acknowledge that part of the line manager's role is to assess others and to provide feedback (see managing your team's performance later), is it not right that we have a decent stab at that in respect of ourselves? Once you're comfortable with and confident you've accurately identified your desired manager fundamentals, there's nothing wrong with keeping them. If you're not, why not try something else?

Leading by example?

Leading from the front was *de rigueur* for thousands of years, being demanded of kings and their knights alike – even though it was recognised as the quickest route to an arrow in the eye, or getting your head lopped off. Indeed, they made it easy for the opposition by wearing fantastic outfits and having a banner-waving entourage! Still today, some seek to preserve the gap – distinctions are made between 'blue' and 'white' collars, overalls and suits. Modern popular thinking is that 'we're all in this together'. That being the case, why does it still seem that today there remain so many not-so-hidden distinctions and demarcations?

Our leaders can seem remote, distant and barely recognisable or visible – taking a 'strategic' view. 'Leading from the front' is a euphemism for setting an example. Einstein said, "Setting an example is not the main means of influencing another, it is the only means." You can set an example without sacrificing yourself to the arrows and lances of competition and challenge. If you regularly turn up for work on time, but looking like you've fought the Spartans to get there, how long will it be before your team starts to drift in, wearing what they like? If you are late acting upon their reasonable requests or fulfilling the requirements of your role, why should they get things done on time? If you don't address anti-social or discriminatory behaviour, why should they refrain from displaying it?

What we would recognise as First-Line managers have always been close to the action. In the police we trained for riots in shield teams, the sergeant (First-Line manager) tucked in close behind the front rank, hands on and sometimes physically steering their team whose view was obscured by their shields and/or an assortment of missiles. From this position the sergeant was afforded a marginally better view of things to the front and sides. Of course the more senior you were, the further back you got! Cynicism aside, there was and remains a well-made case for someone to have a strategic overview of what was going on. Quite often there was little time to discuss the niceties of a particular strategy whilst dodging the bricks, bottles and petrol bombs. Those at the sharp end – whilst invariably complaining – seemed adequately resigned to their lot and content to know which piece of ground required taking or holding.

By properly dealing with testing situations, you grow in stature and confidence. Whilst some types of situation are never easy, you have the opportunity – provided you can be self-aware and learn well from past experiences – to become more confident and able to cope with the emotions they engender.

Which approach?

You always – always – have options. In the 1970s John Heron[21] identified six options or 'interventions'. The first three categories are grouped by being authoritative. The next three intervention styles arguably require more careful and skilful application as they go more to the affective or

---

21   (Heron 2001)

'feeling' side of human behaviour. They are grouped together as 'facilitative' interventions.

Depending on the circumstances of the situation and very much on your levels of knowledge skill and will, you can choose to be:

- Prescriptive
- Informative
- Confronting
- Cathartic
- Catalytic
- Supportive

Being prescriptive is a common approach adopted by new and experienced First-Line managers in operational, structured – maybe disciplined hierarchical structures. It lends itself well to urgent situations or those when little time is available. It often involves quick, short communications. The emphasis is on you giving direction (instructions) to those over whom you have power or influence. Some situations may allow you consult and you may, or may not take heed of the results. However, you take the decision and 'prescribe' what others will do as a result.

Those who have high knowledge or expert power base (see earlier) would often find themselves using an 'informative' intervention, though anyone with more or better information might use it. Managers can also use it in situations when they can allocate or delegate tasks to others. Giving the information then allows the others to go off and get on with the task, make their own decisions or solve their own subordinate situations.

Heron recognises that there will be occasions and situations where as a First-Line manager you would be expected to confront issues and individuals. Please don't be lured into the trap of assuming 'confronting' requires any aggression, rather it is the need to challenge and not ignore.

Being 'cathartic' in a situation will result in you prompting and then managing or helping others to express themselves in a way, or about things that they may not previously have done. Alternatively, you are provoking or promoting a particular (re)action on the part of others.

You might find yourself in situations where you need, or are expected to draw out feelings in a more controlled manner. There may be the opportunity for you to support a person or group by allowing them to find the answers from within (assuming that you understand and believe that the answers are there waiting to be found). In such situations you can be the catalyst. This is the chemistry term now often assigned to us humans – as a person that causes change. However, I prefer to be a 'facilitator' of it, because I can create the opportunity, but the outcomes are more dependent on the willingness of the other parties to change.

Cathartic and catalytic interventions can often be made unintentionally. You might say the wrong thing, in the wrong way and/or at the wrong time. You might say the right thing inappropriately or with bad timing. This can provoke a reaction. Such occasions can result in emotional or irrational responses that make communication and subsequent relationships difficult. However, they can also be planned and managed particularly if as a manager, you assess that an air-clearing exercise is required.

Being supportive and/or encouraging team performance is often high on the list of expectations of a manager. Use them as conscious options. You can choose to apply them to particular situations to focus on and recognise a team or an individual's good qualities and achievements. This intervention can also be used to help 'soften the blow' when dealing with perceived negatives.

Like all theories and concepts these interventions have been identified through considerable research. The psychology behind them is fully explained and often argued. I hope not to have done Heron's work a disservice by simplification to illustrate some of the options available to you. Remember these are <u>types</u> of intervention, rather than styles you should adopt. It's more a cause and effect concept and one that you can apply dependent on a situation and with an eye on the outcome you are working towards.

The 'P' test

It's now time to look at how you wish to be perceived. The idea is to match your self-perception with that of your managers', your team's and your peers' so that you don't send out mixed messages. I believe strongly that you should work on 'being' what others see, or alternatively letting others see what (and how good) you really are.

For this there is my 'P' test. Relax! This does not involve you taking a sample to your doctor! I have categorised the manager types using words all starting with the letter 'P' and will explain why and what I mean by each as we progress. There is no scientific basis for the list, just some personal observations as to the different types of manager there can be. They are:

- Popular
- Practical
- Prescriptive
- Passive
- Proactive
- Proficient
- Progressive

It's possible to mix and match dependent upon the situation, but for the purposes of this exercise we're focussing on a predominant type – the one that others will think most of you.

The Popular manager

'Popular' for the right reasons – these have a power base granted by their colleagues – referent power. Being popular has its advantages, but can also cause difficulties.

On the plus side, you can use your popularity to secure ready and quick agreements; colleagues are more likely to accept you at your word; and communications are easier. You can get the team to go the 'extra mile' with minimum effort.

Problems can occur when the popular manager does things that communicate abuse of power: asking others to do the impossible, or more than is possible for instance. They might shy away from difficult actions, decisions or communications for fear of losing their hard-won popularity. This causes future difficulties not only for them, but also for their organisation. It is also not unknown for subordinates to take advantage of such situations by gradually stretching the rules or blurring the requisite boundaries.

The Practical manager

The practical manager may appear to neither know, nor need to know a lot of theory. They may not need long lists, or detailed instructions. They invariably (but not always) have considerable experience of the same type of problems; have used (successfully) a bank of appropriate solutions; and prefer to get on with the job rather than talking about it. They are a healthy mix of activist – seeking out challenges and dealing with the here and now – and pragmatist: one who is down to earth and enjoys problem solving.[22] These classifications were originally applied to learning styles, but they translate readily into one's approach to dealing with situations.

This type of manager possesses a combination of expert knowledge and referent power, especially from subordinates who feel they can always approach this manager for a quick, effective and workable solution.

Being 'practical' does not mean that they take no account of theory. On the contrary it's quite possible that they have learned it, have since built upon it, and have learned how to translate it in their own environment. They can be self-taught and will have learned through 'trial and error' or been successful by being able to transfer a successful solution from one environment into another.

The Prescriptive manager

The prescriptive manager is comfortable working in environments where they can make, apply and enforce rules, processes and procedures. They may not have an answer for everything, but will tell you it's 'their way or the highway'. Being prescriptive is different to being directive.

The former not only tells what is needed, but how, when and why and in the manner 'prescribed'. They are prone to get emotional when others do not comply.

On the plus side, individuals usually know where they stand and exactly what is required of them as a goal. On the negative side, they may not know the fine detail and how things are to be achieved. They will also have little opportunity to develop themselves.

The Passive manager

The 'passive', or the *laissez-faire* manager leaves others to their own devices or situations to resolve themselves. Some believe that if you leave things alone for long enough they'll put themselves right. However, doing

22   (Peter Honey n.d.)

so is unlikely to endear yourself to your subordinates if they're looking for your guidance and leadership. Neither would your bosses be too impressed.

Some situations benefit from the team being allowed some room to move, especially if they are keen and/or would benefit from using the situation as an opportunity for development, but this is conditional. Both you and they need the correct skills and abilities; there needs to be trust on both sides and you need to be confident that this is the most appropriate way to run the task. Properly managed this can also free up some of your time to address other requirements.

If you use this approach too often though, your team might be asking why they need you and your manager might be asking what it is you do with your time. In the same way that if you throw some of the best musicians in the world into an orchestra pit, they still need a conductor to get them to work effectively together, you still need to maintain control. Being 'passive' or *laissez-faire* suggests that you relinquish that.

The Proactive manager

The proactive manager recognises a situation, acknowledges it, and addresses it. Maybe it's an opportunity for improvement or a problem that should not be ignored. Rather than moving swiftly on, they **ADDRESS** the issue [see Section 2]. Having recognised and acknowledged the situation exists, or is likely to exist, they take responsibility for doing something about it and proceed to take some positive action. This applies equally to crises, non-crises and opportunities. It is a habit that gets them recognised for initiating change and action, rather than waiting for others to. Someone who is not proactive should not necessarily be considered lazy or inactive. It's just that they may be more comfortable and effective being 'reactive'. It is for the organisation to determine which it wants, and for you to work to what is required.

The Proficient manager

The proficient manager doesn't have to be popular. Their power is based on their knowledge and expertise in its usage. They demonstrate proficiency in what is required of them mentally as well as physically in contrast to those who claim to think a lot; claim a lot, but actually do very little or what they actually do, is sub expectation.

The proficient manager is distinguished from the practical manager because the latter may come up with practical if not necessarily totally correct solutions. I prefer the term proficient to 'professional' as the latter is an abstract label applied to individuals we deem to be the former, and who act in accordance with what is expected. Someone who has passed a series of examinations to have post-nominals could be assumed and regarded as a 'professional', but go on to behave in a manner that is far from it. This is especially true of those relying on old qualifications and those who have failed to keep themselves refreshed and up-to-date

Most managers will express their desire to be a *proficient* manager. Many seem to expect this to happen by accident or default. Others think the environment and opportunity has to be created by others and/or their organisation. Others recognise that it is not a 'given', but are unsure about how to get there. Of all the 'Ps' to aim for 'proficient' is the one you should work towards. If you can be this it encompasses the positives of all the other manager types.

The Progressive manager

Somewhat akin to the proactive manager, but distinct in so far as they create the change or opportunity, rather than anticipating it. They are innovators, inventors and initiators. They spend a significant proportion of their time seeking to make things better, more efficient, more profitable. In new, young and high-tech businesses this is a veritable necessity. In well established, highly disciplined or structured and hierarchical organisations the progressive manager can be viewed with suspicion, a nuisance or even a threat as they are meddling with the status quo.

The principal benefit for this type of manager is the growth in themselves, their teams and their organisation. On the downside they can suffer frustration, stress and unpopularity if their environment does not support such a style.

There is another 'P', but I have not chosen to include it in the list of what you can be as a trait as it is more of a feeling. That is to be a 'proud' manager. It is a remarkable thing if you can clock off each day with a feeling of pride. Regardless of the type of manager you choose to be; the style you choose to apply; or the outcomes you achieve – you do so knowing you did all that could be reasonably be expected of you in the circumstances. I'm not talking misplaced pride – the type that comes before a fall – but of a sense of achievement, what Maslow calls 'self actualisation'.

Exercise:

(a) Consider the type of manager you are, or want to be. Do you display traits of one in particular? Is that appropriate? Would you benefit from developing your current style or moving to another? Make notes
(b) What do you need to do in order to display 'proficiency' in the role?

Summary

In this chapter you have had opportunity to examine more possibilities for building on your style of management, whether it's using one or more of the six available categories of intervention or choosing to adopt a particular approach to the situation.

To paraphrase Leon Trotsky, "proficiency is noticed most markedly in those who have not mastered it". Unless you're exceptionally gifted and very lucky, it is also something to which you must apply yourself constantly to stop the bad habits creeping in and to keep up with what's new.

9. What are you good at?

We're almost there – deciding whether the role of manager is right for you and you for it. Here you can assess yourself against criteria I consider essential for effective performance in the role. The intention is that you will produce a self-assessment in which you identify whether there are any gaps between where you are now and where you might like to be. It will also steer you to the appropriate areas in Section 2 to help you in addressing them.

We tend to know what we're good, or not so good at, because we've had a go at it. Some will put the 'not-so-good' to one side and leave it there. Others will keep trying – using different approaches or more effort – until they are good at it.

Then there are the things we don't know we can do because we've never given them a try. This could be because of a lack of opportunity, or some innate fear of doing so. Again, some of us will put off trying. The adventurous will jump in and give it a whirl. Remember the tightrope thing?

Completing an honest self-assessment will highlight the areas that you might benefit from developing. Benjamin Disraeli one of Queen Victoria's Prime Ministers once said "to be conscious that you are ignorant is a great step to knowledge."

In addition you can choose to seek some assessment from those you know and trust to get another perspective. The greater the detail in your picture now, the more likely it is you will be able to target and focus your future activity to the greatest effect.

So are you up for it? Do you have what it takes? I'm now going to pose a series of questions. These are criteria against which I believe the First-Line manager should be assessed. They are distinct from any task or job-related criteria that your organisation applies. The questions relate to your ongoing approach to the role, but can equally be applied to specific tasks you manage. There are 16 questions and I would suggest you need at least two hours to complete them.

1. (a) To what extent do you know and understand the aims and objectives of your organisation, your area or department, your team? You might be able to recite them 'off by heart', but do you *know* them? Why are they as they are, how do they fit together, what would achievement of them look like?

    (b) How would you answer your team's questions about why they're doing something you ask?

    [See 'Knowing your STUFF' in Section 2]

2. To what extent do you know and understand what it is you are expected to produce?

    You are there to ensure your team performs to the extent and standards required by the organisation, but what tops the list? Does the organisation demand a 'happy', sick-day-free team, full of 'self-starters' and serving as a talent pool? Are you expected to develop your team's skills? If so, how do you do that.

    [See 'Knowing your STUFF in Section 2]

3. (a) What do you know about problem solving? Do you work to a tried-and tested methodology for approaching problems and if so what is it? What difficulties do you encounter in applying the model fully? Do your bosses always support your decisions? Are they understood and complied with by your team? How often are your decisions modified or reversed after implementation?

    (b) Do you deal with problems and their causes or pass them around?

    [See 'The ADDRESS model' and 'Knowing your STUFF' in Section 2]

4. How good are you at controlling?

    a) How do you ensure your decisions are complied with? How do you know what the outcomes are and whether your intervention has led to success?

b) To what extent do you manage encounters and meetings so ensuring they have your desired outcome as part of or in addition to the original purpose?

c) Who's rightly spending more time on a task – you or 'them'?

[See 'The ADDRESS model' and 'Knowing your STUFF' & 'Have a CRAFT-T plan' in Section 2]

5. To what extent are you engaged in the processes of your organisation?

a) How committed are you to achieving the organisation's goals, or are you there for other reasons?

b) How much effort are you putting into achieving the organisation's goals? Your own goals? Are you putting in more or less than is required or expected? Are you putting in more than others in a comparable role with different outcomes?

c) To what extent do you take responsibility for what goes on in your work area? Is it shared between you and others upwards or sideways? Who is accountable?

d) What are the benefits to you of completing particular tasks? To others involved?

[See 'Knowing your STUFF' Section 2 & 'Establish yourself' Section 3]

6. How adaptable are you?

a) How willing and able are you to recognise that 'Plan A' won't work or isn't working?

b) How brave are you to switch to an alternative even if it's not your suggestion?

c) How good are you at making quick, sound decisions in the face of fast-paced changes?

d) How do you react to honest, open and accurate feedback?

[See 'The ADDRESS Model' and 'Knowing Your STUFF' & 'Have a CRAFT-T Plan' Section 2]

7. What are your powers of persuasion like – what do you do if your team isn't convinced?

a) How good are you at putting things in context, and translating messages from above into language that your team can accept?

b) How good are you at clearly defining standards, expectations and the benefits of achieving them?

[See 'Manage every encounter' & 'Communicate, communicate, communicate' – Section 3]

8. How good a listener are you? Do you create a suitable environment to be able to get the best information? Can you see behind the words, the emotion, and get the actual message?

[See 'Communicate, communicate, communicate' & 'Watch, listen, feel' Section 3]

9. How good are your relationships with those with whom you work?

a) How many of your relationships exist just because they have to? How many people are dependent on you or you on them? How does dependency affect the relationship? What happens to your relationships when they're tested? Are they strong enough to survive?
b) Do you need to change the standing and nature of some relationships e.g. putting greater distance or formality into them?
c) Do you need to establish some new relationships if so, how good are you at doing that?

[See 'Friend or friendly?', 'Manage every encounter' 'It's OK to be selfish' Section 3]

10. How are you with trusting those in your team and how is that evident? To what extent does your team trust you and how does that show?

[See 'How's your trust meter?' Section 3]

11. What are you prepared to sacrifice for success?

a) You may not need to sacrifice anything, but what about social life and the quality of relationships outside work?
b) Are you prepared, willing and able to sacrifice some of the closeness you had with former colleagues?
c) To what extent would you give up previous views or attitudes?

[See 'It's OK to be selfish' and 'Get a punch bag!' Section 3]

12. How resilient are you? Most of us can deal with the odd knock-back or challenge, but how about when they're coming in threes and fours, from above and below, from inside and out?

a) What processes if any do you have in place to help you deal with any pressure you might encounter?

b) How willing are you to stick to a course of action you absolutely know to be right?

[See 'Remember & persevere' Section 3]

13. How do you deal with rejection, i.e. what do you do when your boss turns down a suggestion or a request or your team doesn't want to comply?

[See 'The ADDRESS model' & 'Have a CRAFT-T plan'
Section 2 and 'Remember & persevere' Section 3]

14. How well do you manage your feelings – do you let it all flood out or can you suppress your true feelings in order to manage a situation?

a) Do you side with the team (implicitly or explicitly) in order to try and make a policy, process or change more palatable?

b) Do you not challenge even though you should, because of your personal take on a situation?

[See 'It's OK to be selfish' and 'Get a punch bag!' Section 3]

15. Are you competent in the role(s) of your subordinates? How well do you know and understand your team members' jobs? Can you do them?

[See 'Know your STUFF!' Section 2]

16. What do you still need to learn or become competent at?

a) Now that you've completed questions 1-15, are you perfect, or do you need to develop some areas? Even if you don't need to, could you become even better if you took on some personal development?

b) Is there anything I've missed?

The qualities being investigated are necessary for you to perform well in the First-Line manager role. There may be more. Some may be more appropriate to your role than others, some not at all. Your (honest) answers will serve to highlight any areas in which you might want to develop.

Consider this: A novice playing a Stradivarius still sounds like a novice.

It won't make them play or sound any better. It will just make them feel good! However, someone with talent, who's taken the time, the pain, and made the effort to become a maestro, will make the instrument – and their heart – sing. Getting there takes application and effort. Tools alone are not enough.

Before progressing to the next chapter please complete the following exercise:

Exercise:

Using your notepad and the section 'Areas for Development' make a note now as to which, if any, of the manager qualities you feel you would benefit from developing on and why.

10. Becoming a manager

If the previous chapters have highlighted some development needs for you, we now consider how you structure and plan a route and activity to achieve personal goals within the role. You have examined why you want the role, the challenges it poses, and it has prompted you to think about the kind of manager you want to be. In this chapter you will not get a solution to every problem, but a framework for planning your development.

What is involved in managing your own and others' development? There is of course 'good practice' and well-tried formats you may follow. To start, you need to understand the purpose of a development plan; know and be able to explain the elements and sequence of a development planning process; and create a **CRAFT-T** (development) plan (see later) to address any development needs you know of now or acquire as you progress.

I know of very few stand-alone learning interventions that you can enter one end and exit the other, fully prepared and ready to be expert practitioners of the content. There has to be subsequent structured application and practice of what has been taught. The same is true of trying to complete '*you*', the manager you want to be. Too often the First-Line manager lands the role and is then left largely to his or her own devices.

Normally we talk of development being needed and addressed in one of five areas: Knowledge, Understanding, Skills, Attitudes and Behaviours. Please get familiar with these. I will be referring to them collectively as KUSAB from now on. Below is one version of how to create a development plan. It follows a cycle:

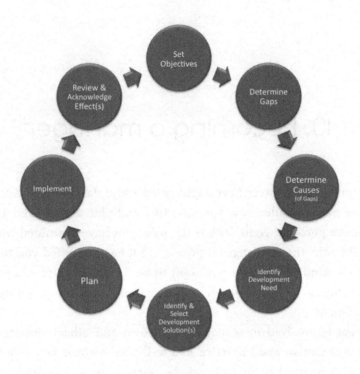

Figure 1: The Development Planning Cycle

The first step is to set **CRAFT-T** objectives for you. By that I mean objectives that are Clear, Relevant, Acceptable, Feasible, Targeted and Time-Bound. You need to be clear on what it is you intend to achieve. Examples might be:

1. In an organisation where you are expected to perform to and are assessed against defined competencies:
    By the end of the financial year my objective is to acquire the Knowledge, Understanding, Skills and Ability in order to display Level 3 Competency in the skill of Analysis and Problem-Solving
2. For an agent in a call centre where there are service level agreements and average call handling times newly out of initial training:
    Within four weeks to be operating consistently and fully with the service level agreement for number of calls per hour, whilst maintaining call quality to the required standard

In relation to specific areas and objectives, step 2 requires you to identify the gap. What is your current level of competence vs. that intended or desired? Very simply: this could be the difference between operating at Level 2 in a particular competency and your intention to perform at Level 3 in it.

In step 3 you determine what is causing the gap(s). It could be you lack a piece of equipment, or you might need to be working in another department or another location – or for someone else! On the other hand it could be that you need new knowledge or a new skill. If it's a 'non-development' cause, you should step out of the development process There are alternative processes that address those more effectively. If the gap is caused by a need for some form of KUSAB development, you move on to the next step.

Step 4 allows you identify exactly what it is you need to develop – is it more knowledge, better understanding, a greater degree of existing skill, or new skills? Do you need to modify an attitude or set of behaviours?

Step 5 is the solution stage. This is where many slip into the trap that 'development need' equals 'classroom-based course'. It doesn't! There is a host of alternatives that can be more suitable to your preferred way of learning; more effective in getting the job done; more cost effective in terms of time and money – for you and your organisation. Examples might be any one or a combination of:

- Observing or shadowing a proficient colleague
- Doing some private research or reading in a library or via the internet
- E-learning or web-based courses
- Coaching
- Being mentored
- It might just be an advice session with an expert
- Learning by doing
- (Or yes) attending a formal classroom-based course

In addition to having set **CRAFT-T** objectives, step 6 requires you to put together a **CRAFT-T** action plan that reflects stages 1, 4 and 5 and goes on to describe *how* you will carry out the development and how achievement will be measured. The latter might be by feedback, or by passing an assessment or examination. If using a combination of solutions, it is important that you apply them in a logical progression, especially if you have to move from simple to complex levels of knowledge and understanding. It is important that you now define what success will look like. You should also set yourself a time limit or target date for achievement.

Step 7: Go ahead and do it! Put your plan into action. You need to be proactive and to be the initiator. You cannot afford to trust to luck and/or expect others to be the driving force behind your development.

Step 8 occurs at the end of the time limit you set yourself in step 6. There is nothing to prevent you having smaller reviews along the way. These can help to keep you on track, refocus or determine whether circumstances have changed rendering the plan no longer effective. It is very important that this specific review takes place. It establishes whether there has been success – in which case celebrate – or whether some further (new) activity is required.

All you're trying to do is get to the stage with any piece of development, where you can apply it readily, easily and almost automatically. I would say "without thinking"; however, I don't want you to stop being conscious of what should go into particular situations. Following the process moves you from unconscious or conscious incompetence to at the very least conscious competence, but hopefully unconscious competence. This progression is often referred to in learning circles, but it's far from rocket science.

It would be beneficial if you could expertly apply a framework unconsciously – only having to consciously insert relevant content into each section. Take the example of cake baking: my mom makes the most perfect fruitcake and I aspire to be able to do likewise, though after many attempts, I'm still trying to get mine to turn out the same way.

At first I had no clue how she made them. All I knew was she mixed a load of stuff, put it in a tin, threw it in the oven and hey presto! I was 'unconsciously incompetent'. Having taken some time to watch her in action, I realised there was a lot more to it (even though she made it look easy). I was 'consciously incompetent'. I now knew what was involved and knew I couldn't do it (yet). So I persuaded her to release the recipe – from where it had been in hiding for years. Then I set about having a go following the recipe to the letter and weighing ingredients precisely. My first attempts weren't half-bad – not as good as mum's but not half-bad. So I put myself down at the lower end of 'conscious competence'. All I need now is to be able to practise until I can turn them out like hers and ultimately to do it like she does –– with 'unconscious competence.' Here's a practical exercise by way of illustration:

Exercise:

Read the set of circumstances below. If you determine it is a development situation, apply the development planning cycle. If you decide it's a discipline issue, note the action you would take.

Situation:

Mary is a full-time agent in a call centre. She has been working for the organisation for four years. She underwent full induction and training to competence and has attended all the required 'top up', refresher and new technology training. Mary has never expressed a desire to 'move up' in the organisation.

Mary is achieving the required number of cases per hour. However, recent call audits have indicated that she is sometimes curt with callers and seems to assume they know as much about products as she does. This seems to be a recent phenomenon.

When faced with a situation like this, new managers often go straight from 'problem' to 'solution'. That solution invariably being that the underperformer must need 'training'! This bypasses the process and runs the risk of not sorting the core issue. This is then compounded saying, "Mary needs training – she'll have to go on the 'X' course." So not only do we lose Mary from the business for the duration of the course, it might not even be appropriate in the first place!

The situation with Mary is, and will always be, one of performance. Mary is required to perform to published standards and in line with her job description (objective). She is not dealing with customers in accordance with organisational requirements (gap).

No doubt many of you considered the cause might be a problem at work or at home After all, she has been fully and properly trained, was previously meeting the standard, and the glitch is recent. However, it is still at this stage a performance issue.

You would hopefully be doing some investigating to find the causes. It is vital you do so accurately, as this determines all subsequent activity.

It could be that Mary had just lost her edge; she feels bored, or lacks challenge. In which case the first could be to tell her to get on with it, pull her socks up. At the same time, make her aware of the consequences of not doing so. There is no development need. You would exit the development planning cycle in favour of a performance-related action plan (still **CRAFT-T**).

It could be a welfare issue. In which case there is a second option: option 2: deal with that. Still no development planning, but again you might create and agree some form of action plan.

There might be something wrong with Mary's equipment – her headset, her touch screen, her screen set up. Option 3: get the 'techies' in to fix it.

If you discover that in fact Mary was OK in simulated environments, or when taking calls with a 'buddy' on hand, but got increasingly nervous if the caller asked too many complex questions, then there's option 4. There is clearly a development need and you would therefore continue on the development planning cycle to identify what was causing these nerves and then see what solution options were available.

If you take nothing else from this chapter, remember that not all situations can or should be solved by 'training'; and that not all training involves yanking your subjects out of the workplace into the (sometimes alien) classroom environment. How do you prefer to learn? Why should they be any different in terms of wanting to learn in a different way or at a different pace (faster or slower) than others in the same position?

Previously you were prompted to list areas for development relating to any functions, activities or challenges that you face as a First-Line manager. If you have none, then feel free to move on. Otherwise it's time for you to create a development plan for yourself.

Your list of what you wish to develop and why (created earlier), forms the basis of this process. If you have quite a long list of needs, I suggest you go through it and rate the components in order of importance. Which are the most important to you (and your role)? Where are the most glaring 'gaps'? Which of the items on your list would make your life in the role more effective, less hard work and more enjoyable? Then pick the top/major three – we don't want this to seem like a very steep mountain! Put each 'need' at the top of a separate A4 sheet of paper.

Clarify how you are going to measure your progress and from where you are going to get your evidence; for instance, are you going to rely on self-awareness and self-assessment? Or will you identify some individuals around you to provide you with feedback? Is there some form of test or assessment you can take?

How are you going to document and use any evidence of or for continued development? I recommend the maintenance of a diary. One in which you note down significant events one side of a sheet and what you did and what the outcomes were on the other. You can include an assessment of how effective your activity was. You can add the anecdotal comments of your peers or others from whom you seek the feedback. There is a definite kick from later revisiting such a diary; reading what you were like at the start, and then noting the progress made.

Subsequent chapters provide a mixture of models and suggestions that you can apply in your role. Working through them you might find that you want to use them but there is a gap because they are new. Use development planning to structure how you gain proficiency and/or unconscious competence in their use.

It's possible you have the potential to be the best First-Line manager ever. If not be the best you can be. If that makes you better than some, but not quite so good as others then so be it!

To paraphrase motivational speaker Earl Nightingale, "picture yourself in your mind's eye as having already achieved your objectives. See yourself doing the things you'll be doing… " And remember that it's up to you to take the responsibility for being the best manager you can be.

It's now time for you to build your own development plan by completing the exercise on the next page. Complete the exercise for each of the three main development areas you identified earlier.

Exercise:

Identify your specific objective(s). What do you intend to achieve? E.g. this might be the ability to use a piece of equipment or application to a recognised level.

What will be the measure of achievement e.g. passing an assessment? Detail how you are going to measure and monitor progress

How will your colleagues react? What will you need to do to bring them on board and/or help you?

What resources are needed, e.g. time, sponsorship, money, a coach, Internet access, etc.? Where are these resources to be found, how much of each is needed, are they available? Are there options?

Set a start date. Does development need to be broken down into manageable stages? Note the proposed duration and completion dates. List in sequence the necessary activities, e.g. getting permission, securing funding/equipment, attending an event etc.

Consider alternatives – what's most appropriate for you and your preferred way of learning?

Can the same plan or part thereof be used to address other areas for development at the same time? There's nothing like 'killing two birds with one stone'!

Leave the plan for a day or two then revisit it and check that the plan is sufficiently clear, targets the need and given the availability of resources etc., is feasible.

Now you can either put commencement on hold until you've completed the relevant chapters in Section 2, or if you're comfortable and eager to do so, start right away on your plans.

Intermission

I have called an intermission here, because – if you haven't already – I recommend you take a break before proceeding. This is for two reasons:

Primarily so that you can re-visit your action plan and confirm it is appropriate. Maybe share it with close colleagues or your manager to get their views as to how **CRAFT-T** (or SMART) it is. Also applying yourself fully to the process will have required a fair degree of concentration and hard work. You might even be working your way through your plan.

Section 1 prompted you to examine your motivation for wanting or continuing to be a First-Line manager. It gave you an opportunity to build up a comprehensive body of evidence as to your current capacity and capabilities to carry out the functions normally required of the role. This is 'feedback', whether from yourself or others, it matters not. Feedback can be solicited – as here – or not; it can be expected, or not; and it can be positive, or not. I discuss the giving of feedback in some detail in Chapter 18 later. However, I'd like to take some time now to look at feedback because you will need it to support *your* development.

Ironically the feedback process involves stages not unlike those identified in the bereavement process identified and explained by Dr Elisabeth Kübler-Ross[23]. The stages she identified are: denial, anger, bargaining, depression, and acceptance. Whatever you do, please don't proceed with the idea that feedback is something horrid that should be avoided.

Denial is probably easy to recognise – and common in those who receive negative feedback delivered in the wrong way. How many times have we seen award winners gush that they "Can't believe it!" or 'So-and-so' deserved it much more than they did? Regardless of the volume and strength of the evidence that supports a particular piece of feedback, we potentially may

23   (Kübler-Ross 2014)

not like it and so choose to write it off; attack the messenger; or deny that the provider understood what really happened. This is denial.

Whilst we wouldn't normally associate 'anger' with positive feedback, it has been known to come unexpectedly and therefore, as a shock. We can easily associate anger with negative feedback. We could be angry with ourselves because the feedback is accurate and we realise we have let ourselves down (and maybe others too). We could be angry that even though the feedback is accurate, it did not take everything into account, or was delivered badly.

Bargaining often occurs in feedback situations when the recipient realises that 'the game is up'. It accompanies a realisation that things cannot be the same in future. They will test just to see how far they can continue doing all or some of the things they used to, whilst at the same time questioning and trying to negotiate how much of the remedy they actually have to take.

Even when positive outcomes are identified and agreed, the feedback recipient might continue to hanker after the 'good old days' when they could do anything as they chose. This is closely linked to the 'bargaining' stage, as there is a realisation that some effort is going to be required. Those who positively solicit and welcome constructive, well-timed and accurate feedback are much less likely to encounter this particular phase, but as a First-Line manager and as someone who is going through a developmental process it helps if you can recognise if this is happening to you or others.

Finally we achieve – what is hopefully – willing (rather than reluctant) acceptance of the feedback. The arguments and evidence have been presented well, received in the right attitude, and recognised as being of benefit. Once this stage has been achieved the feedback recipient – in this instance YOU – can get on and do something with it.

The stages can apply equally to very good positive feedback as they do to negative feedback or what we tend (wrongly) to call criticism.

Feedback can prompt you to **ADDRESS** a situation and if you wish, then to do something about it. A lot depends on the context, content and delivery method and style of the particular feedback – something that along with what it means to **ADDRESS** a situation is discussed in Section 2.

I hope you do not find the process of identifying areas for development too threatening and have emerged from it with some clearly identified areas for you to focus on. Once you have learned about **ADDRESS** you will see that the stages described above fall into the 'A' section, but more of that later.

In Sections 2 and 3 you have the opportunity to examine different approaches. Chapters are linked to one or more of the sixteen self-assessment questions you addressed in Section 1. As indicated there, some of the questions are addressed in more than one chapter.

The purpose is to provide you with a sound foundation. For those of you who have held the role for a while, you can look at these as extensions; though consider whether you need to check your foundations too. You might also be prompted to use the ideas to underpin or amend that which you have built up as your experience accumulated.

I recommend that you read the first two chapters of Section 2 first and in sequence. Thereafter, feel free to pick and choose the ones you wish to explore in whatever sequence you wish. This is because the **ADDRESS Model** is a format for framing all the types of situation you might encounter. The models add support and refer constantly to it. Remember these are intended as foundation pieces and sound buildings rarely survive with large sections of the foundations missing – by design or default.

In the absence of considerable knowledge of you, your knowledge skills and abilities I would never be so presumptuous as to *tell* you what to do. Neither should you contemplate applying anything you read without testing it against what you (and sometimes others) know of your knowledge, skill and capacity to do so.

It's also appropriate that you get into the habit of referring to a framework (even if it's not mine). I could fill another book with different minor variations on a core theme, describing *ad nausea* how the wrong word here, or a different objective there, might generate a different outcome. In preference though, you will be encouraged to take what are offered as frameworks so that you can have structure, maintain control and importantly, minimise the risk of forgetting something important.

Whether a situation is planned or unforeseen, you will benefit from being in as much control of it as possible. For that reason, having a framework that you can work through without thinking (eventually) will help you to manage each situation and maximise the potential for a positive, effective outcome.

The beauty of this approach is that it also allows you to personalise it to yourself and add your own environmental factors. Another good reason for considering all the elements of a relevant framework is that it moderates our tendency to go straight to a preferred solution. This might be one that we are comfortable with, even though it might not be the optimum solution to the particular situation we are faced with.

There are a number of dangers involved in not following a decent framework or model:

1. Not doing so introduces a risk of bypassing the best solution, via the line of least resistance to the easiest. This could be because of our lack of knowledge of facts, solution options, or a good selection process. Even if we do follow process correctly, we might be tempted not to pursue the optimum solution it warrants because we are fearful of some of the outcomes that implementation of the solution might generate.

2. Once we have embarked upon a particular course without following a sensible framework there is a danger that we will stick to a particular solution even when we recognise that it is no longer working as we anticipated, or it is generating some unforeseen undesirable outcomes.

3. Failing to apply the 'review' stage of a process or framework can also lead to us making the same mistakes and having the same unwanted outcomes over and over again.

4. There is a danger of us becoming 'a one-trick pony', only ever having one solution regardless of varying circumstances. This in turn can lead to us being second-guessed by our team or peers who, anticipating our response, but not being in possession of all the facts, as we know them, will go off and do their own thing. This can have disastrous, or less than intended results. In the long term, they could get to know your response so well that they even cease bothering to consult with you. Ultimately you become insignificant to them and unnecessary to the organisation.

5. There is a danger of stepping back too far and not continuing to control and manage the solution by being close enough to be able to make adjustments whenever and wherever necessary.

As we shall see later there is a need for us to know our **STUFF** and knowing what alternatives may exist. You should endeavour to take advantages of the opportunities this offers in terms of building a bank of experiences and in particular, a bank of proven adaptable solutions. We should never be so proud as to discount a good solution that we borrow from others; regardless of whether they are our seniors or subordinates. The more reflection and learning you can take from them, the more resources will be available to you. Rather than having to search for original solutions, time and effort will be saved because you will have a bank of solutions that you can pick and apply with or without some adjustment to meet the current need.

The example situations used in Sections 2 and 3 all happened. The characters however, have been made anonymous. I confess to having been involved in all of them. They span a good cross-section of industry sectors and for that matter time periods. Whilst times, society and people do indeed change, the broad variety of situation that First-Line managers encounter does not. I would also argue that the basic need for an appropriate attitude and high degree of will on the part of the individual to take on the position doesn't change either.

I am not saying, "Do this and all will be right in the world." Instead, I have outlined some real situations that prompted me to consider and evaluate some principles for good performance in the role. What I *am* saying is, "These have worked for me. You might like to give them a try." They may not be precisely what you think you need. I would be surprised if they were, coming as they do straight off the shelf. If, however, you like the basic idea, but think it needs some 'tweaking' for it to work for you, I am more than content for you to do so. I can't *make* you a good First-Line manager and I cannot hope to cover off every concept and eventuality, but I can offer some suggestions – I stress *suggestions* – for you to try.

Very often one model will address more than one development area or competency. This is often more appropriate where the competencies are closely aligned. Models are based on my experiences and so, unless otherwise stated, are not scientifically proven. They provide a framework. Then I will add some muscle and flesh that I will support by the use of case studies and the setting of some tasks for you.

Chapters can be read independently and the models described used on a 'stand-alone' basis. Feel free to take as long as you like over them. If you are seeking to deal with something that's deep-rooted do not expect overnight improvements.

Some ideas may be easier to grasp and apply, for others this is not so easy. After all, all things are difficult before they become easy. If you have decided to address some fundamental personality traits, or beliefs, it will be testing for you. Because you are in charge and control, it should never be painful. Keep some clear, feasible objectives from the outset. If it does get difficult, get into the habit of reminding yourself how good you will feel when you prove successful.

SECTION 2
Models, Solutions & Systems

Anyone who asserts that there is a finite number of steps you can take, or things you must do to succeed as a manager is often thinking more of selling their theory. Pick the right tool for the job. After all, you don't build a house with a pocketknife.

11. Introduction

The aim of this section is to examine and develop your perception of 'situations' and how to deal with them. I want to introduce a framework methodology that can be readily applied to any situation faced by First-Line managers. I also want to give you some other aids to ensure you achieve the ultimate resolution. Here is what you will be examining:

- The **ADDRESS Model** of situation management and how to identify and explain various types and sources of situations
- Knowing your **STUFF** – an aide-mémoire for ensuring you get your facts right
- Applying the **TOP DRAWER** test to potential solutions in order to select the best one
- How to ensure your solution is applied effectively with good planning and application of **CRAFT-T** planning
- How to exercise **CONTROL** once you start to apply your solution
- How to manage all types of formal and informal meetings by applying the **REASON** model
- How to provide effective feedback on performance to team members using the model **A CHEAT'S** guide to feedback.

Each concept comes with an explanation of each of their stages and requirements. For instance, how to identify the type of situation you are encountering and its source. I have included case studies and exercises for you to practise using the models.

I repeat my encouragement for you to believe and understand that not all situations are problems, and that not all problems are bad.

12. The ADDRESS model

A long time ago I was introduced to the 'Problem-Solving Cycle'. It's simple, and for many years I found it useful. Later, as a trainer, I was encouraging others to use it, when I noticed that the title often induced some negativity. Many students and managers associated the word 'problem' with negativity. The fact that problems can also be opportunities is all-too-often lost. So I searched for an alternative, not to reinvent the wheel, but to aid others' understanding and application.

It's vital that in every situation you set out with a clear goal or destination. If you are not clear on your objective, no one else will be; and it is unlikely that any plan you devise or implement will be accurate enough. Similarly, as in any journey, there has to be a start point. If you know these two things, you know the gap that has to be bridged. It doesn't really matter if you intend to take a different route or use a different method than someone else to do so.

Example: If your new role means that you have to visit remote locations to visit sites or supervise your team, you might need to be able to drive. You've had a few lessons, but need to pass your test to be legally qualified to do so. At present all you are capable of is a bit of steering and you know where all the controls are, but gear changing smoothly (manual car, sorry) remains a 'black art'. By identifying what you *can* do, you have created a start point. You can also see the gaps in your skills that need to be bridged. You may have to break it down to bite-sized sessions, or your tutor – if you go down that route – might do it for you. In any event you have a situation, a start point and a goal.

The first thing I had to do was lose the 'problem' word. My alternative word is 'situation'. It's chosen partly for its neutrality and partly because it lends itself to the subsequent methodology I will be promoting. So from now on get used to me referring to 'situations'.

Next, I identified the elements I needed to recall when facing situations and also that I wanted to keep it positive. When forming a mnemonic it's always good to have a word that is related to the issue it is meant to remind us of. The word 'resolve' as in 'resolving the situation' surfaced very readily. However, I took the view this continued the negative connotation. So I sought something less negative.

Using the analogy of reaching a destination or goal led me to the word **A-D-D-R-E-S-S.** So it was that the **ADDRESS** Model for dealing with 'situations' was created. It can be readily linked with 'delivering' something – a solution or result. It can also encourage the frame of mind of getting to a location, or standard that you need or want to be at. As you think about it you are also reminded that whilst remaining responsible, you might not have to implement the final overall solution. It is something you can 'send' to others – a bit like what I am doing now with the concept.

Figure two illustrates the model. Note that it is not in 'cycle' format. We need to acknowledge that, as good as we might become at resolving situations, there will be those when the optimum solution is not achieved and so we might have to revisit it and revise our approach. This would mean starting the cycle over.

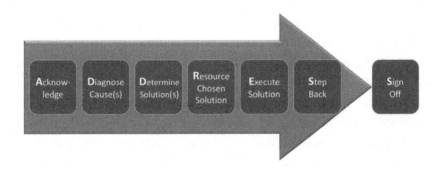

Figure 2: The ADDRESS Model

- **Acknowledgement** is recognising a situation exists AND deciding or agreeing (with yourself) to do something about it, whether this is to proceed yourself, or to plan to hand it over to someone else

It's a 'must' that you first **Acknowledge** that there is a situation that requires your attention. I say '*your* attention' because even if control of the situation is ultimately passed on or around, you will still be involved and must therefore still give it your resource.

You'll examine the influences on this stage and how it might be completed later in the 'Watch, Listen Feel' chapter in Section 3. Acknowledgement involves choice and a test of your decision-making skills. At every stage of this process it is *you* who decides whether something is considered or not, included or not, valued or not. At any given time or with particular types of situation, you may not like being put into the position where you have to make the choice; you may not like the options; and it may be difficult to match the competing interests, but choice it is and thanks to your acceptance of the role (and the benefits that come with it) the responsibility lies with you!

In the first instance you choose – and decide – whether to acknowledge that a situation exists. Lesser mortals may turn and run in the other direction, or cover their ears and eyes. However, it's unlikely you'll be very successful in the role if you adopted this practice as a matter of routine. Many situations present ready and sufficient evidence to enable us to make a virtually instant decision. For instance, flames billowing from a building we know to be unusual and a danger. It's a cut and dry situation. As is the fact that one of your team is late coming into work. Both are fairly immediate situations and in both instances you can choose whether and how you deal with them. Other situations may not have the same urgency, such as one of your team letting you know they've fallen pregnant. This is still a situation, and even though you consider you have more time to deal with the necessary arrangements, the decision to do so still has to be instantaneous.

Once through the first choice you then have the opportunity to make a second quite distinct choice: Whether to proceed and do something about it, or turn away from it. This is what some call 'deciding to decide'. Often it is described as deciding between the options of 'Fight or Flight', especially if the situation involves an element of challenge, some risk to our physical or psychological wellbeing, or to our previously laid plans.

Our prehistoric ancestors faced many fairly basic challenges; not least of these, was the avoidance of becoming another species' dinner whilst looking for their own. Over time, the brain developed and began the use of adrenalin, the chemical that gets pumped around the body once the 'fight or flight' decision is made. This is intended to help equip the mind and body for either option. It is ironic that the same muscle-power and mental alertness are likely to be required whichever choice we make. The eat or be eaten choice called then – and still does – for a more complex thought process and set of decision-making skills than we might at first give credit for, which is why you will be examining your decision-making processes in some depth as we proceed.

When considering this fundamental part of the process though, I prefer 'Should I stay or should I go?' That terminology shifts us away from the concept that all challenges or situations are conflict-driven, or have the potential to do us some form of harm. 'Stay' is about deciding to meet the challenge – to face it; it's about not burying a report, not ignoring one of your team members' rudeness, or dealing with a complaint about one of your staff by another manager. 'Go' is about deciding the situation is in the 'too-difficult-to-handle' box and putting as much distance as possible between you and it. It's about claiming not to have the time or other resources when really you do; it's about recognising that there is a situation, but deciding not to do something about it solely for the sake of not upsetting someone.

So you've acknowledged that there is a situation and you've decided that you are the right person to do something about it, what's next?

Diagnose

- **Diagnosis** requires you to identify the signs and symptoms, eliminate or exclude the presenting issues and get to the core of the matter.

This is the stage in which you look for, gather information about, and identify the central cause of the situation. It comes in two stages: firstly identifying <u>all</u> the potential causes, and then making an assessment as to which is the principal cause that needs to be addressed. It requires you to make some decisions. If you are not accurate or sufficiently inquisitive, there is a risk that you will spend effort and resources addressing a surface or presenting problem, rather than a core issue. Consequently you will ultimately not be successful and may well have to start the process all over again at a later date.

I like the word **diagnose** for its clinical inferences. I recommend you are as clinical as possible when analysing the causes of your situation. Do not be willing to accept 'out of hand' just what is first presented to you unless to completely trust the competence, credentials and motivation of the provider – and even then be wary.

You should be identifying:

- What kind of situation it is – a crisis, non-crisis or opportunity?
- What is the source of the situation, or what are the causes?
- What lies behind the presenting factors?

A weak or inaccurate diagnosis is susceptible to being afforded only a superficial and short-term solution, or one that fails to provide any real solution at all. We shall look at the types and sources of situation shortly. However, once you have accurately identified the cause you can move on to determine the solutions available to you.

Determine

- **Determining** solutions requires that you identify *all* the possible solutions to a situation (or as many that you and maybe your helpers can think of) and pick one!

This is important because it a) gives you choice; b) affords you the chance of getting the best solution; and c) informs your decisions as to what resources will be eventually required. It also allows you to have a 'Plan B' tucked away if later required.

Resist the temptation to jump straight to the first solution that presents itself! As your experience in the role grows, you will encounter similar types of situation and build a bank of tried and tested solutions. However, as no two situations are ever exactly the same, it follows that no two solutions will be either. Thus you will have to make decisions as to what solutions are available and which, under the circumstances and given your available resources, will be the most appropriate.

It will help that you make a conscious, considered decision to actually deal with the situation at stage 1. Doing nothing is always an option. But there are two ways that you can reach that decision: The first is to follow this methodology to ensure that 'doing nothing' is actually the best option. The second is to go directly to that option without 'passing GO'. People do this because early analysis and reaction suggests (for whatever reason) the situation is in the 'too-difficult-to-handle' category. The manager then spends time finding reasons for not dealing with the situation and in the process stores up problems for themselves, their team, the others involved and the organisation.

You may not be comfortable with the situation. It may be new, complex, severe, or occurring at the wrong time. However, we can deal with that! Once – and if – you are confident that you have got to the root cause of the problem, time should be given over to identifying all the potential solutions. Dismiss nothing at this stage. The list will inevitably be headed by solutions you have used before in similar circumstances, or those you know about. You might also have the time and the opportunity to research solutions; possibly seek the advice of others. Ultimately you will be responsible for deciding which solution you are going to apply.

In a following chapter I will talk you through another model for analysing this list of solutions so that you can isolate the one that is most likely to succeed AND most likely to achieve the most acceptable and effective outcome. I call it **TOP DRAWER**. How to do so is described later. For the sake of clarity let's finish this model first and let's assume that you have determined the solution you propose to implement. You then need to ensure you can resource the solution appropriately.

Resource

Consider and list the type, volume and source of resources you would need to implement your chosen solution – and the time (s) you need them for. Resources usually come under the headings:

- People – general labour, or people with particular knowledge or skill sets. They might be in your team or someone else's, at your location or somewhere else.

- Equipment – existing equipment might need upgrading or replacing, or you might need more of it.
- Finance – you might already have budget, or you might have to get an increase in which case you might have to consider a business case.
- Time: is it one person for ten hours or ten people for one hour?

Be careful as you may start 'projecting' and come to an ill-informed snap decision that some essential resources are unlikely to be forthcoming. This may be acceptable, or might prompt you to go to the less exotic solution. Otherwise you might have to put in some extra effort to secure the resources required for the best option.

Once your list(s) is/are complete, you may make preliminary enquiries from the source(s) as to whether what you need is available and/or to put them on reserve or standby. The process of actually confirming and gathering your resources is dealt with as part of the next phase in logistics.

Once you have decided upon a **TOP DRAWER** solution and resourced it, its crunch time! You must now implement your solution. You must 'execute' it.

Execution

- **Execution** entails more decision-making! It's how you put your solution into practice – the planning; the gathering of your resources; and then getting on with it!

Execution has three elements:
    Planning
    Logistics
    Action

It's never a bad thing at this stage to remind yourself of what you're trying to achieve. Having picked what you consider to be the most appropriate solution, it must be that implementing it and bringing it to a successful conclusion meets that aim and those objectives. You need to ask yourself at the outset – and often remind yourself throughout the process – what you expect to come out of this situation and your solution. Will it be more than just resolution of the immediate situation? Also: are your objectives **CRAFT-T**? [The CRAFT-T test is explained shortly]

Your organisation will have expectations of outcomes. Your objectives should always be consistent with them. You may have personal objectives too. If the origin of the situation is 'people' (see later) I can guarantee they will have their own agenda and objectives – explicit or implicit, disclosed or not. If these are consistent with those of the organisation and your own, 'all well and good', unfortunately that is not always the case.

Planning

I have devoted a whole chapter – **CRAFT-T** planning -because failing to plan is indeed planning to fail. Feel free to jump forward if you wish, but ensure you return to finish this chapter.

Logistics

The logistics element has no unintentional military connotations, which are pursued in planning. It concerns the gathering of your resources. It's about having the right kind of resources in the right place at the right time. It's one thing to have identified the resources in the earlier phase. You need to actually get hold of them and get them committed to your task. You cannot trust to luck, especially when your solution is significantly dependent upon a person or a piece of equipment for success. This is the time for you to get everything in place – including your contingencies.

Logistics covers the procurement, distribution, maintenance, and replacement of equipment, materials and personnel. Consideration should be given as to how you're going to manage these resources, especially if the solution is complex. An essential element of this is establishing the framework for coordinating and communicating between resources. You will need to 'Communicate, Communicate, and Communicate!' (See Section 3) This is something else that warrants its own detailed chapter. So it joins **CRAFT-T** planning in being examined more fully later.

Action

So you now calculate that you are sure you have identified the root cause of the situation; chosen the optimum solution under the circumstances; your plan is **CRAFT-T;** and that all your resources are organised. Having done all of that, should you appear hesitant to your bosses or team it will lead to uncertainty on their part – something you can do without. It's time to act. Don't put it off.

Step Back

- **Stepping back** requires **CONTROL**. Not only control of others, but self-confidence and control of yourself and ensuring that whatever happens, your aim and objective(s) are achieved.

Stepping Back is not the 'stepping back, rubbing your hands with glee and basking in the glory of success process that you think it might be. That may come later when all evidence confirms that your solution has worked. Rather this is the process of stepping back and taking an overview of the execution of your plan; monitoring and recognising progress; and not interfering if it's working.

Even the finest, most beautifully crafted machines, require care, maintenance and lubrication. Often, the more complex the machine, the more it requires check-ups and supervision to maintain its fine-tuning. The most useful and best-designed pieces of computer hard – and software still require 'patches' and security updates from time-to-time (to the point where the provider gives up and comes up with a new version altogether). So if that's the case with machinery and software, why shouldn't that be the case with your plans?

You may well be involved in some of the specifics and at the sharp end. However, it's your solution, your plan and your responsibility; you need to be able to 'step out' to control the other elements – if indeed there are any. It can be difficult if you're leading from and/or focussing on driving forward your solution. This is because you can't see what's going on behind or to the side. Similarly if you're 'getting your hands dirty' with the team – showing them you're feeling the pain too – it's difficult to maintain the necessary control.

Stepping back is a process that requires effort and above all self-control – resisting the urge (sometimes) to get stuck in yourself because a) it is quicker to do it yourself (or so you think); or b) you know you can do it better. Exercising control is a key First-Line manager responsibility. It is not as simple, or easy as telling everyone what you want done period! OK.

Stepping back is about having the intelligence (information or feedback) coming back to you as to whether things are going according to plan, the capacity and confidence to acknowledge that a revision may be required, and the courage to do so. When suddenly the unforeseen happens for which there may or may not be a prescribed solution you have a contingency.

I use phrases like confidence and courage because in my experience it takes that to reverse or change a plan, not least because of how we think others will perceive it. It's different if one failed to take into account something one should have, or should have foreseen something that wasn't. This indicates a solution out of a lower drawer. Other than that, it's a bad plan if it can't, or won't be changed regardless of any changing circumstances. Personally I'd rather be embarrassed briefly than ashamed for a long time. For as long as I am taking decisive actions to remedy something – even if it involves reversing a previously well-founded decision – I'm OK with that and I can usually take the feedback.

An even trickier decision as to whether or not to step in comes when things are going well – even though your plan is not being strictly adhered to. Should you step in – risking a failure – to ensure conformity? Should you let it ride? If you do the latter, is it worth raising the issue in the 'wash-up' afterwards? I suppose it all has to come down to an accurate assessment of the situation, what was done and its outcomes.

Say you'd carefully and fully briefed your team. You gave them all the information, all the resources, and had secured their agreement to complete a task. Then say, having agreed (to keep you happy), the team had gone off and done their own thing with an equally successful outcome. What would you do?

You might take the view that there's no harm done. After all there was a successful outcome: the job got done! Looking at it on a more long-term basis however, think of the potential dilution of your levels of authority, respect and power if it happens next time, and the next. If the group knows that it can say one thing to you and then go off and do another in planned activity, what about those when you are not directing them closely – such as day-to-day routines?

This isn't about 'loss of face'. It is about the long-term impact on you and your ability to function in the role. At the risk of sounding self-perpetuating, you have been presented with another situation to **ADDRESS**.

There should come a point when it is apparent that the aim and objectives (organisation's, teams' and individuals') have been achieved, it's time to consider finishing and signing off.

Sign Off

- **Sign Off** requires accurate, open and honest assessment as to whether the aim and objectives have been achieved; noting performance and learning to apply in the future; and celebrating the positives.

In many organisations, in non-crisis or opportunity situations, policy may dictate that your plan must be 'signed-off' before you proceed. This is approval *before* execution. This is different from 'sign off' here. This is signing off the situation, challenge or project as complete. It is a time for one of two things: either it's "time to think again", or it's time to celebrate successful completion, put the situation to bed and move on.

Before you can justifiably sign off, your performance in the situation and that of your team can and should be assessed. You need to review the execution to determine if it has worked. You should never forget this important process. Apart from establishing whether the situation has been resolved, or whether you need to start the process again because fresh situations have arisen as a result, it will help you learn from the experience. Doing so can add something to your toolbox for the future.

Remember you are not the only source of performance information. Depending on the relationships you have with those above, below or around you, you may have to seek this out. Paradoxically this is especially true if all went well. How often are we readily and quickly informed if it didn't?

Before 'sign off', scrutinise what happened and how successful each stage and indeed each contributor proved to be. The event as a whole might have proven successful more by luck than by judgement, or because plans had to be urgently and/or critically revised during the process. Conversely, the event itself might not have been successful, but some elements when taken in isolation were.

The purpose of having a 'debrief' is that we don't want to repeat the same mistakes in future. We do want to repeat success! We don't want to beat ourselves up – or anybody else. We do want to learn and promote best practice! Debriefing can be a solo affair or with others; it can be impromptu or at a scheduled purpose-built session. Whatever the environment or who is present, the best results are achieved when the process is structured.

Figure 3 shows one version (there are others) of a typical debriefing cycle. The model will also be more closely examined in the Feedback Scenario chapter later, as it can be used in individual and personal development debriefing and feedback scenarios in a similar manner.

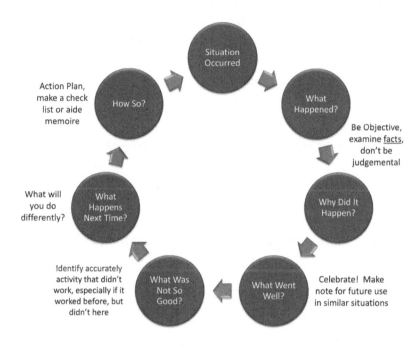

Figure 3: A Debriefing Cycle

Let us look at a simulated example and get you to identify the stages of the **ADDRESS** process:

CASE STUDY: Available for comment

In a high-profile community organisation, Kerry, whose job it is to manage the office of a couple of full time staff and a number of contractors, receives an email from a local news reporter with whom she and the organisation has previously had a good working relationship. The reporter has asked if they could meet for a 'chat' regarding some disturbing information they have received. It would appear that one of Kerry's contractors has been acting improperly in dealings with suppliers by seeking and accepting inducements whilst representing the organisation.

Given the nature of the organisation's work and its profile in the community, this is a potential 'public interest' story. The email has some verifiable facts and Kerry knows the paper goes to press in three days' time.

After some enquiries it is apparent that if the allegations are true, it could be very embarrassing for the organisation if the information gets out in the wrong way. Kerry agrees to meet the reporter tomorrow morning.

Case Study 2: Available for comment

Exercise:

What is/are the principal situation(s) Kerry must deal with and are they crisis or non-crisis?

How would you plan to **ADDRESS** the principal situation(s) you have identified?

Note down your own solutions before moving on.

Perhaps you recognised two main situations that need to be **ADDRESS**ed:

A. That with the reporter. It's urgent because of the impending press deadline and important because of the potential damage that could be done to the organisation's reputation and therefore, its future earning capacity. Above all this is a communication situation, one that necessitates a **REASON**ed encounter (see later).
B. That with the contractor. It's important for the same reasons as (A) above. It's only marginally less urgent than A because, if true – and we have to run with the presumption of innocence – it is behaviour that has to be stopped. This too is a communication situation, but overriding that is the fact that this is a discipline or performance issue.

Consider whether either situation presents us with an opportunity. Might the situation be used to demonstrate how honest and trustworthy the organisation is and how appropriately it reacts to crisis – maintaining confidence? Might this be an opportunity to dismiss the contractor early?

The exercise has inherently completed the 'A' for Acknowledge element of the system in both cases. I've given that first situation first priority because it is as important as the second, but more urgent. Let us follow the rest of the **ADDRESS** process:

Diagnosis: One of Kerry's contractors seems to have been acting inappropriately, but we'll deal with that in due course. What has caused the first situation is that: the information has found its way to a third party-in this case the press; the reporter has, not unsurprisingly, decided to follow up on it; and has (fortunately) decided to give Kerry the opportunity to respond prior to going to press. Kerry does have a range of potential solutions to this particular situation.

Determine Solutions: She could take the view that this is an internal matter, nothing to do with the press and go with a 'publish and be dammed' approach. However, the information supplied suggests this approach would do nothing for the press-organisation relationship, or the organisation's reputation. Kerry could haul the contractor in straight away, and commence disciplinary procedures. This would provide Kerry with some ammunition, or evidence that she could give to the reporter to prove the organisation's probity and willingness to address the matter. Alternatively, she could make some informal enquiries with the suppliers involved and indeed with the contractor to gather as much information as possible. The meeting with the reporter would then be more of a 'fact-finding '.

The latter two possibilities require Kerry to devote her time to the situation, but little other resources would be required at this stage. Whatever her choice, Kerry would be well advised to use the time to plan her strategy for the encounter. One method would be to use the **REASON** approach discussed later. This would provide her with an idea of the potential directions that the conversation with the reporter could go in and with a range of responses that are appropriate to whatever points she anticipates the reporter will raise.

With regard to the subsequent stages of the model: the remainder of 'execution', 'stepping back', and 'sign off' stages all require Kerry to guess how the meeting will develop. This is because the situation will be being dealt with a little in the future, not immediately. So this is about as far as we can go with the **ADDRESS Model** at this stage for this particular situation.

Looking at the second situation: If the allegations turn out to have some basis, we need to look at why the situation might have arisen (Diagnosis). Did the contractor know the rules, have they been fully made out and explained and was evidence to hand that they were understood? If so did the contractor choose to deliberately ignore the rules, or was this an innocent misinterpretation? If the rules have not been properly explained why was this?

Determine Solutions: However unrealistic given the circumstances, Kerry still has the option to do nothing, though for the same reasons as earlier this is unlikely to have a very beneficial outcome. Any of the remaining potential solutions revolve around the organisation's disciplinary procedure (assuming such exists). I must stress that invoking any disciplinary procedure is not and should never be a determination or suggestion that anybody is automatically guilty of some breach. Such procedures exist to ensure that individuals are treated fairly and that both they and the organisation are protected throughout the process.

Remember this is only a small organisation. So it is unlikely to be able to support an HR or legal services department. Kerry will need to know her **STUFF** to know in the first instance what the rules are and, if proven to be true, how the behaviour breaches those rules. She needs to be aware of her options; for instance, do the same rules apply to contractors as they do to full-time regular employees? In the absence of any experts' support, she is likely to require time resources to be able to do some research and get her facts right and then further time to follow any relevant disciplinary process through to a conclusion.

Having considered the possible causes of this situation in an earlier phase of the model, Kerry can begin to formulate a plan to manage any information gathering exercise she might choose to undertake with other potential witnesses and indeed subsequently with the contractor. For instance it might prove difficult to deal with the contractor for a breach of any rules if they were genuinely and proven to be unaware of what the rules were. Similarly, if it was a genuine and honest misinterpretation of the rules it may well be that the full weight of the disciplinary procedure might not result. Obviously, if this was proven to be some form of dishonesty or malicious activity on the part of the contractor the most serious consequences i.e. parting company might ensue.

As a cautionary note, the fact that there is now press interest in this story or situation, should in no way influence the outcome of any disciplinary procedure even though it may have instigated it. A lawsuit for breach of contract could be equally if not more damaging to the continued functioning of the organisation, than a piece of short term adverse publicity.

There is an opportunity shortly for you to apply the principle of **ADDRESS** in your own working environment.

The Sources of Situations

As promised we can now look at the types and sources of situations. Being aware of where they come from and what they are can help us develop personal contingency activities to implement as and when they occur. There are three main types of situation: the crisis, the non-crisis and the opportunity.

The Crisis

A crisis can be viewed as a crucial or decisive point, usually sudden and unexpected; often involving a degree of uncertainty and instability; with risks and accompanied by heightened levels of emotion or stress.

An objective of mine is to help you avoid crises as much as possible, or if such is unavoidable, provide you with some tools to deal with them effectively. You are most likely to encounter and to be expected to deal with crisis situations involving your team. You're the first port of call for welfare or discipline issues; their processes, when they or machinery break down; or because being a point of escalation (dealing with more complex issues than those you manage) is a requirement of your role.

Some people can acquire a reputation for maintaining a cool head in a crisis. Others will take a crisis on, but may not be so successful. They might acquire a deserved or underserved reputation for 'going to pieces'. Still others might avoid crises altogether.

Crises often require an urgent solution. You might think following the processes and tests outlined above would preclude that. However, as stated above it is your knowledge, understanding and skill in applying the tests effectively in the time available that are key.

What do the cool, calm, collected managers do, that their opposites don't? Firstly, maybe they are not being exactly cool, calm, and collected inside, but are able to control their non-verbal communication. Wouldn't it be great if that were all it was! They probably have a plan, or system that can be applied to any given situation. They have the capacity to work through it irrespective of the situation's complexity or severity and notwithstanding any interference. Maybe it's courage, which I agree is not the absence of fear, but the quality of thought and consideration that allows one to persevere, because on balance it is the right and necessary thing to do, even though this might result in harm to oneself or others.

It is not so difficult to put a positive slant on a crisis, though when we're negotiating one it might not feel like that. We must wait a while before we are emotionally and physically able to look back and accurately appraise our contribution. In the words of Victor Hugo, "emergencies have always been necessary to progress. It was darkness, which produced the lamp. It was fog that produced the compass. It was hunger that drove us to exploration. And it took a depression to teach us the real value of a job."[24] Crises are nothing new and this quotation points to the reassuring fact that they invariably have solutions. The right solution can inform and positively affect life forever.

In Section 1 we talked about proactive managers and those who are reactive. A proactive manager might well avoid most crises as they think ahead, consider possibilities and consequences, and introduce contingencies into their existing plans. They may even create work for themselves when recognising an issue that no one else has, or for which no one else has yet found a solution and electing to do something about it. Having said that, a proactive manager may be able to do all of this, but even they cannot predict with certainty what the future holds. They cannot predict the exact moment a piece of IT or production material breaking down, nor when a team member might have an incident at home that prevents them coming in. All they can do is have a plan in place to deal with that. Such plans help to render what might be a crisis for others into a non-crisis for them.

The Non-Crisis

Sharing many of the attributes of a crisis, a non-crisis can be just as important and cause just as much impact, but usually without the urgency or so much risk. These are the situations you know are coming and that will require your attention and some activity. You will probably have time to plan for them.

24   (Hugo 1802–1885)

Opportunities

Both crises and non-crises carry opportunities with them and in a perfect world you would only have to deal with the latter two. In that same world you would also be able to turn crises into opportunities with the deftness of an artist's hand. Unfortunately when embroiled in a crisis situation it can be difficult to acknowledge the opportunity, still more so to be able to take advantage of it.

The type of organisation you operate in, the culture, your length of service in your present and previous role, and the nature of the situation are all variables that affect the levels of expectation that both your subordinates and seniors have in respect of you resolving the situation. So in order to inform your decisions in this stage it's important that you get to 'Know your **STUFF**' at an early point and continue to maintain and develop your knowledge, understanding and skills. Think of all the training a doctor undertakes to recognise an ailment as often symptoms are shared by a number of ailments, but only one ailment has all the symptoms.

Conan-Doyle's Sherlock Holmes famously asserted in several stories, such as *The Sign of the Four*, that "once you eliminate the impossible, whatever remains, no matter how improbable, must be the truth". And so it is with situations: once you eliminate what are merely presenting issues or symptoms, what you are left with (however unpalatable or difficult to deal with) is the core problem that needs to be addressed.

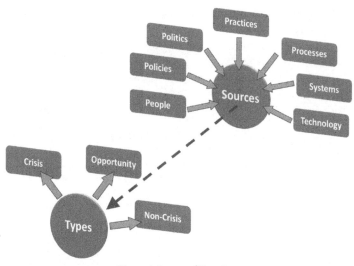

Figure 4: Source of Situations

105

Optional Exercise:

Select a time frame for this activity – One week would be appropriate:

After dealing with a situation at work, take ten minutes out and review that situation and break it down into the stages identified by the **ADDRESS Model** then, using your diary if you are keeping one – otherwise a sheet of paper will do – answer the following questions:

How clearly did you define the stages?

How effective were you in completing the requirements of each phase?

What will you do differently next time to ensure you complete each phase effectively?

Repeat the exercise twice leaving a day between each.

In this chapter you have examined the source of the situations that you deal with in the First-Line manager role and how to **ADDRESS** them.

You have had a small insight into **CRAFT-T** planning, which is described fully later. You can leave this chapter with this thought offered up by the American politician Rahm Emanuel: *"Never waste a crisis. It can be turned to joyful transformation."*[25]

25   (Emmanuel 2009)

13. Know your STUFF!

As a First-Line manager, you're expected to know: your staff – not only those who report directly, but also those over whom you might have temporary control; your peers; your task responsibilities – what's in your job description (and what's not); and the understandings and customs that are practised in your workplace. For each situation you deal with you are also expected to gather as many facts as possible, to have a good idea of how you want it to develop, and what the end product will look like. In other words you're expected to be able to forecast the outcome. The aim of this chapter is to identify and explain a way to remember what types of information are needed in order to manage any situation to best effect. Here I introduce you to the aide-memoire known as '**STUFF**'.

In this chapter I highlight the benefits of gathering as much information and evidence as is practicable and using it effectively. It also outlines a simple test you can apply to gauge the extent to which you and your team are involved, engaged and in control of what's going on and affecting you in your organisation. This might well highlight some personal issues/situations for you to **ADDRESS.** You are encouraged to do so through end-of-chapter exercises for the workplace.

Some argue you can never have too much information to support the decisions you need to make. Nineteenth-century British Prime Minister Benjamin Disraeli asserted, "As a general rule, the most successful man in life is the man who has the best information".[26] Note he says the 'best', not the 'most'!

There are numerous factors that affect our capacity and capability to obtain information. Time is a major factor, as is the urgency of the situation. You may not have the required knowledge of how, or the resources to

26   (Disraeli 1880)

gather it. Too much information coming in all at once, or in a confused or unrecognisable format can be just as harmful as not enough information. Therefore, we have to manage the source, quality, volume, and timing of information. This then, is about knowing your '**STUFF**'. You need to know:

S	Staff
T	Task responsibilities
U	Understandings and Customs
F	Facts
F	Forecast

With all this information you should exercise care that you interpret it accurately. It is easy to allow it to adversely influence a decision through its support of a particular 'bias' that you might apply (see Managing Team Performance). So far as is possible you should be gathering, collating and analysing this data/information with a high degree of objectivity and neutrality. Consider the following:

CASE STUDY: Party Boy

A few months into role, Bassey was asked to supervise another team whose manager was going to be on long-term sick leave. This team had only been recently formed, whereas hers was well established and self-sufficient. A senior member of her team was going to substitute for her and get the opportunity to get some much-needed developmental experience.

The absent manager liked being 'one of the guys' and was known not to bother too much with minor transgressions of policy. Everyone was aware that this manager was very supportive of his or her team in times of personal, non-work-related difficulty. Bassey knew many of the faces in her new team, but did not know them very well as people.

Gil has worked for the organisation for about three years. He is one of the younger, livelier members of the team, with a bit of a reputation for enjoying a party.

The first week passed off without incident, but then on the first day of the second week Gil arrived 25 minutes late for work.

Gil sees the questioning look on Bassey's face when he arrives and in an initial encounter with her he admits to having been late on a "few" occasions before, but insisted that his "real" manager had always treated it as a bit of a joke, as had everybody else in the team. It was never a problem so long as he made his hours up

Case Study 3: Party Boy

Exercise

How would you apply the **ADDRESS Model** in this situation?

I assume you acknowledge there is a situation and that you will decide to deal with it. At the very least and regardless of the other manager's attitude and preference for dealing (or not) with it, there is the issue of personal credibility and future exercise of control if *you* did not. There would also be the difficulties you would encounter in dealing with others in the team who took it upon themselves to transgress in other similar or more serious ways. When looking to 'Diagnose', there are a number of potential causes for this situation:

Some are related to the previous manager's conduct:
   A *laissez-faire* approach to discipline generally that keeps the team happy and has them working well, but causes his peers difficulty.
   Not dealing with Gil more formally under the organisation's disciplinary procedure

Others are linked directly to Gil:

He knows the rules but chooses to disregard them for whatever reason:
   (a) Malicious
   (b) Non-malicious
He does not know the rules:
   (a) He's never been told them
   (b) He's been told them, but it was so long ago, or they've changed, that he's forgotten
   (c) He is having difficulties of some kind
       i. Personal issues of some sort
       ii. A lack of self management

Maybe you were thinking along the lines that Gil is having some personal problems that are driving him to drink. It's good you should be thinking along those lines, but there is nothing in the information currently available to support that theory. It is often the case, and it's a trap easily fallen into, that we spend too much time looking for something that isn't there. Alternatively when all the evidence points to a particular conclusion, we choose to dismiss it. In this instance could it not be that Gil is fully aware of his responsibilities, has no excuse and has just been getting away with stretching the rules under the previous manager? Diagnosing and determining solutions require you to know your **STUFF**:

S – Staff

I'm not suggesting that you should know everything there is to know about your staff. However, each and every time you deal with a situation involving a colleague, you will get to know a little bit more about them as individuals. For instance, their knowledge of their role and tasks, their knowledge of 'the rules', their capability and willingness to abide by them, the things they enjoy doing-and those they don't. You might also find out some more about their attitude to the organisation, to their colleagues, and to you. All this knowledge can affect the manner in which you choose to approach situations involving them and also the potential outcomes.

You must also consider whether or not you should be a friend 'to', or friendly 'with', all or some of those whom you work with. This is a sensitive area, as this too will have an influence on how you deal with the situation. This is a complex issue and a difficult thing to get right. I have afforded it its own chapter later.

Lao-tzu the Chinese philosopher said, "People are difficult to govern because they have too much knowledge." You might replace the word "because" with "if" to make the sentiment more relevant for the twenty-first Century. However, the extent to which your team knows, understands and applies the rules they are supposed to, has a considerable impact on *your* capacity to be effective. For instance, it could make your life easier as you don't need to constantly explain the reasoning for a particular decision. On the other hand, it has been known for some staff to deliberately become experts with the rules so as to manipulate them to their own advantage, which of course can be a source of situations for you to deal with. However, if they do transgress and you deal with the situation appropriately, they have no excuse!

I'm not sure that modern thinking is entirely in line with Lao-tzu as especially in the area of change management, it seems the more quality information people have, the more likely it is they will accept the change and contribute what is required.

Another consideration when it comes to knowledge of colleagues is that of their capabilities; their knowledge and understanding; and their current levels of skill and ability. It's very counter-productive to be asking them to be doing something from the outset that they are totally incapable of, though situations can be used to develop latent skills on a simple-to-complex basis.

On top of that is your understanding of their willingness to participate in the process and whether any explanation, persuasion or direction is going to be required in order to get the job done. This is commonly called staff engagement. A good way to illustrate this concept is to put you through an assessment of your 'engagement' and then encourage you to ask the same questions of your team at your leisure. You will have this opportunity once you have familiarised yourself with the **STUFF** aide-memoire.

T – Task responsibilities

Your 'task responsibilities' fall into two areas: the first is that of knowing your organisation's policies, rules, and systems. If you are in a heavily regulated environment this could also include elements of law and regulation that govern your organisation's operations. Most First-Line managers' job descriptions contain an element of enforcing the rules, controlling, or ensuring compliance. So that knowledge of the rules is your 'technical knowledge' (or task). Not only are you expected to know the rules, you are expected to apply them and to know how to apply them to best effect.

Secondly, you need to know about the task or job at hand. This would include: the purpose – aims and objectives; what resources were needed, and which were available; the plan, how achievement is going to be measured and how long it should all be taking.

Knowing your task responsibilities can also include knowing the role of your subordinates. In many environments, when the customer demands 'to see the manager' it's going to be you. In many instances they know that the answer will not change, but they derive some satisfaction from having heard it from 'the manager'.

In many other situations however, they expect you to have more room for manoeuvre, more information, more authority; and so to be in a better position to sort the situation out. Also, if a subordinate encounters something from the 'too-difficult-to-handle' box it's highly possible – if not probable – that they'll gladly pass it to you.

Whilst that raises a question over the levels of knowledge, authority, training and attitude of those subordinates, it also implies that you need a good working knowledge of what they should know and be able to do.

For those 'promoted in house' from within the area over which they now command, this is normally less of an issue. However, if you are 'parachuted in' – say from outside the organisation or from another department – your induction and orientation learning should/would include time given over to familiarising yourself with what it is your team does.

U – Understandings and Customs

This is about what local arrangements and customs exist in your new environment. They are the things that don't tend to be talked about until you ask, or until a situation crops up. Very often they are unofficial. In some institutions it is highly likely that the organisation itself is a beneficiary -senior managers tend to turn a blind eye to them taking place if it's good for business.

It could be that to go against custom could result in unwanted confrontation and team de-motivation. There's a very apt scene in the film *A Few Good Men*[27], which, if you haven't seen it centres on the trial of two American Marines for conducting the informal punishment of a colleague. Such informal punishments, though previously ruled illegal were commonplace and customary though senior officers deny this. They were aware it was being done – even on some occasions with their support. However, either they had lived through the regime themselves, and did not like the fact the custom had been banned, or they saw it a good way to enforce team-shared responsibility.

In the scene in question – intent on proving that if it's not in the book

27   (Sorkin 1992) *A Few Good Men* (1992) Castle Rock Entertainment, Columbia Pictures. Dir. Rob Reiner

it doesn't happen – the prosecution asks a Marine, a series of questions based upon regulations that were readily located in a procedure manual. In response, the defence then asks a question – the answer to which cannot be found in the manual, i.e. "Where do you go to eat?" – He responds, "I just follow everybody else, I guess."

The points were extremely well made. Some things are carried out in the workplace as a matter of habit, some of which are acceptable, and others that are not. Secondly, not everything that happens will be found in the manual!

As a manager you are expected to adhere to and apply the rules and practices of your organisation as contained in a rulebook somewhere. But I suspect most of us have experienced situations where:

- Some rules are enforced more than others
- Some 'rules' are conveniently ignored or side-stepped if doing so is perceived by the person doing so, to be to the advantage of the individual or the business

All too often rules are created and applied to everyone as a reaction to the errant behaviour of a rogue individual who's transgressed in some way. This is to try to prevent others following suit. More often than not, such rules don't prevent the activity; just provide the organisation with a sanction if it occurs again. Very often rules have been in place for so long that people have forgotten why they are there, or they have failed to keep pace with the world. So why are they there at all?

After all, if rules are appropriate, necessary and properly written and enforced, why does the threat, or implementation of 'working to rule' (as an industrial dispute weapon) cause such an issue? If working to a rule causes the effective operation of an organisation to break down, I would suggest there's something not quite right. The same applies if a business cannot function without the systemic breaking of a rule. If either applies, shouldn't that organisation be taking a serious look at the rule and re-writing it?

If you are promoted in-house, there could be an expectation on you to know and apply these customs in your new role. However, given that they are not universal, you could well be promoted into an area where a custom you are used to does not apply, or vice versa. Furthermore, now that you are a manager you could well encounter some new understandings or customs that are peculiar to you at that new level. Even if you're fortunate enough to go through a comprehensive induction process, the rules might well be communicated to you, but not the fact that particular ones are not enforced as a matter of custom.

It's not hard for you to be placed in a moral dilemma. Custom and senior management acquiescence to a particular custom or practice can imply that it's OK to break the rules so long as the organisation benefits and/or no one gets hurt (too much). Unofficial practices can often be to the detriment of the organisation otherwise they would be openly spoken about and all included in staff terms and conditions. Wouldn't they? This dilemma applies especially if/when you were 'one of the guys'. Then you were a beneficiary of some of these customs -even some of the dodgy ones – and now your new team knows it! Would you expect, or be expected by your peers and your new team to perpetuate these customs? If you now decide you're going to change things, including your approach to, or acceptance of these customs or understandings; does that make you a hypocrite?

It's not easy! You must balance your responsibility to your organisation with the difficulties that implementing all the rules, all the time might bring. Knowing the rules and relying on them as your sole method of controlling the team can make you appear robotic and autocratic.

Perhaps it's appropriate to draw the distinction between what are organisational rules and what is the law of the land. If the former are customarily and habitually, broken, bent or ignored with the tacit agreement of the organisation, you are unlikely to fall foul. If you did, you might well have a good defence. Even then however, if something goes wrong, you have to be prepared for the common scenario of the organisation suddenly remembering the rule and deciding that (as things went wrong) it should have been enforced.

Compare this to breaches of what is your country's law: The potential defence of ignorance; or the fact that 'everyone else was doing it, so you thought it was OK', do not apply. Not only will you be culpable, but in many cases so will your organisation. The flexibility you may have with rules just isn't there with the law.

There is no golden answer regarding rules and how you apply them. It is a matter of conscience, comfort and personal standards. At the very least you should know what the rules are and how they are applied within your organisation. This will very much inform the decision as to which line you take. You should always, always work within the law.

F – Facts

The more you rely on weak, inaccurate, old or unsubstantiated facts, the greater the risk of any decision being a weak decision that will need subsequent revision or reversal. That is not to say you can, or should put off making a decision, or initiating some action, until you know all there is to know. That's a recipe for inertia and can send out a message that you are indecisive.

This is more about using the time that you have before embarking on a decision to gather what facts you can about the situation. Think about a good doctor seeking to diagnose an ailment: the more symptoms they establish, the more likely it is they will be able to narrow the problem down to what it is they need to actually treat.

When I had my own small health scare, the consultant rattled off a list of three or four things that my symptoms could be evidencing. However, he then explained a need to investigate further. In this case, with a short spell on an operating theatre table, before he could be certain. So this is directly and fundamentally linked to the 'diagnose' phase of the **ADDRESS** Model.

You should try to think of a list of 'facts' you might need about any given situation. Be realistic about the ones you're likely to get in the time available (and whether you can legitimately delay a decision pending the desired facts coming to light). Think also about the quality of that information and the reliability of the source. Separate facts from conjecture and opinion.

There are a number of sources that you might get your facts from:

- Individuals involved – if necessary though formal/informal meetings, or 'fact-find' interviews – I refer you back to the 4Q-4A model
- Other individuals such as HR specialists, technicians, recognised experts, lawyers etc
- Written company policies, procedures
- Technical manuals
- Observations
- Research – libraries or online
- Your own knowledge/notes of past behaviours on the part of the individuals, machines or similar types of situation already dealt with

Given the comments made in the later chapter on questioning, I would also recommend that where possible, you take an appropriate amount of time to verify the facts. Does every individual provide a matching version or are there significant variations? Are the policies up-to-date and in line with current law? Is it the right manual for the model in front of you? Has the model in front of you been tinkered with so that it's now different to the original? Are you confident that what you observed is what happened and/or to what extent does it need checking out? Does a previous experience you intend to apply, actually lend itself to this one; or are there some significant differences requiring some modification of the original before it can be implemented?

• Just like knowing your **STUFF** generally, it is important that you get your **facts** right so as to avoid you or them being discredited.

Once you have identified the facts, you should then give some time over to clarifying what you expect or need to come out of the situation.

F – Forecast

Once again we have an eye on the outcome. This element looks beyond the immediate situation and focuses on two things: a) what you want the outcome(s) to be; and b) what impact your action is going to have.

As with all aspects of your planning, you temper the amount of time you spend completing this phase according to the importance and urgency of the situation. Just because you have a limited amount of time, doesn't mean the time should not be used wisely and to best effect. Forecasting is influenced by your experience of dealing with similar situations, your knowledge of appropriate techniques and their common outcomes. It is not uncommon for someone presented with a particular situation to go into 'automatic pilot' and go straight to a method and solution that they have used successfully (or not) previously. This can be a legitimate course of action – indeed the whole concept of development is that we do build up a bank of solutions – providing you do not ignore any variations that exist currently. So in the first place when you forecast what you want the outcomes to be, you are setting yourself a goal that becomes the focus of your **CRAFT-T** plan.

Forecasting will also inform the quality of your solution: for it to be **TOP-DRAWER**, it has to consider the reactions of your organisation or bosses, and those who will be implementing it with you. At this stage you can include others who might be the target of your solution. Typically this group might include direct customers, consumers or communities, outside but with an interest in the situation.

In any event you are seeking to test whether the objectives and outcomes contained in the task plan are sufficient? What if you want to use the situation for a broader or more long-term purpose? For instance, if the situation warrants it, might it be used to give participants an opportunity to develop skills? Is it an opportunity to build a network or reputation? Would buying one piece of equipment in particular mean that production could be speeded up elsewhere? Is this an incremental situation – one necessary to complete on the way to a greater objective?

Consider the outcomes YOU want to see come from the situation. Some situations allow for everyone to come out a 'winner'. In others it's sometimes difficult to see, or impractical to deliver that. Someone will come out a loser. If you think about it, it's much easier to walk into a team meeting and declare that if production is 'upped' by 10% over the next week everyone will receive a bonus, than to take a member of staff to one side to talk about their current poor performance, with the prospect of dismissal if they do not do better. However, as difficult as it may seem in the latter case, both situations have the potential for win-win, both can be positive. We would naturally see the second situation as being negative, but what if in the first situation your team was already working at what they considered and was generally acknowledged to be full capacity? Demanding more could be equally as negative, even though the potential win is obvious.

- **Forecasting** is about using your knowledge, experience, understanding and skills to project beyond the immediate and to determine one or more likely or intended outcomes for the situation.

Knowing your **STUFF** requires you to be inquisitive and receptive to information. Gathering the information to answer the questions is best done in advance. However, there is nothing to stop you putting the brakes on during a situation if you believe it will afford you the opportunity to do so. Remember, that this process is there to help you and others get the best from any situation.

Be realistic! You may never be able to get all the information you think you need at the right time, in the right format or in the right quantity. This has the potential to affect the quality of your decision and maybe, the need for you to alter it once any missing information is obtained. In these circumstances balance the need for a decision against the risk of not making one because of the lack of detail. You do not wish to appear unnecessarily hesitant and uncertain as this can create a similar feeling in those reliant upon you.

Secondly, recognise that you are confined by the degree to which you can remain objective through the process; I confess that occasionally I have used the 'facts' in a way that helps me to achieve my goals, when I have been selective as to which facts I have used. I have placed greater emphasis on the favourable facts than the less so. Similarly, it is possible for the 'facts' as we learn them, to affect our emotions and judgement in a manner that does not project the greatest of impressions.

Maintaining impartiality when one has a passion for a particular project or argument is not easy – some might say impossible. Having some passion – showing what you believe in and why – can be an argument-winner, but often only if the facts and evidence are there to convince your audience. Too much passion can breed suspicion and subsequent resistance on the part of those who don't know you and what you do.

Knowing your **STUFF** is applicable equally to your general day-to-day operations as a manager as it is to the circumstances and components of individual situations you will be called upon to deal with.

There is nothing wrong with not knowing something, though it is a lame excuse for doing something wrong. If you realise that you don't know something that you know you should, it only becomes a problem if you do nothing to rectify the ignorance.

Exercise:

In consideration of the Party Boy case study above, what **STUFF** would you consider it necessary to know?

Engagement

As promised, I want to expand on the word 'engagement'. Maximum possible team 'engagement' is considered essential to successful outcomes. A substantial requirement of effective engagement is effective communication. However, communication alone does not effective engagement make! Much of what follows is based on the work of Jonas Ridderstråle and Mark Wilcox who established clear requirements of engagement in order to re-energise organisations. Of necessity I have amended elements so that they can be applied to your operations as a manager.[28]

If I walked up to you and straight off asked, "So how engaged in the process do you feel right now?" you'd probably tilt your head to one side and give me some kind of disbelieving or inquisitive look. Put yourself in the shoes of your team members and consider how they'd react to you asking them that same question. It's a little too abstract for many. So to gauge the levels of engagement generally or for a particular task, consider approaching it a little more subtly.

I believe that effective and realistic engagement involves members of your team having:

- Knowledge of what's going on, the plan, the intended outcomes and the effects
- Knowledge of the benefits for them and the organisation, and possibly the negative consequences of not doing something
- A real feeling – based on evidence – that their views and contributions are heard, and taken into consideration.
- A firm commitment to the process and its outcomes – agreement to fulfil what is expected of them
- Appropriate rewards and/or recognition for contributions
- Trust and confidence in the leadership generally and you in particular

Some argue that some form of emotional involvement is also required. That may be true, but I remain unconvinced whether it is essential, or whether you can expect it to be so. I would also argue that if the other elements are present, you are providing the environment for emotions such as 'pride in

28   (Ridderstårle 2008)

a job well done' or 'loving' one's work to be generated and nurtured.

Your team needs to have certain knowledge and feelings, what about you? In addition to knowledge of the task, don't you also need knowledge as to whether the team are engaged and some confidence that this is the case? Furthermore, don't you need confidence in yourself and your own abilities – preferably based on good experience and practices?

I am always reluctant to try and measure 'confidence' as a stand-alone trait, mainly because confidence is born of and influenced by other traits, such as knowledge and its application. 'Confidence' is an impression we gain, based on what someone does and how. We can recognise confidence in others. So what makes you think that others wouldn't recognise it or its absence in you? If you don't believe what you're saying or doing and/or can't for whatever reason implement something effectively, how can you expect or assume that your team will follow? Consider the person you think of as being confident:

- Are they good at challenging – picking the right time, right argument and right person?
- To what extent do they appear comfortable in situations you consider are 'difficult'?
- What do they do when they don't have an answer – retreat or admit it and work to find one?
- What do they do when they realise they're wrong – argue, plough on regardless or readily admit it?
- What relationship do they have with their team and networks, e.g. are they trusted with sensitive information from above or below?
- What attitude and behaviours do they display that gives the impression of assuredness?

Now ask those same questions in relation to yourself.

We deal with relationships and in particular, whether you should be a friend or friendly, further down the line; however, relationships are not just about that. You need to consider the size and strength of your 'network' or support; what evidence do you have that those you work with see you as an excellent communicator and someone whose judgement they trust; the amount of time you spend talking to others at work, listening to their ideas generally and in relation to specific projects or problems; how caring are you of the way in which you are perceived by those at work and the extent to which you are willing to work at that. If you're the type that likes things laid out and evidenced numerically you could rate your own level of engagement in something you've been assigned to do, or that of your team for something you're leading on.

Exercise

Pick a situation you are currently engaged in considering a solution for and then simply score it between 1 and 10 with '1' being 'Not at All' and '10' being 'Fully'.

This can be a self-assessment and/or you can put yourself in the shoes of your team members (i.e. how are they thinking?) If you're feeling brave you could then do it for real with them.

Score

1	You/they understand the scope and target of the situation/ project	
2	You/they understand and agree with the need for the activity	
3	You/they believe that the advertised benefits will be achieved & there is benefit to them	
4	There are clear goals, success criteria and measures of success	
5	You/they know the chain of command and who is responsible for what	
6	You/they know those with responsibility are willing and able to deliver	
7	You/all others affected have had adequate time to study and comment/contribute.	
8	You/they know that a clear, achievable plan has been drawn up	
9	You/they believe any risks have been identified, assessed & accounted for	
10	You/they accept the risks	
11	You/they think the task or project is value for money	
12	You/they understand and accept the disruption that will come with the project	
13	You/they know and accept that support will be given to acquire new knowledge/skills	
14	You/they believe obstacles have been identified and steps being taken to remove them	
15	You/they understand how this piece fits the overall strategy of the organisation	
17	You/they believe top management is fully committed and supportive	
18	You/they believe that those in charge can solve problems and be decisive	

Add the numbers that you have circled to produce a score between 18 and 180. What does the resultant score suggest?

18 – 58	You/your team are unsettled and likely to resist the solution considerably.
59 – 99	The solution has a lack of support and a lot of work will be required to get it to work.
100 – 140	It's a good well planned solution, there's room for still better communication.
141 – 180	You/your team know the solution and believe in it. It has good levels of engagement and a strong chance of success.

Summary

This chapter has illustrated the benefits of knowing as much as possible about the people involved: their personal agendas, motivations and objectives; what is expected of you; the customs and environment in which you are operating, in particular with any given situation; the facts of the matter with emotions removed so far as is possible; and a forecast of what is likely, or what is desired will come out of the situation.

You have also looked at the benefits of being impartial when gathering and analysing the facts of tasks and the people involved. You may find yourself called upon to justify to others – your bosses, a tribunal, the civil courts for instance – why you acted, made the decisions, and caused what you did. If you can show that you worked with the facts and acted impartially and within the law, rules and guidelines you can make out your case with confidence and secure in the knowledge that you acted correctly, no matter what the ultimate outcome.

End of Chapter Activity:

The next time you are presented with a problem complete a self-assessment based solely on the extent to which you feel you knew your **STUFF.**

To what extent do you feel knowing your **STUFF** helped you to deal with the situation?

Where and to what extent do you feel there were gaps in your knowledge?

How did that affect your management of the situation?

What would you like to do differently next time?

If there are areas for development you can repeat this exercise as many times as you like.

When we're talking about what the acquisition of knowledge is all about, you can think on the words of eighteenth century writer Dr Samuel Johnson[29]: *"Knowledge is of two kinds. We know a subject ourselves, or we know where we can find information upon it."*

29   (Boswell 1791)

14. TOP-DRAWER solutions

TOP DRAWER is a method for helping you to match the best solution to the situation. When it comes to determining solutions, knowing your **STUFF** includes knowing your options. You need to decide which of the available options will best suit the situation at hand. It applies easy to remember criteria that can be scored in respect of each of the possible solutions. In theory the option that scores best should be the right one.

There may be some extreme options you can discount almost immediately. Others may be more difficult to eliminate as they have some characteristics that could work.

This is a framework to use with whatever brevity and at whatever speed you deem appropriate. It 'sanity-checks' your solution options – anything from 'doing nothing' through to a fully comprehensive proposal. It lends itself to any situation: those where you have to think on your feet – in which instance you can practise working through it in your head – to those non-crisis and/or opportunity situations that afford you the time and resources to search for and select the optimum solution.

'TOP-DRAWER' aims to select the most effective option that also balances the needs of the situation with those of your organisation, your team and (last but least) *you*. **TOP-DRAWER** solutions are those that are:

T	Time bound
O	Opportunity – taking advantage of
P	Politically acceptable
D	Decisive
R	Resourced
A	Acceptable to the team
W	Workable
E	Economical
R	Reversible

Let me explain what is meant by each of these criteria:

Time bound

An effective solution must have start and finish points. It should take notice of any time implications, i.e. is this matter of urgency, or is it one we can take some time over? Some larger tasks can be broken down into manageable elements, each of which has a 'due by' date (a milestone). There will be interdependencies, e.g. one stage cannot start before another is finished or has reached a certain point or until a resource working elsewhere is freed up.

Whatever the time frame and/or constraints, they should be stipulated and communicated from the outset. Whether things get done on time is one of the common measures of successful performance and one of the elements that needs to be controlled.

Timings need to be realistic. Generally speaking there is a relationship between the volume of work, the number of resources and the time allowed. Crudely put, if the time allowed is four days and the number of staff ten, you could say that for the job to be delivered two days early, you would need twenty staff. The ratio might not be so simple, but if one element changes, the others will probably need to do so in proportion.

Opportunity

Does this situation present an opportunity to deal with or address another (connected) situation at the same time? Examples of this would include using the task:

- As a means of exposing one of your team to some development
- As a means to practise a technique for your own development
- Reinforcing a policy or process that had been allowed to slip
- Introducing a new working practice or piece of equipment
- Assessing members of the team for coaching or quality assurance purposes or against competencies for a review
- Raise the profile of you or your team
- Reinforce or establish a power base

I'm sure you can think of others and after reflection it may be that no such bi-product opportunities exist, but the point is that you make a conscious effort to look for them.

Politically acceptable

Is the solution one that would be acceptable to your organisation and/or your boss? You may already have sufficient knowledge of your organisation, your boss and the accepted ways of working and customs that prevail. Alternatively, you may be fresh to any of them and have to undertake some additional activity to learn the ground-rules. After all, you might come up with the most innovative, practical and effective solution, but if for any reason it cannot or will not be accepted, there is potential for a lot of implementation and communication effort going to waste. That's not to say you should be put off pushing the boundaries where and when appropriate.

You may use the situation as an opportunity to challenge the status quo, but if doing so, you should consider where your power lies and which approach to challenge is appropriate to the situation, e.g., is successful completion of the solution more important than trying to get an archaic practice revised right now?

Decisive

Is this solution comprehensive, and complete? Is it, or does it need to be one of a series that would need to be implemented to achieve a long-term goal or task? There is such a thing as incremental decision-making, which is often likened to a ripple effect. It occurs in circumstances where you make one decision and embark upon a course of action that then requires subsequent decisions to be made by yourself or others.

Very often this occurs when the original decision is based upon a lack of knowledge of technique, or without the full facts of a situation. So what we are assessing is a quality of the solution, not your decision-making skills. The test is, is your solution beyond doubt and unmistakable?

Note that terms such as 'set in stone' and 'inflexible' have not been applied. You are not being told that decisions and solutions should be irreversible (see below), or that some incremental decisions might not be necessary where information is absent or patchy. The 'decisive' element of the mnemonic addresses other requirements for it to be a '**CRAFT-T**' solution (we covered off 'Time-bound' above). The things to consider are:

1. Does the solution clearly and specifically target at least one of the clearly stated, specific goals? If you don't have clearly stated goals you need to go back to the drawing board.
2. In view of the availability of resources, the time available and desired outcomes, is your solution feasible in so far as it makes best use of the resources?
3. Is the solution capable of being properly communicated to those who will be tasked with implementing it (see Communicate Chapter in Section 3)?
4. Does the decision demonstrate a consideration of all the facts and circumstances currently to hand and recognise and make clear any future related decisions that will be required.

Items 3 and 4 are additions to the '**CRAFT-T**' criteria. Demonstrating that you have considered these factors will provide substance to the solution. So that not only will it appear to be decisive, it will be!

Resourced

Consider whether the resources necessary to implement the solution will be readily available in the quantity and quality required or will some work need to be done to acquire them?

You not only have to assess whether the required resources are available, accessible or obtainable, but also whether they are affordable. If the best piece of kit, or person for the job costs more than you have or more than you can afford, you might have to go for second-best and amend your plan accordingly. If the alternative is slower, or takes up more room, you might have to extend your time frames, or relocate within the department to a suitable space. Similarly if you need six people with a certain level of knowledge and skill to complete a task, having access to fewer – or more – will impact on delivery. If the resources are not currently available you may even have to postpone until they are.

Cost is relative and dependant on what the organisation can pay or is willing to pay. Even though the costs may be affordable – and here we're talking finance, time, and effort – this is an appropriate time to consider whether those expenses are appropriate and justifiable given the desired or expected benefits that implementing the solution are likely to reap. Once again if they are not, you should give serious thought to revising the solution.

Acceptable to the team

What is going to be the likely reaction of your team to the solution? Is it going to be resisted, or is it a solution they are comfortable with or used to implementing? This is no less important than the solution being acceptable to your bosses. The level of anticipated acceptability influences the language, tone and methodology of how the solution is communicated. A lot depends on the source of your power and the style you intend to use to approach the challenge as discussed in Section 1.

This might be the type of challenge and solution the team is used to. Irrespective of that, you might be new to the role or well established. Importance and/or the urgency of the situation might mean that you have to push through an unpopular solution – omitting some of the customary niceties, or at least putting them off until the challenge and situation has been addressed.

Later you are prompted to test whether your solution is economical in financial terms. Here you are encouraged to do so in human-cost terms. Is the cost to staff-manager relations and long-term effectiveness applying the solution with/without force actually acceptable?

It is quite common to second guess incorrectly. You can assume that something that you considered the team wouldn't like, or would resist, actually goes through relatively easily because the prevailing environment means they knew it was coming. Conversely, something you thought they would welcome could be resisted because it comes as a shock, disturbs well-established customs, or is perceived as a threat in some way.

You will be asking your team and possibly others to commit not only to achieving the goal, but also the manner in which it is to be achieved. Both you and they need to be accepting of what is expected. Questions will be raised: why they're the ones doing it; what support will there be, when, where from and how; what will happen if you're not successful; and what's in it for them if anything?

You may find it difficult to commit when you consider you have insufficient information. Your team is no different – especially if the plan is clearly not feasible, or the pain is likely to outweigh the gain. Commitments can be discussed and agreed at this stage, but will only truly be tested when you get round to the actual execution of your plan.

Checking out acceptability early on has the potential to save a lot of effort. A scheme – no matter how wonderful – that cannot be put into practice because of operator resistance should be discounted early. Doing so also fulfils and contributes to the consultation and communication requirements of an effective plan (if consultation is required, expected and appropriate).

Workable

Is the solution practical, given the surrounding circumstances and environment in which you are working? This goes directly to the 'Feasible' requirement of a **CRAFT-T** solution. It is closely aligned to the need for your preferred solution to be adequately and properly resourced. If you do not have the required resources, you have the option to reconsider or – if your solution is by far the best – work towards getting the resources you do need. Knowing your **STUFF** – or whether similar solutions have worked in the past can influence and assist in you reaching a conclusion about this aspect.

Economical

Is there a financial and/or time cost involved? Consider the requirement for extra labour, technology, or equipment. If not readily available, what is the likelihood of you having access to the necessary budget?

During an economic recession, sales of goods and services are unlikely to rise. Such periods cause organisations to review their cost lines and to make cuts to preserve the bottom line; or even keep them afloat. Consequently if your solution costs money, you'll have to put forward a pretty convincing argument and business case to get it through. Usually this will involve demonstrating that a 'spend' now will save costs, or drive profits in the medium to long terms.

A £1, €1 or $1 saving is worth ten times as much in sales, primarily because of the extra effort, raw materials and resources that are required to drive those sales.

The point is that as a First-Line manager, your awareness of cost implications and how the prevailing economic climate is affecting your organisation needs to be higher than that of your team. There will be an expectation placed on you by your managers, or from those whom you must gain approval and support for your solution, to demonstrate you have considered the costs and proved the value.

Reversible

Once implemented, would it be possible to reverse this solution, or at the very least stop it if you realise part way through that all was not as predicted, or something happens that requires a rethink?

Illustrating the TOP-DRAWER model

Let's say in the case study scenario that Kerry faced earlier she had considered a number of options. There's no need to run through them all now, but let's use a 'for instance'. Suppose Kerry considered that one of the solutions would be to ask the reporter for a delay in publishing so that she could make some enquiries and come back with a definitive answer.

Exercise:

Kerry decides to make some informal enquiries with suppliers and the contractor and secures a short delay with the reporter. Apply the **TOP-DRAWER** test to Kerry's chosen solution.

What do you think might influence Kerry's determination (decision-making) as to how the solution meets the criteria?

You might have wanted some further information, before critiquing Kerry's potential solution. However, I wanted to keep it simple and get you used to applying the test. So how '**TOP-DRAWER**' is this solution likely to be?

T Time Bound? At the moment it's not. Kerry has not stipulated how long it's going to take her, not negotiated (yet) what delay the reporter will accept. Can she start straight away; or does she have other more pressing matters taking priority? When will her enquiries be completed? When will she have analysed the information and come to a decision?

O Opportunity – This as an opportunity to build or strengthen a relationship that could be useful for good publicity in the future, or did you only see the threat?

P The solution probably would be acceptable to her boss. It would allow a more positive image of the organisation. That said, would the bosses expect her to have the information anyway and not risk an allegation of at best being incompetent, or at worst trying to 'cover up'?

D On the face of it this is decisive, though we acknowledge that a series of further decisions would have to be made once the information is obtained, e.g. how it is to be packaged and given to the reporter.

R Kerry needs to apply time and possibly other resources to doing what she is committing to do, i.e. get the information and get back to the reporter. Think about the implications and repercussions if – having managed to get an agreement from the reporter, Kerry failed to deliver.

A The team would probably view this as Kerry supporting and even protecting them by ensuring that false information did not get out. On the other hand, they might be unhappy and/or resentful that she is even co-operating with the reporter.

W Given that the reporter would be under pressure to get the story in, they would probably be facing similar pressures to refuse a delay. Similarly, if Kerry does not have the time or other resources to get to the bottom of the allegations, or is likely to be 'stone-walling' when she does, it may be that she is just putting off the inevitable.

E This is not a test of the indirect impact of the solution on the long-term balance sheet. Having said that, she might choose to consider the economic cost (in terms of future revenue).

R Were a delay in publishing to be agreed, the paper would most likely give the space over to other matters. So unless it was a really juicy story, they would probably not 'hold the front page'. So replying early wouldn't be so helpful. This solution is probably not reversible, as altering it might again be perceived as either indecision, or incompetence.

Remember that this is a subjective test. You may think differently and that's fine, so long as you thought it through and did so by applying each element of the test appropriately. You have the option now of applying the same test to any solution that you believe you would 'run' with in respect of any situation.

Using the TOP-DRAWER Model Process

If you have a number of solutions under consideration, you can consider scoring them against each of the criteria. Doing so now, could well save time in future. Tradesmen use the adage 'measure twice, cut once' to try to avoid costly mistakes.

You could use a table. The left-hand column lists all the solutions using either a number or a brief description. There is then a column for each of the criteria. A score from -5 to +5 could be applied. For instance a solution likely to attract a high level of staff resistance might in your opinion receive a score of -4; or a solution likely to be highly acceptable to your bosses might score +4. This enables calculation of an overall score. At the end of the process you could end up with one solution that stands out with the highest score. Theory has it that you should proceed and adopt this solution.

For support or double-checking, you might get a trusted colleague or colleagues to apply the same testing process and see whether they come up with the same scoring as you.

The test will not guarantee the best solution, but it certainly helps your choice. Take for example the following situation:

Your organisation has decided to branch out into another product or service related to those you currently provide. All necessary training will be provided. It is anticipated your volume of business will increase by about 15%. You will not be getting any additional team-members.

The regional manager as asked all team managers to submit their proposals as to how this increase in volume will be dealt with.

Below I have identified a number of potential solutions – there may be others. These are scored according to an agreed scale. If one would work more in your environment, vary the scoring. It's a process of objective scoring, not one of engineering the process so that it reflects your original/preferred thought. In my table -5 is a rating reflecting the lowest potential, +5 the highest.

You may disagree with the outcome, especially if you tailored the exercise to your own organisation, but there follows some reasoning.

Possible Solution	RATING (-5 - +5)									
	T	O	P	D	R	A	W	E	R	Total
Do nothing	5	-5	-5	5	5	-3	-5	5	5	7
Send an email to your team announcing the impending change, inviting comment, with a deadline	4	3	3	3	3	4	3	4	3	30
Leave it until the next team meeting and discuss then	4	3	4	4	5	4	4	4	2	34
Pick a couple of trusted/proficient team members, meet them and discuss ideas	5	3	4	5	5	2	4	3	2	33
Call special full team meeting with all who can attend doing so	5	4	4	5	4	4	4	2	4	36
Develop your own solution(s) without any consultation & report back to your manager	5	-3	4	5	3	2	3	3	4	26

Figure 5: Solution Scoring Format

Firstly, you should recognise that consciously or otherwise, your manager is in the second 'D' phase of the **ADDRESS Model** in determining albeit through you, possible solutions. Regardless of their motivation for doing so, or whether you recognise a particular reasoning, they have created a separate situation; one that *you* must now **ADDRESS**. This is a new situation for you to deal with. This is the case even if you have a legitimate reason for saying 'No'.

We have determined the 'gap': your manager needs information you don't currently have, or have ready. You are now in the third phase of the process (the second '**D**'). To complete the task you must aim for a **TOP-DRAWER** solution. You should consider a range of options even if you think you already know what the solution will be. For you, 'execution' will be putting together the information; possibly one or two solutions with an evaluation of each; a recommendation as to which you think is best; and delivering it. 'Step back' will be just that – affording your boss the time to make a decision in line with, or discounting your suggestions. You can 'Sign-Off' as and when you are informed by your manager that they have reached their decision and (at your request if necessary) provided you with some information or feedback as to the effect and quality of your contribution to their process.

So! Your manager has given you a legitimate task. You cannot do 'nothing'. That would be detrimental to all concerned, especially if in the absence of you providing an acceptable solution, your manager comes up with one of his/her own and imposes it. Consider the difficulties it will cause you; the breakdown of trust and the extra effort you'd have to put in to the eventual change management. If you did nothing, you're probably not too 'pro' change-management.

Working on your own ideas without any other consultation and reporting back to your manager is denying your team members any opportunity for development and any sense of control over their environment. If time permits, there's the opportunity to develop staff engagement. Otherwise, when it comes, they are unlikely to have any ownership of the solution and are more likely to resist it. Taking this all on your shoulders may ensure a solid solution, but your capacity to do this whilst juggling all your other responsibilities is open to debate. What would happen to this task, if something similar came along the next day? What would happen if you went off – sick?

Sending an email round to your team announcing the impending change and inviting comment with a deadline may be time bound, but it is one-way communication. If you did not understand a respondent's comments, or thought that it was a good idea, you would need to invest further time and resources to getting additional information and maybe even circulating it to the rest of the team for comment etc. The email could also be hastily deposited in recipients' deleted box without reading. This methodology is weak on engagement and wastes an opportunity for you to give a full explanation and to answer any questions, before solutions are offered.

There is a danger in picking a couple of trusted/ proficient team members in that if you're not careful it is always the same trusted/proficient individuals that get selected even though they may not want or need to participate. This can breed resentment amongst the remainder of the team; result in some who are deserving and need of development not getting it; and you may lose some valuable contributions. Don't forget the rest of the team would also have to provide cover for the lucky ones who could be seen as having a soft time of things.

Leaving it until the next team meeting has many of the positive attributes of the highest scoring solution, provided of course it is due well in advance of your deadline for submissions. You also have to consider what else – if anything – has to be discussed at that same meeting. Will there be enough time to get quality responses and to discuss ideas? Or once you've got some ideas, might you have to have some follow up (time-consuming) meetings to develop them?

The highest scoring option would (of course) be based on your experience; your knowledge of the situation, the operation, the team; and what the goals are. It carries a time cost, but it affords an opportunity for all those who want to get involved to do so; it enhances the potential for team development, team engagement, acceptance and application of the ultimate solution. You can call it at a time that suits the business, but also gives you as much time as possible to collate responses and come up with a presentable response for your boss. On the basis of the scoring therefore, the manager should probably run with that.

If having completed this exercise the manager is uncomfortable with the highest-scoring solution they must ask a couple of questions: 1. Did I score everything accurately and objectively? 2. If I did – and I believe the outcome – what do I need to do in order to make myself more comfortable? Similar questions can be asked in the eventuality that two solutions come out with the same score, as you would need to pick just one. As an option you might then revisit the scores for the two main contenders and run it again.

In different situations it may be opportune and you may have the time, to consult colleagues, peers or knowledgeable subordinates to 'sanity-check' the solution that comes out on top. Give them a blank version of the same table and options and get them to score using the same process. A useful by-product of doing so also affords you the opportunity to manage your emotions – if such is required – and to determine the most appropriate style of approach to challenge that would best suit the situation. Once you have a solution that fits your requirements, you should consider the resources you'll need.

15. CRAFT-T planning

If you have followed **TOP-DRAWER**, you will have included contingencies, so it is important that once you have set the solution in motion, you maintain appropriate levels of control activity a) to ensure the original plan continues to be appropriate and b) to step in with a contingency as and when required.

CRAFT-T (pronounced 'crafty') operational planning and decision-making are inescapable necessities for the First-Line manager. They operate at a very personal level with a relatively small team. In the short term and in close proximity, your decision-making may only affect a small number. However, recognise and accept that your decisions can have far-reaching implications.

It is very possible to over-plan, or stick too rigidly to one's grand scheme. Whilst everything you do beforehand feeds into the plan, planning for real starts when you enter the **Execution** phase of the **ADDRESS Model**. The aim of this chapter is to outline some simple processes for facilitating the optimum outcome. You will be encouraged to identify the components required of any plan and then to apply a test to any plan you decide upon before you go ahead and execute it. Thus even if it is not the optimum solution, it has a chance of being the most effective one that could be applied with the resources available.

You should be able to explain to others what a **CRAFT-T** plan is and apply it to your future plans.

The **CRAFT-T** test IS applied to your planning using the criteria of:

C	Clarity
R	Reaction
A	Adequately resourced
F	Feasible
T	Targeted
T	Time-bound

On the face of it this appears to be repetitious of the **TOP-DRAWER** test you have just learned. It is important to stress that just as you are testing your solution, you then need to test any subsequent plan. I am also conscious that you might be thinking that I'm making the process too laborious, and that consequently there is no way you would have the time to complete it all.

So far I have not stipulated precisely how long each of these activities will or should take. Those of you with experience of facing challenges will have completed many if not all of these tasks unconsciously. Maybe even in an appropriate sequence too. On occasions you will have done so in a matter of minutes – the whole process! On others you may have needed a day or two. Those who are new to role, or who are still building their experience bank will benefit from getting into the habit of following a process.

The more experiences you have and the more you learn from them, the more potential solutions get stored in the old grey matter for you to consider. This reduces the time searching for or assessing solutions that you know have worked previously. Remember though, to tailor the solution for the particular challenge in front of you. No two situations are ever exactly the same, hence the benefits of using the aide so that you don't forget anything.

If others are involved in delivering your plan, you will have to communicate it to them. This communication needs to be as clear and concise, yet as comprehensive as possible if they are to know and understand what is required of them – and go on to do it as expected.

Providing you keep an open mind, applying the test will illustrate whether your plan will work in practice. You may think you thought of everything and work hard at planning out the problems and barriers you foresee. It is often the case that not everyone is as committed as you; they don't do as promised; a vital piece of kit may not arrive, or may fail immediately; and there's always the mouse that chews through the cable! If you have contingencies you may be applying them. The key thing to remember is that once you have started to enact your plan you will have started a series of events – a chain reaction. You will have initiated a series of subsequent situations each of which may require you to **ADDRESS** another situation.

In earlier chapters you got a hint of what **CRAFT-T** planning is about.

Keep in mind that it is an *optional* test. If you have taken the trouble to identify and apply the **TOP-DRAWER** you need to plan to implement it as best you can. No matter how much time you have, it is your responsibility to ensure that anyone else involved knows what they have to do, that the necessary resources are gathered and ready and that you have in place some measures of success.

The test explained below is similar to others available and is provided as an alternative, not a replacement. As it is a test method, it identifies not only what is to be tested, but suggests the criteria that should be applied. Remember, the identification of a solution is one process; planning to put it into practice is another.

Why Planning?

American General and statesman Dwight D. Eisenhower commented, "In preparing for battle I have always found that plans are useless, but planning is indispensable."[30] No matter how long we take to create a plan, no matter how detailed, how well resourced, or how polished and impressive it looks, that plan requires human input and most humans are fallible. Someone, somewhere will be in the wrong place at the wrong time; or in the right place but without the piece of equipment they need; or even in the right place, at the right time, but without the necessary skill or will to do what is expected of them. We then introduce IT and other machinery that doesn't know and doesn't care about the users' feelings yet has the uncanny knack of breaking down when it is most needed.

There needs to be some balancing: between the time available to plan and the complexity of the situation; between the resources that are, or can be at your disposal and those required for the most effective solution; and around just how many contingencies you cater for, the likelihood of them occurring, or your control over them.

The **TOP-DRAWER** model is intended and best used when you have a range of solutions and you are seeking to distinguish between them and select the optimum. There is nothing at all to stop you using the same criteria and applying them to your chosen plan. However, once you have reached 'Execution' in the **ADDRESS Model**, you are no longer seeking to compare several options against each other. You have chosen a solution

---

30   Quoted in (Nixon 1962)

and need a test that focuses on the qualities of your plan. **CRAFT-T** is an alternative, possibly quicker option. As we move ever more closely to action, we should be focussing on that and have confidence that we have completed the previous stages effectively. This is a framework to test the plan regardless of the time available.

Good Planning

There are benefits of identifying a logical ordered sequence of activities. The military are very good at it. Without wishing to scare you – I want to reference the nine Principles of War as set out in ARTEP[31], the US military Army Training and Evaluation Programme. I am not suggesting every encounter and situation should be entered into as a 'battle'. But, to paraphrase ARTEP, I do recommend the concept of having:

- A clearly defined, decisive and achievable objective
- Your resources concentrated in the right place at the right time
- The initiative or lead
- Applying only the minimum of resources to secondary issues – not essential to the task
- One person in charge and
- Clear, simple plans and clear, concise instructions to ensure thorough understanding

I have omitted three of the nine as I don't think 'Striking when the enemy is unprepared', 'placing the enemy in a position of disadvantage', and 'never permitting them to acquire an unexpected advantage' are appropriate for our purposes, but then I don't know your organisation. Maybe the language might be varied according to the nature of your business and what you are trying to achieve.

You may recall me talking of the role of the First-Line manager in police operations. Very often in stressful situations, such as the dawn raid or policing a demonstration, the detailed content of the pre-operation briefing could be quickly or easily forgotten. Alternatively, if it was remembered, it could be abandoned in the face of unforeseen circumstances; speedily amended when the circumstances 'on the ground'

31   (Army 2011)

140

changed; or when the foreseen type of circumstances proved more or less extreme than anticipated. It is very often in these circumstances that the strategists and tacticians are dependent and rely upon the knowledge, skill and ability of the operational manager to think on their feet and maintain control. For this to happen the operational manager requires a good knowledge of the overall aim and objectives and must also know their **STUFF**.

Too much preparation can be just as bad as not enough. As Napoleon is said to have said, "Over-preparation is the foe of inspiration". If things are too constrained by a script or over-detailed plan, the situation breaks down when something that was not in that plan interferes; or something in the plan doesn't follow the rules. That's why so many organisations require varying degrees of initiative from their First-Line managers. Unfortunately many of the same organisations are too quick to jump on said managers if the initiative is not as successful as desired.

By identifying a sequence of clear (and clearly allocated) activities, a plan facilitates the translation of desire and intention or aim into reality. You are encouraged to recognise that not doing everything in the plan can be OK. We talked about 'confidence' earlier, and if at the planning stage, you can test the plan to breaking point and make corrections and compensations, it stands more chance of giving you confidence as to its likely success.

So how do you test your plans – to see whether and how effective they will be? To what extent would your plan expect or require you, or others, to act in a manner that questions, or stretches their values? Is this acceptable? To what extent will your plan develop you and the others involved and make everyone better at what they do?

For you, the latter may be minimal, especially if it's a routine situation that you've dealt with many times before. But that doesn't mean to say the others have been involved in something similar before. The point is to look for the opportunity and if it is there, to take advantage of it.

The next case study could be used to test application of the models outlined so far. For now focus on the planning that the manager has to conduct. It matters not whether you agree with the manager's choices, nor if you can think of a better one. Just need come up with a plan!

Exercise

Remembering the conditions mentioned in the case study introduction, put yourself in Bryan's position: create a plan to ensure you get the best Senior Advisor possible.

CASE STUDY: Who to choose?

Bryan manages a team of fifteen specialist contact centre staff, based in a business park unit about five miles from the city centre. This is one of several units in the region and is part of a national group. As part of expansion to meet demand, Head Office has determined that Bryan's team will be enlarged. Consequently a post of Senior Advisor will be created for each of the sites affected. Bryan will be responsible for this post holder at his site. The expectation is that the Senior Advisors will be recruited from within the organisation and all agents past probation are eligible to apply.

Head Office HR has templates and well-established processes for recruiting the agents. These have been set in motion with a target date for them to join the business and commence their six–week training in three months' time. Training takes place at a regional centre. Bryan will be expected to take part in the recruitment process for these agents. However, the senior agent position is new to the organisation. HR has put together a role description, but because they are recruiting the agents nationally, they do not have the resources to assist with the Senior Agent recruiting process. As with other centre managers, Bryan has been tasked to conduct this process. Bryan was himself promoted 'through the ranks' and has recruited agents before. Head Office will be publicising the Senior Agent vacancies in five days' time.

Bryan recognises that in the long term the Senior Advisor will be able to help and take off some of the pressure from him. He knows that there are a couple of good candidates in his team and would rather one of them was promoted than getting an outsider in.

Bryan also recognises two situations that he has to deal with: He has to take part in the testing, interviewing and recruiting of five new agents; and he has to manage the recruitment of his 'deputy'. He decides to leave the former to HR to organise and will rely on them to let him know when he is needed. He is confident that his participation in the task phase of the agent recruiting process will secure the right people. He will put his energies into getting a good Senior Agent.

Case Study 4: Who to choose

Ensure you have attempted a solution before reading on.

In your planning you may well have resorted to a format you have used before – nothing wrong there – and you may have been influenced by the contents of the lead-up to the case study.

Your goal should be consistent with recruiting the best-possible Senior Agent. Bearing in mind you will not know if you have been successful until the successful candidate has been in place for some time, the measurement of this goal becomes – if not vague – certainly protracted.

You may have focussed on the inference that Bryan wanted someone from his own centre to get the job. This suggests he might well skew the process and his plan accordingly. If you did immerse yourself into the role of Bryan therefore, you might well have created a process that was biased towards internal, local candidates. I'm not going to comment either way on that for the moment. If you couldn't bring yourself to go that far, your plan will probably have included some form of 'paper-sifting' (Bryan might sift out all those not from his centre for instance); and either a series of practical tests or exercises, or interviews (competency based or otherwise), or a combination of both.

Once identified, you probably wanted the successful candidate to be appointed and settled in advance of the new agents arriving. Hopefully, Bryan will allocate time to the various stages of the process and will complete some research to see if he can obtain recruiting materials from previous processes that he can use straight away or with some minor amendment.

Moving on and without criticising your plan, because you will probably have used a method you are familiar and comfortable with, I want to explain what is meant by the **CRAFT-T** test. It is a test that can be applied to any plan, no matter in what format it was drawn up. I will refer back to the case study and to the plan you created

Clarity

Does the plan you devised for Bryan have **Clarity**? When considering **Clarity** you need to confirm whether it is clear as to: why action is necessary

– are the aims and objectives explicit, specific, relevant and achievable; who does what; when and by when; where; and how (you may already be familiar with '5WH'). Does your plan have clearly defined stages (if appropriate) and target dates for each to be completed? Does it specify who is needed to do what? [Note that at this stage we are saying what is needed without prejudging whether a particular resource is available, willing and/or able to support].

If I was to pick up your plan cold, would I be clear as to what you intended to achieve and how? That's clarity!

In the case study your overall goal should indeed be to recruit the best person for the job, but given the difficulty and delay in measuring this, applying the **CRAFT-T** test suggests we need to be very specific about the goal. In this instance the more immediate goal would be to "Put into effect and to follow through on an effective recruitment campaign to ensure that candidates are properly and adequately examined and that the best candidate is identified." You will be able to measure this, as there will be records of any tests applied and/or interview responses provided.

Very often clarity can be supported when depicted by a project sheet or Gantt chart e.g.

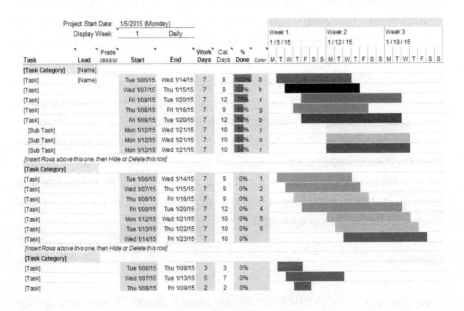

Figure 6: Sample Gantt chart

144

Reaction

How would your boss or organisation **React** to your plan? In **TOP-DRAWER** earlier, acceptability of a solution to the organisation and to those who would be tasked with implementing it, were treated as separate considerations. In this model they are combined.

You need to test the likely **Reaction** to both the plan *and* the likely outputs by a) those on the receiving end and b) those that have tasked you with the job.

In the case study Bryan must gauge what the reaction of his bosses and the organisation would be if the plan he implemented led to recruitment of an individual who (a) took up the post and 'flew', proving to be excellent or (b) was one of the weaker candidates, but got the job because of Bryan's patronage and went on to cause the organisation some serious industrial relations problems?

A question he and you can ask is based on your knowledge of the organisation: "Would the outcome of your plan justify the plan itself?" Would they care so long as the right person got the job?

Adequately Resourced

Whether or not a plan is **Adequately Resourced** will have considerable influence and impact on the extent to which execution is successful. An under-resourced plan could take longer than is required, or if money is tight, be of a reduced standard.

In the case study, not only does Bryan have to recruit a senior agent, he will also be called upon to help with the recruitment process for the extra five agents; he also has the 'day-job' and must continue to ensure the service is still delivered. Bryan needs to identify how many and what type of resources are required for administration and for the performance of the actual chosen processes.

Would he be expecting to 'paper-sift' himself? Arrange all the appointments himself? Run any assessment centre and interviews himself? I suggest he needs some administrative support at least. It would be unwise for him to conduct any process such as interviews on his own, especially when operating with internal candidates. He would need some support to keep things going in business as usual. Perhaps this is an opportunity to bring in some of the existing team to assist with the administration? Perhaps once he is aware of any of his team putting themselves forward, he might delegate some of his existing tasks to them to allow him to focus on the recruitment and them to get some experience in a supervisory role?

Unless we are in very creative organisations, or those in which the environment and culture encourage and support innovative approaches and 'thinking outside' the box, it is unlikely that this is an opportunity for Bryan to be creative. For this reason it is less likely that something we come up with would be a 'flight of fancy' that could never be implemented.

Especially at the First-Line level, there is a predominance of use of experience and what knowing our **STUFF** tells us, stands a good chance of working. Many of the solutions and plans we come up with will invariably have been previously tried and tested. This might be by us, when we call on past experience, or by others from whom we have learned. After all, if it worked then, provided it is applied properly (with or without any necessary modification for the current circumstance), there is no reason for it not to be appropriate now. Caution is necessary though. You still need to check the proposal and even though it worked before, there is absolutely no cast-iron guarantee that it will automatically do so now.

Feasible

This is a step beyond that of the test applied to potential solutions. The latter tends to be more hypothetically based and the former more founded on the planner's knowledge of the circumstances and the environment. Similarly, there could be more than one way of applying a particular solution with some being more feasible than others.

In the same way that you were required to test your solution for its cost-to-benefit ratio, you should be testing your plan to ensure that the costs fall within those anticipated. If your plan has generated costs that are now more expensive than budgeted for, or some new costs that were not initially budgeted for, you will have to revisit either or both. A plan cannot be considered feasible if it is too costly or if any cost though affordable, will not generate the benefits desired or intended.

Targeted

Review whether the proposal actually addresses the stated aims and objectives. 'Targeting' the plan is dependent on accurate goals from the outset. So this and **Clarity** go very much together. If you are not clear on your goal, how can you expect to communicate it clearly and accurately? How can you expect anyone else involved in the plan to fully achieve what is expected of them?

Yes! Bryan's goal should be to get the best person for the job. However, his objectives in the case study should be to (a) devise a process that is fair and appropriate to identify the best candidate; (b) gather, organise the resources necessary – including those required to free up his time and (c) implement that process.

Time-Bound

Apply specific timings to distinct phases: start times, duration and expected due dates. This provides you with measures and helps to manage expectations.

In the case study some specific deadlines are inferred: The agents will be starting in three months' time, but will not be ready to operate in the business for a further six weeks. Good practice would then suggest that Bryan wants the Senior Advisor to be selected, appointed and reasonably settled into the role in advance of the agents coming in. In other words there is little time to waste, as, whatever process for recruitment he selects, it needs to be started as soon as possible. It would be quite easy to allocate time deadlines to each of the phases. The earlier Gant Chart illustrates these across the top.

The Unforeseen Spanners

No matter how good the plan, whether or not it's a **TOP-DRAWER** solution and has passed the **CRAFT-T** test, the potential for unforeseen eventualities is ever-present. It would be impractical to attempt to plan all these out. In the case study, some spanners that could be thrown into the works include:

- Bryan's choice of candidate from his team skews the process because he applies for other similar roles and goes through the respective processes concurrently. He is successful in another application too and, because it was closer to home, decided to take that one

- Whoever gets chosen decides that they don't want the role after all
- No one reaches the benchmark criteria or 'pass mark'
- The successful candidate is found to have been less than truthful in their application
- The successful candidate was good at getting through assessment centres, but proves less good in practice
- The successful candidate is in an accident and goes long-term sick shortly after being appointed
- Before the successful candidate is appointed, they are found guilty of gross misconduct and dismissed from the organisation

There could well be more – any of which could be more predictable than others. What they all boil down to, however, is that Bryan would have to start the whole process over again. It would be interesting to see if he then applied exactly the same plan, or whether he learnt by this experience and where appropriate, and if necessary, changed it to factor out any of the causes.

There could well be reasons for doing or not doing things in a particular way: there could be local agreements, legal reasons or customs, which influence process. But I hope the point is well made, that there is a need to be objective in your planning.

Communicating the Plan

It's time to look at what you do next with your plan. Alexander Hamilton (1755–1804) suggested that, "Men often oppose a thing merely because they have had no agency in planning it, or because it may have been planned by those whom they dislike." Hence the need to get people involved and engaged by way of effective communication of your proposals.

Earlier on, I touched upon the inevitability of you having to communicate your plan to others involved, whether this is upwards to gain approval, or sideways and downwards to get co-operation and participation. Aside from the general qualities of good communication, you want to be able to ensure that all concerned know amongst other things: the background to the activity; what its purpose might be; who is involved and what is expected of them. This is where having a format or aide-memoire to follow can be of use. There's no shortage of them. Many contain the same principles and requirements, but change the name, or the sequence. I include the following selection for you to try and pick one you feel comfortable with:

- IIMAC – used in military briefings
- **REASON** as a briefing is another form of encounter (see later)
- BRIEF
- GUIDE

I reiterate that these are all offered as alternatives. You can give each a try; stick to one; or use a variety according to the nature of the situation you are planning for.

IIMAC

This relates to:

Information: The background to the event and current situation

Intention: The aims and objectives of the plan

Method: How it's going to be done, by whom, when and
                        where (the why is covered off above)

Administration: How is it going to be organised, who is doing
                        what, what's the chain of command and
                        responsibility

Communication: What the channels of communication are

REASON

In this context **REASON** can be utilised as follows:

Relationship: Introducing yourself and your role generally and
                        within the current task

Explanation:	What is the briefing for and what format is it going to take
Account:	Used in this situation 'Account' is split into up to three parts:

Part 1 correlates to the last four elements of IIMAC. It is sub-divided into
- Background as in 'Information' above
- Aim and objectives
- Method – using who, what, when, where and how, administration and communication
- Measures
- Controls

Part 2 is led by you and is the opportunity for questions and (if appropriate) suggestions from the audience

Part 3 involves you asking the number, type and complexity of questions you feel is appropriate to confirm that the right information has got across and has been understood [Part 3 would be omitted in an approval seeking circumstance]

Summary	Is the opportunity for you to reinforce the key points of the method
Outputs	Would be confirming that all participants have been made aware of the aim & objectives and methodology. It relates to the encounter more than the method
Next	Reinforces the 'kick off' date and also the time and date of the next time the group will gather again.

BRIEF

You could use this for less complex situations or those in which a speedy briefing is required. It is made up of:

Background	As described in the previous models
Rationale	The purpose of the plan and the Aim and Objectives
Indicators	What the measures of success will be and also any stages/milestones
Execution	This is the same as 'Method' described above
Follow-Up	What controls will be run and once the aim and objectives are achieved to the extent possible

GUIDE

This is my final offering and as with BRIEF above, is best suited to quicker, simpler situations. It consists of:

Goal	What are you intending to achieve (as per aims and objectives)
Utilisation	What are the resources involved
Indicators	What the stages, milestones and outlines are
Delivery	This is subdivided as per the 'Execution' or 'Method' elements of the earlier described models
Evaluation	When and how will the process and its success be assessed and reported on

Summary

You have been introduced to a **CRAFT-T** method for testing a plan. Even if you don't use *this* testing method, find one that works for you and get into the habit of applying it objectively. If your passion for the task or its intended outcomes hinders objectivity, get someone else to test it too or instead.

These aide-memoires will help you to communicate your plan to others. These are not tests of the efficacy, suitability or prospects for a plan. Rather, they are ways of you remembering what and how to communicate about your plan.

Napoleon advised not to over-prepare, "Take time to deliberate; but when the time for action arrives, stop thinking and go in."[32] Balance this with the advice of writer Florence Scovil Shinn that, "If someone asks for success and prepares for failure, he will get the situation he has prepared for."[33]

End of Chapter Activity 1:

The next time you plan something, test it using the **CRAFT-T** criteria.

To what extent is the solution **TOP-DRAWER**? What effect did that have on your planning?

What effect did the amount of time you had have on the content and quality of the plan?

If there are areas for development you can repeat this exercise as many times as you like.

End of Chapter Activity 2:

Prepare to brief your team on a plan. Pick any one of the formats described.

Deliver the briefing and seek feedback as to its clarity etc, from those being briefed.

Feel free to source or construct your own aide-memoire if none of these work – it's important that you have something that works for you.

---

32 (Bonaparte n.d.)

33 (Shinn n.d.)

16. Exercising CONTROL

What does being in control require and look like? There are a few things to remember, all of which may help you acquire the air of a manager in control of any situation.

Firstly, once your plan is 'in flow' you should **check in** regularly to monitor how things are going. The frequency at which you do so depends on the nature of the situation and the complexity of the plan. A simple solution with a long time frame, few participants and not much at stake, might require a check-up once a week or so. Whereas a more complex plan with high/serious consequences of failure, may require more frequent check-ups. It's for you to decide and early on in your role there may be an element of trial and error. If you sense your team needs more support, you can do more. If you sense they think you're interfering and not trusting them to get on with it, you should consider backing-off a little. The latter however, should not be to the point that you're abrogating your responsibilities.

Observe what's going on. This includes asking for progress reports or feedback. And if you're going to allocate time to doing this, and pull them away from the task also, don't waste the opportunity. **Note progress** and achievements so that you can check them off against the plan requirements. There is more on this in the subsequent chapter Watch, Listen, Feel.

If something is not going according to plan. Consider it as a fresh 'situation' and work though the **ADDRESS Model** anew. **Take action** as required – based on what following that process tells you. This is equally as applicable to when things are going well and ahead of schedule, as when they are going poorly or falling behind. For instance, if a finished product is made up of several interdependent components or stages and one is finished too early; what do you do with it and/or the team that is now idle waiting for the rest to catch up?

If you do change or 'tweak' something, always **revisit** the original plan to determine the effect on the rest of it. Minor changes to the plan may not be an issue. Indeed they might be beneficial! You might in the example above for instance be able to bring everything else forward if one part is finished early. But major changes or technical issues might have a significant effect on the whole. In which case you would be looking at maybe another **TOP-DRAWER** solution and possibly re-assessing the plan to see if it still meets the **CRAFT-T** criteria.

Like a machine, your plan will need to be kept moving and so will require some lubrication or **oiling**. I'm talking about recognising good work, keeping up morale, smoothing over issues, and removing anything that might cause the plan to seize up. You might need to bring in new personalities, remove under-performers, or light a fire (metaphorically) under those who are dragging their heels.

However, if all is going according to plan, aside from encouragement, **leave it** alone! Give it chance to work and resist the temptation to make unnecessary or cosmetic changes that might serve only to unbalance or confuse those tasked with completing it. Do this, and you will be exercising **CONTROL**. It is to be applied during the 'Execution' and 'Stepping Back' phases of the **ADDRESS** Model.

To be concise, **CONTROL** equates to:

C	Check regularly
O	Observe and ensure plan requirements are being completed as required
N	Note and recognise progress
T	Take action to remedy issues (good or bad) as required
R	Revisit the plan and realign if necessary
O	Oil it! – Reward good performance, keep participants engaged and motivated
L	Leave it! If it's working as it needs to, don't tamper.

Exercise

Answer the following questions in your note pad:

How do you currently check on the performance of your team? Is it too much, too little, or about right? ADDRESS this as a situation if necessary. Devise a plan to develop

When you observe, from where do you get your data and how reliable is it? Do you record it, analyse it appropriately and use it to take action?

Do you recognise progress and good performance?

Do you take appropriate decisive action as and when required to deal with variances to any plan? Can this be improved?

To what extents are you willing and able to revise plans (if they are your own); or influence changes in others' plans?

How good are you at motivating?

How good are you at resisting the temptation to interfere unnecessarily?

17. Have a REASON for every encounter

Interaction between any First-Line manager and others, both inside and outside the organisation is inevitable – some would say essential. Even if you only interact with machinery as a 'day job', doubtless you'll still have someone to report to, and must also deal with the repair engineer.

When following the **ADDRESS** process, you may have meetings to help 'Diagnose' causes and 'Determine' solutions. Almost certainly there will be interaction to plan and implement the 'Execution' of your solution. Think of the many other encounters you might have when **CONTROL** is required. You will also have day-to-day issues to deal with.

How many times have you left an encounter or meeting, wishing you'd asked a killer question, or not got your point across effectively or not at all?

It is important to be able to properly prepare for all encounters, not just scheduled meetings. They can and should be approached methodically and with **REASON** so as not to waste anyone's time. That's what this chapter is all about. I will also introduce my '**4Q-4A**' model, which you can use to structure inquisitive encounters such as interviews. Both models will help you manage encounters at any level. **REASON** is a system for controlling encounters, ensuring they are as effective as they can be, resulting in the outcomes that both you and the other parties intend and require.

Your working time is limited and so, precious. You only have so much time in which to fulfil tasks and meet expectations. It is both logical and sensible therefore, to reduce waste of that time and of 'you' as a resource. You will be perceived more favourably if perceived as a manager who is practical, decisive, and efficient. *You* may not mind your time being wasted, but others almost certainly will mind theirs being.

Unplanned, unscheduled meetings – bumping into a long-lost colleague in a corridor for instance – can be equally as important as the scheduled variety. Just because they are unscheduled, doesn't mean they can't be structured, even if requires you to think very quickly on your feet.

Whether you're responsible for a meeting or responding to an invitation, there can be little worse than turning up unprepared and/or minus the information you need, or are expected to be in possession of. A lot can also depend on your power-base; for instance, are you the 'expert', or are you expected to be there because of your position?

To ensure you maximise a planned meeting's potential, consider the following checklist. Working through it might involve quite a lot of work. But remember it is intended for meetings for which you have sufficient advance notice. Also remember that 'prior planning prevents a pretty poor performance!' You can trim the list according to the circumstances, your environment and the time available. Having tried to answer the questions, it might give you grounds for postponement.

- What is the main purpose? E.g. is it your performance review, or that of a subordinate? Is it project-related, a crisis or an unforeseen opportunity?
- Why has the meeting been called? E.g. could the subject be handled in another way? Was it scheduled or unexpected?
- Why are *you* attending? Obvious if you're the subject or in control. Alternatively you might have accountability within a project; your expertise/knowledge may be required to advise a discussion. Then again you might just be on a distribution list.
- Is it formal or informal?
- What is your contribution expected to be?
- Can you meet any expectation already, or will you need some preparation? Maybe you're not the right person so could or should send someone else.
- What are *your* objectives for attending the meeting? They may be indirect, e.g. networking
- What do *you* expect to come out of the meeting?
- What will *you* do if neither transpires?
- What other benefits/drawbacks might there be in you attending?
- Under the circumstances do you have the time to be present?
- If you cannot be present do you need to be represented, or can you supply

157

any required information in advance and/or answer any questions in advance?

The REASON Model

A lot of what follows is dependent on good preparation and so is of particular relevance to scheduled and planned encounters. However, the elements are still usable in other encounter-types; I'm thinking of those corridor encounters: bumping into a colleague at lunch and having a 'chat', or the unexpected or short-notice 'phone call. Whatever the encounter it can be divided into the following distinct phases:

R   Relationship
E   Explanation
A   Account
S   Summary
O   Outputs
N   Next

Let's look at each of these elements in a bit more detail.

Relationship Phase

This contributes to setting the tone of the encounter. It is as an optional element and is as applicable to difficult encounters as it is to the easy. If one already exists, you are encouraged to look at the relationship you have with the other participants and how it might be affected by the encounter. If no relationship already exists, you should consider whether building one is necessary to make the encounter more effective. Consider too whether the encounter will initiate or build upon a mutually beneficial relationship for the future?

You may believe you have a sound working relationship with and understanding of others in the encounter, their views, feelings, understanding and knowledge of what is going to be the topic or subject of it. However, some encounters may well test that relationship: misunderstandings, topics likely to heighten emotions, or situations that are unexpected, could lead to totally unexpected reactions from others. If no prior relationship exists, if it is in its infancy, or has been previously difficult, then it is easy for either side to be nervous, or even suspicious of the other.

In any event, a well-managed encounter involves an attempt to establish, reinforce, or maybe repair a relationship. Done well, this helps to establish ground rules and rapport. It may even help to reduce some of the emotion in the situation leading to a more effective encounter. Done poorly it can serve to reinforce the negative gaps that exist between the person in control (you) and the other party or parties; for example, a half-hearted attempt to ask about the 'family' or 'the wife', when everyone knows you don't really care, or they don't actually have a 'wife'!

When considering including some relationship-building, you must assess whether the activity is necessary; whether there is a need for a professional interest; or whether under the circumstances, it would be being overly and/or falsely interested. Unpractised and clumsy attempts are quickly interpreted as such. Not a good start to the encounter! Be genuine! If you know virtually nothing about a person's hobby, don't ask technical questions about it. If it's a mutual interest such as a shared love of a particular sport, make sure you can be non-partisan, or partisan in a friendly manner.

If you can't or don't want to build or reinforce a relationship you should consider skipping this stage. But don't do so 'out of hand' as I have seen the phase used to lighten a difficult atmosphere, or soften the forthcoming blow. You will have another opportunity in the next explanation phase, as the words and messages you incorporate then can certainly establish, or help to reinforce an ongoing relationship between the parties, or one that exists for the purposes of this particular encounter. If the encounter is to impart some bad news, a good pre-existing relationship is very beneficial. So care is required with this first stage in such an encounter.

This phase can easily be completed on the way into the meeting venue. It doesn't want or need to be too long. Getting involved in a long discussion about your team's current dismal performance in the league may do wonders for the relationship, but will eat into the time set aside for the encounter. You will be at risk of not achieving your objectives. The relationship phase shouldn't take longer than three-five minutes.

Seeing how someone acts and responds when they are answering easy or non-challenging questions in this stage helps in the account phase later as you will be able to pick up on the differences in them when they are put on the spot – if that's the purpose of the encounter of course.

It's usually inappropriate for you to use terminology such as "We're having this discussion because I'm the manager and you're not!" or "I want you to remember that I'm the boss!" Such an opening may well reinforce the relationship, but it's hardly likely to get the other parties to open up or be as responsive as you would wish later. It must be more subtle than that; containing acknowledgement that both of you have a role within the encounter and an attempt (depending on the purpose) to put the other party at ease – if that is appropriate. Wherever possible you want to be reducing any 'threat' levels and removing potential barriers.

Similarly, good practice suggests you don't want to be starting off on a negative, or potential negative such as, "You look tired is everything OK?" "How are things at home?" (When you suspect they're not going well); or "How's 'it' going (whatever 'it' refers to)?"

Examples of good relationship building are where:

1. There is some normalisation of relationships; e.g. "I haven't seen you for a while, what have you been up to?" or "Are you still involved with the (whatever) group?" Consider making a reference to a previous (even if unrelated) good piece of work. "I see… is doing well in the league, what do you think about them buying 'so-and-so'?" "I saw a programme on (whatever subject you know they're interested in) on TV last night. I didn't know about… " This subtly tells the other party that you know your '**STUFF**' – or at least that which relates to them and that you have also registered things discussed in your regular one-to-ones or from previous meetings.
2. In meetings of new groups or where some of the participants don't know each other, getting everyone present to identify: who they are, what they do and why they are there might well suffice.

Go for neutral, non-confrontational territory. You do not want it to be robotic, rigid or staccato, as it will look like you're working to a script and only doing it because you have to. You're working to a structure not a script! If possible, use something that also sets the scene for the explanation phase. For instance: "Last time we discussed a few activities you said you would have a try at." This subtly reinforces the relationship, i.e. that you are the manager and in this instance coach, and that the other party is the coachee.

If, however, you don't feel comfortable with 'small talk', if you don't actually care, if the circumstances don't warrant it or aren't right, then don't pursue this phase rigidly. As an alternative you might consider blending this and the next phase together, especially if you correctly assess that there is no requirement to build or maintain a relationship, or where the nature of the encounter is such that it does not lend itself.

- Consider using the **relationship** phase to build or reinforce an ongoing relationship for the encounter and how the encounter might affect a relationship. Along with the explanation phase, it can set the tone for the whole encounter and the foundations for success.

Explanation Phase

If you are in charge of the encounter, two activities are required in this phase: the first is to explicitly acquaint the other party or parties with *your* purpose for the encounter and what you expect to get from it. The second is to define the ground rules for it – the rules of engagement if you like. From the start it will greatly assist your control of the situation if everyone knows why they're there, how long they have, how the encounter will be managed, and what each person present should get from it. Who better to establish that than you?

Even if you did not initiate the encounter, you may at this stage be able to take some control of it by clarifying these points. A good meeting manager will – if time permits (and subject to the purpose of the meeting) – provide an opportunity for others to outline whether they have a particular need. All present being clear now about your expectations, will save time later! This is the point at which you outline the purpose (as YOU see it) for the encounter.

Perhaps you can recall occasions when you've unexpectedly encountered your boss in the corridor, or in the car park and they've launched into a dialogue with you. You've stood there wondering 'why is he/she telling me this?' or 'I know why I need to know this, but why is it happening in the corridor or car park?' Maybe you've been the initiator and maybe you noticed the bemused look or frown on the other person's face, but you decided to plough on regardless.

No encounter needs a long-winded explanation. Neither must they all be completely formal. In purely business-related encounters, having a good relationship in the first place will help. So will (when there's time) circulating in advance, an agenda, and a proper statement of the aim and objectives of the encounter. Giving the other(s) some forewarning should lead to a shorter explanation phase (as a reminder is generally all that is then required). In the corridor or car park, it might be worth checking out whether it's OK to stop and detain the other person, and then just a sentence to inform them what it is you need a quick word about.

The explanation phase comes into its own more in formal meeting or interview situations. Some participants might be nervous, apprehensive, emotional, or expecting the worst. Of course the opposite might be true. In either case, both relationship building and the explanation phase can serve to 'level the playing field' and establish clear expectations for all concerned and even allay some fears. It also gives you a baseline to measure the effects, outcomes and benefits of the encounter at the end of the process.

This is predominantly a 'telling' phase and if you're in charge, the one in which you can establish answers to some of the questions outlined earlier. You can be telling the other participant(s):

1. What area of work the encounter is about
2. Why a meeting has been called
3. Why you and they are there
4. Whether it's formal or informal
5. What your contribution is going to be
6. What you expect from them – if anything
7. What your objectives are for the encounter
8. What you expect to come out of the encounter
9. What will happen afterwards (so far as you know now)

Remember, it would be polite, and usually helpful, to establish what other participants want or expect to achieve too. If an unscheduled encounter, you wouldn't lose marks for skipping questions 2–5, and maybe 6.

- The primary function of **explanation** is to set the ground rules for the encounter and provide structure.

Account Phase

What happens now very much depends on the purpose and nature of the encounter. Is it to impart information – you to others? Is it to gather information – others to you? Then there are those that could be included in the latter, but which are probably best kept separate. These are the kind of meetings intended to bounce ideas around, or discuss a theory when no one really has dominance or priority. No matter, they all require some control. If it's you that are the cause/initiator of the encounter, you should be in control even if, as in the latter type of situation, your style is less directive and more facilitative.

In a planning meeting, for instance, the leader of the meeting may provide background, objectives and then propose any options that are then open to question and discussion. In a workshop situation, all involved might contribute their account and/or appreciation of the situation. In a performance review, an attendee might be invited to give an account as to why their performance might be falling below acceptable standards, which is then open to questioning by the manager.

Whatever the purpose of the encounter, it will have an account phase that involves opening general statements. These are expanded upon, honed, clarified later and understanding agreed. You may have heard expressions such as 'drilling down' to the detail. These illustrate the process of trying to get as much of an accurate answer or item of information as you need. There are well-publicised conversation-management models such as the 'conversation funnel'. And in a moment I will be describing another method I call '**4Q-4A**'. Whichever model you choose, the process necessarily involves questioning and equally – if not more – importantly, *listening* to the other parties' contributions and actively hearing all the messages as well as the surface information.

Initially maybe before consensus is reached, there can be several different perspectives of an issue. Groups of participants can hold the same/similar views, whilst others present may be diametrically opposed. We can each apply different weighting or importance to different criteria. Wide variations from a 'norm' for a particular situation should prompt some examination to test whether your perception is likely to lead to the best outcome. To that end, consider how you gathered the information upon which you base your decision – and the quality of it. Thereafter, it's how you proceed to act upon *your* perception of the situation.

The brain is magnificent at gathering information and then editing it into what we consider to be important and necessary to use. Have a go at completing the next exercise *without reading further*.

Exercise:

On a blank sheet of paper, write an account of your most recent journey to work.

Does your account extend to no more than a single paragraph of no more than four or five sentences? Why is that? It's probably, because you do the same journey very often. You're probably on 'auto-pilot' when you do it. Most of us are invariably thinking of, or doing other things at the same time (especially if using public transport), and we probably don't often vary the route.

So we can take some things for granted, ignore others, and don't take notice unless something out-of-the-ordinary happens. Yet your senses will continue to feed information to your brain. It's just that *you* have conditioned it to discount much of the data as not being required.

In business or in meetings however, you need as much information as possible upon which to base your decisions. Even if you choose to discount it later, if at first, you do not consciously gather it; there is a substantial risk that you might miss something important. Yes! You are encouraged to achieve 'unconscious competence' at applying the framework, but that doesn't mean you should leave bits out. Carmakers are proficient at making cars, but they don't leave the brakes out of a model. Architects won't take for granted the need for appropriate foundations, nor tell the builder to leave out a structural girder.

Have a go at the following:

Exercise:

On another blank sheet produce an account of the same journey as before. This time imagine you are making a video diary that you will be sending to a pen pal.

'Freeze frame' at three key stages of the trip:

i.   As you leave the building you live in
ii. Halfway through your journey; and
iii. As you approach your place of work

For each stage picture yourself standing still and make a note of what you see, hear, smell, feel and even taste.
[It may help if you close your eyes and take some time to picture before you commit pen to paper]

Your account should now extend to at least three paragraphs each of a good few sentences? If not, you may need to re-visit the exercise.

If in the course of an information-seeking encounter you get from the other party, something resembling your first account above, how do you secure a more detailed and comprehensive account such as that in your second attempt? This could be especially difficult if the other party is especially shy, is a subject-matter expert who expects you to be at the same level as them, or is a reluctant participant.

Before looking at a model for structuring account conversations/ interviews – a note on questioning and question formats and one on the use and recognition of non-verbal communication.

Questioning

With regard to question types, it's a question of 'answer' vs. 'explanation'. Most people are aware of the concept of 'open' and 'closed' questions. Very often, there is a misconception that 'open' questions are always right or best. Surely, the 'best' question is the one that gets the right answer (note that I don't say 'the answer you want'). If that happens to be a 'closed' question so what? The closed question "Did you do it?" might well get the response

"Yes!" This can save an awful lot of time trying to drag the information out with a series of perfectly crafted, 'round-the-houses' open ones.

You may be short on time or temper, and you want or need a straight answer. A 'closed' question such as "Did you...?", "Have you...?", or "Will you...?" is likely to suffice and elicit the response you're after. If however, you're not pressed for time and you want, or need an explanation, an open question is more likely to secure the desired response. Most 'open' questions involve my six good friends Who, What, Why, Where, When or How. There is no hard-and-fast rule for this. For instance, a 'closed' question posed using an inviting, interested tone may well elicit an 'open', explanatory response, especially if the respondent is willing and operating on the same wavelength as you. Conversely, an open question posed with menace or recognisably as a trap, can easily shut the respondent down.

Non-verbal communication

Non-verbal communication (NVC), or 'body language – I love it! There's a saying that goes "they leak before they speak". Usually – I stress usually – someone's NVC will 'leak' what he or she is actually feeling and sometimes thinking before they actually vocalise it. It's actually a multi-tasking issue. For many of us, we either display NVC that matches what we say – no problem generally; or we display NVC that is at odds with the words. This is most often either involuntary or unconscious. To do it purposefully, however, takes an awful lot of concentration and effort.

To use what you 'hear' from NVC effectively requires: recognition – seeing it in the first place; acknowledgement – noticing any match or mismatch; interpretation – why the match or mismatch; and reaction. It's the last two that usually get the novice practitioner into difficulties.

For one thing they don't know or understand that a particular NVC – folding one's arms being a common 'for instance' – can mean several different things: relaxation, boredom, defensiveness. What you must do is compare the words, to the occasion, to what you know about the individual. If you're not sure why the mismatch has occurred, check it out before reacting.

This could be by asking the question another way immediately or later. It might be 'parking' the knowledge for later on. Problems may occur when you react immediately, based on an incorrect example. Say you see 'arms folding', believe 'defensive', and react with a question like "Why are you going all defensive now?" Maybe the interviewee was just relaxing! By misinterpreting and reacting incorrectly, you have communicated to the interviewee that you don't know what you're doing – even if you do. You have also potentially caused a change in their attitude to you and the situation. You invite the negative "No I'm not!" You bring about a self-fulfilling prophecy because they will now clam up.

A key requirement is your ability to listen effectively and actually hear the answers. This concept is developed further in Chapters 22–24.

It is wise to remember that someone who is mistaken can be very passionate, persuasive and convincing. Similarly, just because you hear the same or a similar version of events from more than one person, it doesn't necessarily follow that they are all correct.

An individual's account or contribution can be coloured or contaminated by physical and psychological influences as indeed, can how one chooses to hear, or react. We have preferences or prejudices. Alternatively, a contributor might be easily and readily influenced to change their view having heard the strong perceptions or points of others. They go on to agree with them, even though they know deep down that the other is wrong. One can be influenced by one's personal morals, one's long-held views on the subject matter, or by a misplaced desire to please the other party. Remember! You are seeking accurate, correct, timely information; the truth as it is, rather than how you want it to be.

Be mindful of asking 'leading questions', the type that include in the question an element of the answer you want. "How late was he?" suggests you believe 'he' was actually late. Whereas "What time did he get here?" elicits the information allowing you to determine whether that time made him late. Then there's "What colour was the car, red?" Individuals have been shown to say "yes" even though the car was more accurately maroon or even blue!

Emotion

Consider the physical and emotional state of others and whether it's conducive to an effective encounter. Someone who is tired, upset or nervous, or in a rush to be somewhere else might say anything and/or just what you want to hear in order to get it over and done with. Someone 'caught out' might wish to stall, divert or prolong the encounter to delay the inevitable. Someone who is over-keen or 'on a mission' might seek to prolong the encounter until they feel they've got what they want from it.

With those general points addressed I want you to consider how you might structure and control the account phase.

4Q-4A

4Q-4A is based on what investigators use in what are known as cognitive interviews and conversation management techniques that I was taught as a police officer. They are amended to take account of the more general types and variety of usage it can be applied to.

The account phase is divided into four distinct parts each intended to get more and more accurate and/or detailed information.

'**1Q**': The first/opening question. Don't confuse it with any relationship phase questions. It can be a straightforward 'closed' question with or without the kind of tone that solicits a longer response, or an open question.

'**1A**': The first answer is likely to be a general, un-detailed account containing all the responder thinks you need to know – or wants to give away on the subject (recall your first account in the exercise earlier).

'**2Q**': Now pose some non-challenging questions that develop the respondent's first account. You must have listened to and – more importantly 'heard' – the initial response, not only hearing the words, but also checking out the NVC that accompanies them. You may have been able to predict the actual response because of your preparation. Predicting is not assuming! Be prepared for something unusual or unexpected. You may also have had the opportunity to prepare contingency lists of follow-up questions for this phase, based on the potential different answers that the responder could make.

'**2A**': Responses and the information gained here depend on the quality, timing, pitch and accuracy of your 2Q questioning. The respondent/interviewee should remain comfortable and not under any sort of pressure to justify a previous response. They shouldn't feel challenged, or get the idea that you do not believe what they are saying.

They may focus purely on the incident and what they consider to be the important points. So you may want to be asking things such as "What else was happening in the store at the time?" "Who else was around?"

168

"What had you been doing immediately before?" or "What did you do immediately after?"

'3Q': Is where you drill-down to get the fine detail. It is most unlikely that you will have been able to predict the 2A responses very accurately. So this can be a testing stage for you. It's essential that you listen to and hear the previous responses and be able to formulate effective subsequent questions if they are required – thinking 'on your feet'. This is still not the time to be overtly challenging the other party's account.

For instance, if you were going through a customer complaint letter which the member of staff complained about: They could say: "The customer was really out of order and rude." So you would be asking: "What did the customer actually say or do that you thought was rude?" They might say: "I let the customer know there was no way they could have a refund." So you might ask: "What did you actually say to the customer?"

'3A': The interviewee/responder may well now be feeling a little more under pressure. Maybe because they realise that you are 'on to them'. It may be that even though they have done nothing wrong, they are having difficulty in recalling what actually happened. If they can remember, they're maybe not articulating it very well. You may find yourself asking 'closed' questions. Things like "Are you sure that's what the customer said?" "Could you have misheard them?" "Did you say anything else?" or "Why do you think the customer/ your colleague believes you were rude?"

'4Q': Is your opportunity, if the situation warrants it, to challenge, or confront what the respondent has been saying. If you have supporting information, you can be challenging by making statement-questions such as "There were two other members of staff who heard what you said and they both agree with the customer," or "I've checked with the train company and they say your train was on time this morning." If you use this type of question, you would need to get the tone correct and also remember to leave a pause to get some response or reaction.

'4A': Answers are not without risk. The respondent might have a moment of realisation and not wish to say anything further or, they might realise the game is up and reach out to you for 'rescue' by laying their cards on the table so to speak.

This model is for use in any type of interview, not just negative ones. In a recruiting interview, for instance, I have used stage four to try and pin the applicant down to what *they* actually did or contributed within a team effort, rather than allowing them to get away with referring to the team performance as a whole. Similarly, it is not uncommon for individuals to whom doing something very well comes naturally, not to realise they've done a good job, or why.

In order to pass on the good practice to the rest of the team, you might wish to isolate what exactly it was that made an event so successful. Be careful that you – and they – don't get frustrated if this can't be done.

Remember too that you might have several topics to discuss or cover in the course of one encounter. If that is the case split them, make them distinct and go through the sequence above for each of them. This will avoid confusion both during and after the encounter when you assess whether the objectives and desired outcomes have been achieved; what else if anything needs to be done, and how well you performed.

The framework allows you the flexibility to amend it to the relevant encounter. There is no set length or duration for any of the elements. It is entirely possible that you cannot, or do not need to pursue every phase. Do not be a slave to the model, or to every part of it. If you secure all the information you want or need after stage '2A', why pursue the next stages for the hell of it? Apart from risking a very unwanted reaction from the other party, it's a waste of time!

Remember! You might ask the best questions in the world, but unless you have listened to and heard the responses, they will be wasted. Whatever the meeting's duration, it is a 'must' to make note of the salient, important points especially if they contribute to the encounter's objectives.

Summary Phase

You may not have secured all the information you wanted, all the desired outputs, or done so to the quality you wanted, but once you are satisfied you have addressed the objectives of the meeting as far as possible, it is always advisable to sum-up.

Timing the start of this phase is important. You want to have given all present the opportunity to make the contribution expected of them. You want to have secured as many of the objectives as possible. There usually comes a point where everyone recognises that no further progress can be made. You don't want to repeat the whole meeting; neither should you provide a verbatim account of who said what. So include the main topic areas that have been discussed – yours and theirs, items that were on the original agenda and those introduced within the encounter. If when you summarise, you find other parties wanting to reopen discussions, or make further points of clarification; if you get any challenges, or questions, this is actually good feedback. Either you've started the summary phase too soon, or perhaps the other party has not got what *they* wanted. It could also of course be that others aren't working to the same rulebook as you.

- **Summarising** accurately and concisely sends out powerful messages that you have heard and understood what the other contributors have offered and what has been discussed. This gives others a very final opportunity to clarify something. It also serves to signify that discussions are at an end at least for the time being.

Once you have provided a bullet point summary of the key topics you can move on.

Outputs Phase

This is kept separate from the summary phase so that it can focus all parties to the encounter on what it has or has not achieved. If all the objectives have been met, closure can be included in the final phase. If not, participants will be focussed on the need for further activity. This could be that you got the message across that certain actions were decided upon and allocated (but not yet to whom). It could be agreement as to a particular course of action. It is also an appropriate time to note particularly good contributions or benefits and to celebrate them.

- **Outputs** affords you the opportunity to check off whether or not the encounter objectives have been achieved

Next Phase

Make it clear what actions now follow, who is responsible for them, and when they are due for completion. Of course this is dependent upon the purpose of the encounter and whether it was one that necessitates anything more. I dislike meetings that leave issues hanging, or have items on the agenda that cannot be finalised. Especially if this is because previously required action hasn't been done. If items are constantly postponed to the next meeting, and the next, it feels like 'ground hog day' and any impetus is lost. If something cannot be dealt with and finalised at a meeting to the extent necessary, it should be taken off the agenda completely. For instance, if a particular project or piece of work was expected to be finished in time for a particular meeting and for legitimate reasons it hasn't been – why have the meeting? If there were less than legitimate reasons, would you be dealing with that in the original meeting or a separate, more private one?

Don't forget to say "thank you" and don't forget to review how successful the encounter was in achieving its planned or generated objectives. Use the 'debrief cycle' headings described later as a format.

Applying the REASON model in a working environment

You might say "How does this help me at work?" Well, as a First-Line manager, one of your roles is to fight 'fires', to **ADDRESS** root cause of issues. You should take prompt action to resolve the situation. At this level, the time frames available are usually considerably shorter than those at higher tactical or strategic levels. If you're going to get it as right as possible, the more good information you can gather in the time available, the more likely you are to make a sound decision.

There is another major influence in dealing with situations effectively: your knowledge and understanding of the situation and your skills, abilities and application. Let's say you've been called in to deal with a crisis on the 'shop-floor'. You ask your colleague "What's happened?" or "What's wrong?" or even (sometimes) "What have you done?"

Often, the first response you get will be akin to your first attempt at telling me about your trip to work. There are a number of reasons for this. Possibly an assumption on the part of your colleague that: You speak the same language technically; respect and understand that there's an established working relationship and understanding of roles; and can actually do something about it! You may or may not be able to make an instant decision. So you need to secure the information you need.

As your experience grows, it's possible to store learning and apply it to future – similar – situations. You can build a catalogue of potential responses.

Don't automatically dismiss those that may not have worked too well in the past. They may now, under ever-so slightly different circumstances, be totally appropriate. This requires you to conduct effective reviews of how you handle significant situations so that you can maximise the learning (see 'evaluating' later).

Summary

In this chapter I have covered what to include when preparing for an encounter; having a '**REASON**' for every encounter; and how to structure the account phase using the **4Q-4A** model.

End of Chapter Activity 1 – Formal/pre-arranged meeting:

You have two options. You can complete either or both.

When you are due to have a planned encounter, take some time out to plan for it, determine your intended content so that the encounter will run with the **REASON** format. Then apply the format to the encounter and try to work to it. Don't forget key questions that you want answered if appropriate

After the encounter (and regardless of whether you completed exercise A, take some time out and complete an assessment of the extent to which you managed the encounter in line with the **REASON** and **4Q-4A** models

If there are areas for development you can repeat this exercise as many times as you like.

End of Chapter Activity 2 – Informal/unexpected meeting:

When you next have an unplanned encounter, take some time out afterwards and complete an assessment of the extent to which you managed the encounter in line with the **REASON** and **4Q-4A** models. Did you initiate it or did someone else? Regardless of that, did you get what you wanted out of the encounter?

If there are areas for development you can repeat this exercise as many times as you like.

Leave this chapter with this thought:

The imp on one shoulder believes the satisfaction to be had from approaching a meeting fully prepared can only really be beaten by realising that your opponents are not. The angel on the other will be satisfied when you walk away from it with your objectives achieved.

18. A CHEAT'S Guide to Feedback

Most managers must at some time engage in the very particular form of communication that is the process of providing 'feedback'. This much-used word is often a euphemism for giving someone a dressing down, or letting them know how you feel about a particular situation or course of events. More positively, it is an opportunity to improve relationships; build networks; develop not only your team, but you too; and ensure quality and effective performance. There's a Chinese proverb that says, "Do not remove a fly from your friend's forehead with a hatchet".

Unlike revenge, feedback is not best tasted cold! Feedback can be a very powerful, very positive instrument. Properly offered, it will be accepted and acted upon. Improperly offered or delivered, it can be resented, resisted and ignored. In the words of US management writer Ken Blanchard: "Feedback is the breakfast of champions!"[34]

So I want to bring together elements of managing situations, communication, and being 'adult'. At the same time, I want you to consider what the qualities of good feedback are and also how, by using some of the models described previously, you can get the maximum benefit from a feedback encounter.

All the previous models can readily be applied to a feedback encounter – it's planning; ensuring subsequent development is the best solution, properly planned and implemented; ensuring the encounter is structured. However, this must be based on high quality feedback in the first place.

This chapter is structured to explain and to get you to adopt, principals of good feedback. By examining the qualities of feedback you will be provided with a simple way to remember them – **A CHEAT'S** guide. I will use two scenarios for you to test yourself. A key component is a methodology or

---

34   (Blanchard n.d.)

sequence for you to follow when considering providing feedback, thereby maximising the likelihood of it being accepted and acted upon.

The test often highlights the difference between what is expected and how we seem prepared, or able to deliver it. Many incorrectly associate feedback with criticism, and criticism with negativity. We need to move away from that! Remind yourself how do you expect to get your feedback?

The qualities of feedback are that it should be:

A	Accurate
C	Constructive
H	Honest
E	Evidenced
A	Actionable
T	Timely
S	Supportive

It's '**A CHEAT'S**' guide to feedback. This apparent misnomer is a good way to remember and check your proposed feedback.

Whether or not you have people reporting directly to you, you will doubtless be involved in delivering feedback of some kind. Yes, it can be the delivery of difficult messages regarding others' performance. This, coupled with the natural reluctance to be the bearer of bad news, can lead to those giving feedback being more apprehensive of the reaction, and more nervous throughout the process than they need to be. Somewhat perversely, it also results in those same managers having similar difficulties when it comes to delivering positive feedback (or praise). It can be difficult to get it right without sounding patronising. It can also unnerve the recipients if they're not used to getting feedback at all, let alone of a positive nature. This in turn could lead them to be suspicious of your motives. **A CHEAT'S** guide to delivering it can increase the chances of feedback being effective; positively received; and the necessary benefits to everyone involved and the organisation being accomplished. So what does effective feedback look like?

Accurate

It has to be **accurate**. If you're not accurate, you will dent your personal credibility and that of the feedback. You communicate that you have got your facts wrong (not knowing your **STUFF**); or that you have not been paying attention; or that you have put the wrong interpretation on something. You also open the door for the recipient to belittle or ignore altogether the feedback, even though it was well intentioned and an important matter to be dealt with.

Constructive

Feedback is not there to destroy. It may be provided to stop someone doing something, or do it better. It might be given to praise or encourage someone to continue 'as-is' because of the positive effects their actions are having. It should never be a 'removal of a fly with an hatchet' exercise. **Constructive** feedback communicates that you care about the recipient, what they are doing and about your organisation. It communicates that you are willing to match the time and effort the recipient has, or needs to put in to address a situation.

Honest

Honesty is always the best policy. The worst-case scenario is the one in which the recipient believes that you have an ulterior motive. If they get that feeling, no matter how well you fulfil the other qualities of feedback, it is likely to get a less than positive reaction.

Evidenced

Some of the most common responses from those receiving feedback can be: "Why have you said that?" or "Why should I?" Nowadays, the response "Because I said so!" rarely suffices – not that it ever has, other than in very authoritative environments when there were serious repercussions to be had for non-compliance. Even then it was resented. There is a need to watch, look and feel for information – your **evidence**. There is a need to check the quality of the evidence. Does the evidence support or contradict the point you are trying to make?

Actionable

Maybe the feedback allows you – the person offering it – to 'let off some steam'. However, offering feedback to someone on anything about which they can do nothing is counter-productive. It's like saying "I wish you weren't French" [I have absolutely nothing against *Les Francais*]. It's something you can do nothing about! So feedback has to be **'actionable'**.

Timely

It has to be **timely** for a number of reasons: if *you* do something that warrants feedback (positive, or negative) today, wouldn't you prefer to know about it today – when maybe you have time to do something about it or can enjoy it? How about when you next see the observer, which could be in three or four weeks' time and when you'd actually if not forgotten all about the situation, moved on? Given late, feedback is more likely to be ill received and un-actionable.

Supportive

I reiterate. Feedback should never be destructive! It is NOT a tool for you to let off steam! It is not to deliberately upset the recipient, though upset can be a result. In such cases your prior knowledge of the recipient can be invaluable in managing the process. For instance, just because the provision of otherwise sound feedback might lead them to be temporarily upset, it should not prevent the feedback being offered, rather the manner in which it is.

The requirement to deliver some feedback is certainly good **REASON** for an encounter. Someone once advised me that: "If you can tell someone their body odour is a cause for concern (feedback), you can tell them just about anything." I want you to consider the following two situations, testing combining the feedback criteria and then planning to deliver that feedback using the **REASON** model.

Exercise:

For each situation consider how, when, and where you would be delivering the feedback. Apply ALL elements of the test (use 'A CHEAT'S' guide if you wish).

Then plan out both of the encounters using the **REASON** process. Both scenarios are discussed afterwards, but try producing your own solutions first.

A. This morning – as a result of some other colleagues' comments – you notice one of your colleagues is (not for the first time recently) emitting unpleasant body odour

B. This morning you observed one of your team dealing with an argumentative customer demanding a refund. They resolved the situation very well. You are aware they have been working on conflict resolution as part of a development plan.

Looking at Scenario A:

Other team members have raised an issue. You should acknowledge the situation. It's not life threatening, but it does have the potential to affect organisational and individual performance (if no one will work with them, or customers start complaining). It needs to be dealt with positively and quickly.

Don't confuse the causes of the situation with the causes of the colleague's body odour. Determining the possible solutions also determines how you are going to deal with the situation – not how you are going to make things smell sweeter. Sending the colleague an email? Not good. Putting up a notice on the staff notice board reminding all staff of the organisation's standards on personal hygiene? Not too hot either. Leaving it until one of the team gets fed up of waiting for you to do something and confronts the colleague? Well it might sound better coming from a 'friend', but there's no guarantee that it would be. It's equally likely to be a hostile delivery. Of all your possible solutions, the most likely to succeed and be best received, would be to confront the issue face-to-face and on an informal basis in private.

Not many resources are required, just your time, that of the staff member and a private area. Remember execution has three elements the first of which is planning. Plan your **REASON** and plan how you're going to deliver the feedback, as this is likely to be cropping up in the explanation phase.

I'm going to assume that you have arranged to see the team member the same day. Is the information accurate? Is it something you honestly believe, and something the team member can do something about? How

179

are you going to deliver the feedback in a supportive and constructive manner? There's the direct approach, variations ranging from the very blunt "You smell! Sort it out!" to the not so blunt, but equally direct "I've noticed your personal hygiene is not up to the standard I expect. Come back tomorrow with an improvement." Aside from the fact that neither variation has afforded the recipient an opportunity to explain, either is likely to be somewhat catalytic and elicit something of a cathartic response. They also involve a level of uncertainty as to the likely reaction of the recipient. That it is not to say that either is wrong. Your style might be very direct and you might be well equipped to deal with the recipient's response, no matter what it is and how the feedback is delivered. Your knowledge of the individual might lead you to the direct approach if you know for sure they prefer it and would do so in this particular scenario. Some people don't like beating about the bush. All things considered, they could respond equally directly with a "Yeah OK. Sorry." Then go away and act positively – job done!

Alternatively, you might prefer a more indirect approach, to be more supportive and constructive, and look for the underlying reasons for this presenting issue. Body odour could be a sign of trouble at home etc. A less direct approach opens up the possibility for a deeper problem to be sorted, and the opportunity for longer-term benefits to the recipient's self-esteem and your standing. Whilst still addressing the issue and having the potential for a cathartic response an indirect approach is less likely to become a drama. One of the most common routes is for example: "Is everything OK at home?" as an opener, seeing what the response is and then if nothing is offered up start to steer the conversation with something along the lines of "I've noticed that you're not as spruced up as usual".

Whichever route you opt for, it should be based on knowledge of your **STUFF**. Situations like this warrant a subtle mixture of the direct and indirect. The recipient might be unaware and when you ask to meet with them they can get worried. So the gap between asking for 'a word' and actually having it should be kept to a minimum.

The relationship and explanation phases should be short and can even overlap. Depending on the STUFF, your opener could be "I need to have a word with you about your personal hygiene. I've noticed it isn't up to your usual standard. It needs to be sorted as it could lead to difficulties for you with the rest of the team and also we have to remember what the company expects." Pause – the recipient might volunteer a reason straight off the bat. If not you can follow up with the Account phase with an opener like "Tell me why your standards have slipped recently?" I know that's technically an instruction rather than a question, but with the right intonation can do the trick.

At this point the floodgates can open. Of course you will have prepared for the most likely responses: There'll be the simple and obvious such as "My hot water system's broken." "The alarm clock has broken." to the more complex yet potentially equally obvious: "I've been thrown out by my partner." "My new partner is keeping me up all night." "I've been caring for a sick relative." It's often the case that the least frivolous, most complex causes are less likely to be offered up easily – not through stubbornness, but because the recipient is aware of the situation and embarrassed.

Once you know the true cause, you can apply the most appropriate solution/response. Your primary objective is to stop the person upsetting others and to ensure the organisation's needs in terms of standards and continued performance are maintained. If by resolving this situation you help the recipient with other issues then that's a very useful by-product.

Your chosen response should match the style of your approach and the attitude or response of the recipient, which may be equally direct and prescriptive. Giving the recipient fewer options, less control and therefore less ownership could lead to reluctant or malicious compliance. You may discuss a series of (available) options and allow them to select one and agree to it. This has more likelihood of success. It also gives you more recourse if it is still not complied with. If the reason is more serious and deep-seated, you still need to address the presenting problem before moving on. You might find it necessary to take a pause and arrange/rearrange your diary so that you can **ADDRESS** that.

To sign this situation off, you should be agreeing a time-bound course of action that will lead to the specified objective. How will you measure whether the recipient's body odour is now acceptable, is it your opinion, theirs or someone else's?

For Scenario B:

The scenario illustrates a principal occasion for the use of feedback – addressing individual performance – especially after an observed incident of some kind. It is very similar to the debriefing cycle discussed in **ADDRESS** – Sign Off, but here I am overlaying the process with the use of the '4Q-4A' process. It's a managed conversation with the purpose of getting the feedback subject or recipient to identify the circumstances, gaps, causes, or behaviours that are the subject of the feedback and which therefore, form the bases for future development.

There is a situation to acknowledge – a good one! It's an opportunity for you to bolster the esteem of one of your team – and your own. Indeed it is likely to have a positive effect on the rest of the team too if it's done in the right way. I've seen positives mishandled: feedback given too late when the recipient has forgotten what they did; delivered too quickly and/or without explanation; or given frivolously.

You observed one of your team dealing with an argumentative customer demanding a refund. They resolved the situation very well. You know they have been working on conflict resolution as part of a development plan. Be aware of your **STUFF** and in particular why this was a good performance. Why store it up to their next one-to-one meeting, or call them into the office to do it? Remember what an unexpected call to the office can induce and that this is a GOOD situation.

Relationship and explanation phases can overlap here. Put them at ease by explaining that you are impressed, or pleased, that their work on their action-plan seems to be paying dividends and that you just want a couple of minutes with them to discuss that. This signals that you are taking a personal interest in their development and that you are recognising their work. Use the account phase by asking them why they dealt with the situation in the way they did. Make sure they don't gloss over things and make sure they understand why things happened as they did. Provide evidence as to why *you* believe it was good. You can still ask if there was anything they would do differently next time as some continued development might still be required. The 'next' phase can be an undertaking on their part to carry on approaching similar situations in the same way.

Whatever the feedback, manage the environment in which this takes place. Think of the tightrope walker. If you create a 'low wire' safe environment, i.e. one where a fall is likely to be painless, the recipient is much more likely to try the process, as they don't perceive there to be too much risk. If however, you infer that a fall here would be fatal, i.e. 'if we don't sort this, you're out!' you can guess the likely outcome. Having said that, you shouldn't shy away from making it clear that certain levels of performance are required and expected and the consequences of not achieving them. This is only fair. It is the manner in which that message is delivered that is crucial.

Another key factor is your willingness to devote the additional time and effort required. In the short term, teasing the right information out of the subject might seem laborious. Their previous performance might make you reluctant to make that effort. You might genuinely not have time. In the long term however, the fact that the solutions come from them, means they are better founded and stand a greater chance of success than those imposed by you or anyone else.

The diagram below illustrates a feedback cycle that can be followed by an individual in self-assessment; colleagues in peer assessment; or a manager. It overlays the depth to which the **4Q-4A** conversation might develop at each phase. Steer the subject through the cycle, using appropriate questioning. You'll have a good idea of the causes and also the subject's desired future behaviour, though be prepared for surprises. Once the *subject* has disclosed the information needed, you can build on it. If you are considering giving feedback to reinforce or contradict their self-assessment, consider why, and how. Will it be cathartic or catalytic, prescriptive or informative? In any event will it be constructive?

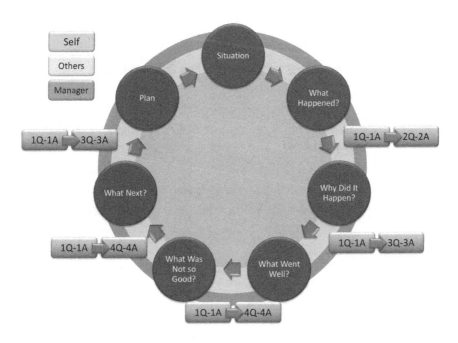

Figure 7: A Feedback Cycle

Feedback Summary

Good feedback? Always ask yourself, 'Who is this for and why am I giving it – my benefit or theirs?' How and where is it going to be delivered in public or private? Is it quality feedback?

End of Chapter Activity 1 – Assessment of a feedback session:

After you deliver feedback to a subordinate, peer, or manager. In retrospect, test it using the qualities for good communication. Did it fit the bill?

Using **A CHEAT'S** guide, were all the qualities of good feedback present?

Did the session comply with the feedback cycle? If so how did that work, if not why not and what was the impact? How good was your **4Q-4A**?

End of Chapter Activity 2 – Planning a feedback session:

In advance of delivering some feedback to anyone, test how you propose to deliver it against **A CHEAT'S** guide and plan the encounter using **REASON**.

Take time out afterwards to assess how you performed. You can also get feedback from the person(s) receiving the feedback.

SECTION 3
Being a manager in practice

The approach you adopt to management permeates throughout all you do and affects you and those around you far beyond the immediacy of the situations you face.

19. Introduction

If other distinguished authors on the subject are to be believed – and some, such as Dale Carnegie, Kenneth Blanchard, Stephen R Covey and Peter Drucker, are definitely worth reading – there are many 'principles' involved in being a manger. Some things you *must* do if you are going to be effective in the role. I have selected some key activities and practices that you should become accustomed to adopting. There are many ways to apply them that do not lend themselves to being condensed into models or acronyms like those described and explained in Section 2.

In this section I describe some activities that can help to make your time as a manager – at any level – more effective and consequently more rewarding. The aim is also to minimise the difficulties and stress that *not* practising them could lead to. This is what you will be examining:

- Establishing yourself in the role
- Being the most effective communicator
- Managing performance of others – Deal with it!
- Managing encounters
- Watching, listening and feeling
- Distinguishing yourself from your subordinates
- Learning to trust
- Looking after yourself and being selfish
- Perseverance
- Dealing with the stresses of the role

This section is intentionally pushing you from learning theory-based concepts to actually putting them into practice.

20. Establish yourself in the role

How do you 'put down some roots' – create and then adhere to some principles of your own? How you should 'start as you mean to go on'? Here you will examine the importance of communicating your style, standards and limits of acceptability from the outset. This is to support you in setting off on the right foot; in short how you should go about establishing yourself in the role.

If you are in the role already, you can appraise your early time in it. How did you go about establishing yourself? Is it timely, or appropriate to *re*-establish yourself? Perhaps it's time to refresh some of the foundations on which you operate and the relationships that exist between you and your team, or those you report to.

If new to role, use this chapter as a basis for testing the pros and cons of 'setting out your stall' at an early stage in your role in *your* organisation. We should consider too, the benefits of sending out clear messages about your operating principles and personal standards.

There's no 'golden formula' for achieving this. But there is 'good practice' that can be adapted to your individual circumstance. I will outline common tasks that are involved in establishing yourself and encourage you to apply the models from Section 2 to deal with these tasks – or situations – in a prioritised, logical sequence. I encourage you to apply the ideas to your own situation. As it is often a key expectation of the role, I will also use this chapter to examine your responsibilities for building and/or maintaining 'the team'.

I remember reading that the first seven seconds of any encounter will determine the nature of the relationship of those involved for the rest of their lives. Regardless of the accuracy of this statement, most would agree that 'first impressions' count. So what can you do to negate or minimise confusion, contradiction, and future conflict?

Poor reputations can be earned in seconds; good ones lost equally quickly. A poor reputation is only lost over time and a good one built that way. Edward Flom, CEO of Florida Steel, is much quoted as saying, "One of the hardest tasks of leadership is understanding that you are not what you are, but what you're perceived to be by others."[35] You can replace 'leadership' with 'being a manager' but it still rings true.

A good reputation takes a succession of sound performances and demonstrations of competency and trustworthiness to build. Yet it can be lost very quickly due to just one significant lapse. That lapse does not even have to be workplace-based. Think how often the peccadilloes, addictions, or activities of so-called celebrities and politicians, once published, have led to their removal from a pedestal. The reverse scenario can be just as bad. Where no reputation existed previously – say a new manager – a poor reputation can be created off the back of just one – albeit fairly significant – *faux pas*, fairly early on in their tenure. It then would take a succession of improved performances to 'up' one's political capital.

If you were not aware of the phenomenon, or indeed how it could be applied to you, then you should be! You would also be wise to bear it in mind when establishing yourself. A lot has to do with your principal reason(s) for wanting the role as discussed in Section 1 earlier. If you are setting yourself up as a 'high flier', how are you going to set, and then achieve consistently, the highest of standards? You'll need performance levels that distinguish you from your competitors from the outset. This would be particularly applicable if like most of us, you are not lucky enough to have a sponsor who can mollify the outcomes and/or evidence of those moments when perfection is not quite there. This is not to say that you should never make mistakes, or that you should be held back from trying something for fear of making one.

There is a lot to be said for thinking about why mistakes are made. The honest variety will usually be acceptable to, and accepted by, the majority of your network, provided there aren't too many repetitions or the consequences are not too great. Furthermore, it is one thing to recognise and accept a risk for yourself, where you are likely to be the only one to lose out in some way. It's entirely another when you're creating for, or accepting risk on behalf of others. This is especially true if the others involved do not have, or have not been given the opportunity to accept

35   (Flom 1987)

the risk for themselves (see staff engagement in the Communicate chapter later).

Get into the habit of constantly focussing on what your ultimate goals and objectives are until it becomes second nature. Look ahead and try to remove the negative elements of hindsight. Please practise establishing and feeding the roots of being a good First-Line manager, whilst dealing with parasites and pests.

The following case study is based on one of my first days in a management role. But first I want to explain what I perceive to be the benefits of having a plan for your early days. To make sense of it we must first confirm the circumstances of your promotion. What you are moving from and what you are moving to? This will inform the broad areas in which you must establish yourself. This will also help to prioritise them, establish objectives and expectations. It provides you with a checklist of what needs to be done.

When promoted, the lucky ones receive some form of effective, formal, structured induction programme. This should provide you with what the organisation believes you need. But invariably this will be limited to introducing you to rules, regulations and compliance issues. No doubt, you will hear more of its philosophy, vision, mission, policies and procedures. If joining the organisation as a manager, there may well be introductions to peers, colleagues and seniors with whom you will be working, often accompanied by a 'tour of the building'. There could also be some technical elements relating to the job(s) carried out by your team. I have found that due to the length of time it can take, the latter is often left until after the set-piece induction.

My experience of this process, however, is that much of the information fails to register immediately because there is too much of it to be effectively absorbed. Especially as it is competing with your feelings and emotions that could include excitement, trepidation, nervousness or plain euphoria at getting the job at last! You might have moved home (or country), or even still be in the middle of doing so. You might be trying to reunite the family, or trying to get all your domestic needs sorted. These latter factors can certainly adversely affect your ability to absorb all that knowledge.

Some people naively venture into the role with an assumption and expectation that the organisation will provide everything needed in terms of knowledge and understanding. However, things such as getting to know the culture and operational customs 'on the ground' are very often omitted from official induction events. Very few induction programmes will overly focus on pitfalls and weaknesses of the host organisation. I've not yet experienced an induction process that I didn't come out of the other end still feeling something akin to a sacrificial lamb. Even if you are fortunate enough to be in, or moving into an organisation that takes manager induction seriously, the odds are that they are time limited – they need you up and running as quickly as possible. Consequently they may not be able to do a complete job on you.

Consider the change(s) you experience when you're promoted. There's a host of permutations. Dependent on the nature of the move will be the list of things you will need to consider. If you're not careful, you can find yourself trying to sort them all at the same time, with the inevitable consequence that some will be achieved more effectively than others. You should take as much control as possible. Once you have identified the tasks involved you can begin to **ADDRESS** each; come up with some **TOP-DRAWER** solutions and **CRAFT-T** plans.

In the table below I have listed some typical promotion situations and the tasks that the new incumbent should consider. If you've been in the role some time, try assessing the extent to which you completed these tasks and whether you should address them now.

You'll notice the cluster of activity around the centre of the table, which suggests that no matter what the circumstances of your promotion, there are some common elements to be **ADDRESS**ed.

You will have to get to know and become proficient at manager-specific tasks such as: conducting one-to-one or performance-related disciplinary events; gathering evidence for and preparing management information reports; dealing with escalated incidents. It would be rare for you not to need to increase the size, content or nature of your network of contacts. Finally, you might also need to acquire new knowledge and skills – task and technical.

If your move circumstance is there and has a line full of ticks, it can be difficult to prioritise. It's not uncommon for there to be a self-imposed expectation that one should know everything immediately. Consequently you try to do everything immediately. The result is that things get omitted, or don't receive the level of attention they require. Very often the new manager can be so focussed on trying to impress their new boss and their new team, that they forget the domestic elements.

Unfortunately, only *you* can determine what takes priority. Only you know what your attitude and approach to each related activity is or can be. Remember what works for one person may not for a whole host of reasons work for you.

It helps to recognise some tasks cannot be completed overnight: acquiring skills or building a network, can take months if not years. For each of the tasks you deem necessary, conduct an **ADDRESS** exercise. This automatically confirms you acknowledge a need. Determining causes may identify a common thread. This can save time, but remember there may be underlying causes too.

Note: This is an illustration <u>only</u>. There are other promotion situations and other variables might be introduced for instance the new role might bring new working times or shifts that mean you have to make new arrangements to look after dependants at home. You should also remember that being promoted internally is not necessarily an easy option as others' expectations, opinions and attitude towards you can change.

When determining solutions, you will be tempted to pick one that you think will address several tasks at once. This could be a mistake, leading to the dilution of application that I warned against earlier. Best practice suggests you should first identify a separate optimum solution for each task.

Apply **TOP-DRAWER** to your solutions in turn and amend as necessary. When you go into planning, take particular care over the use of 'you' the resource and your available time frame. There is only so much of 'you' to go around!

Once you have a plan for each element, you can lay them out and identify the overlaps; those that can start together without interfering with each other, or those that could be combined.

Resources are important: not only time, but your presence too. The resources of your manager and team – especially if you agree priorities and plans with them – and those of your social circle are also important.

Having looked at the clutter that can come with a move into the role, it's time to consider what I mean by 'start as you mean to go on'. Your promotion is not a green light to stamp your authority onto things from the word 'go' like the proverbial new broom. Give yourself time to assess what's going on, what works, and what doesn't. This is unless of course, you have been brought in to manage a crisis wherein things have to be changed and

Type of Promotion examples?	What needs to be done (examples)								
	Familiarise with new organisation	Familiarise with Area/ department etc.	Familiarise with Team	Policy & Procedure – 'Manager Knowledge'	Learn Job specific Knowledge	Learn Organisational Culture (s)	Build a Network of Contacts	Sort out your Domestic arrangements	Build a Social Life outside of work
Internal – Same region/ technical specialism		✓	✓	✓	✓		✓		
Internal – Different region/ technical specialism	✓	✓	✓	✓	✓		✓	✓	✓
Internal – Same Team/ Organisation Structure				✓	✓		✓		
Internal – Different Team/ Organisation Structure		✓	✓	✓	✓	✓	✓		
New Organisation – Same technical specification – no relocation	✓	✓	✓	✓	✓	✓	✓		
New Organisation – Different technical specification	✓	✓	✓	✓	✓	✓	✓	✓	
New Organisation – Same technical specification – no relocation	✓	✓	✓	✓	✓	✓	✓		✓

Table 2: **Promotion Circumstances & Required Tasks**

changed quickly. Then use, support or reinforce the good practice and be able to provide evidence as to why the not so good can be done better or to better effect. Don't change things for change's sake. To do so is often poorly received by those who know the original version/method worked perfectly well and they were used to it.

Exercise:

Please read the following case study and answer the following question BEFORE considering my comments:

If you were Nino, how would you **ADDRESS** the situation?

CASE STUDY: Early Drift

Across Nino's organisation it is customary in some areas that, when it becomes very quiet on a night shift, one or two colleagues are allowed to go home early without loss of pay (known as 'the early drift'). It is usual for this 'perk' to be shared out fairly between the team. However, circumstances could lead to some colleagues missing out when it comes to their 'turn'. This unofficial, but tolerated benefit is never recorded anywhere. To a large extent it relies on the supervisor's memory to ensure fairness. It is also open to further abuse as and when it is seen that only the more senior members of the team seem to be allowed off early. This is Nino's first series of night duties in charge of his new team. The second night evolves into a very quiet shift. Two relatively senior members of the team approach Nino and say, "So are we getting an early drift then?"

This is one of those customs and local practices that were not discussed during Nino's induction into the position.

Case Study 5: Early Drift

Firstly, **Acknowledge** that there is a situation that Nino needs to deal with: members of Nino's team are asking for a benefit to which everyone knows they are not entitled, but which 'custom' dictates they are used to receiving.

In **diagnosing** the possible causes and source of the situation Nino has to consider, is the situation the request by the senior team members, or is there an underlying agenda here? Could it be that in asking the question (the presenting situation) those team members are trying to enforce an unofficial perk? This is something they know they are not really entitled to. So they cannot make any form of official complaint if they don't get it.

Another possibility is that by asking the question, they are seeking to test Nino to see whether he really is 'one of the guys', or whether he's going to be the source of some problems for them in the future. An accurate diagnosis by Nino will be a significant influence on what comes next. Nino must now decide whether or not he is going to do something about it. If he chooses not to, what do you think the implications would be?

Nino isn't like that and also doesn't want to make a 'snap' decision. Neither does he wish to appear indecisive. He wants to get this right as he realises the implications. So he buys himself a little time. In this instance, he points out to the colleagues that he believes it's a little bit early to be deciding right now, but that he will monitor the situation and get back to them in thirty minutes.

Having given it some thought – and being new to the team – Nino takes the view that there is nothing sinister behind the request. He acknowledges that any solution he applies will inevitably affect his relationship with the whole team. Any solution has to take that into account, together with his responsibility to the organisation and himself. So he uses the time to **determine** a number of possible solutions to resolve situation a few of which I have listed:

- Refuse the early drift and make it clear they would not be happening now or in future
- Refuse the early drift this week, but endeavour to consider it in future
- Allow the early drift for those requesting it
- Allow an early drift, but as there is no record, draw lots to see who gets it

In this situation not much time needs to be spent on gathering **resources**.

He calls the two colleagues together in order to **execute** his plan. Remember this is an 'encounter' and if he wants it to be effective – and to get his message across and the outcome he desires, Nino needs a **REASON** to it. He needs to begin with the end in mind. A potential **REASON**ed meeting is described shortly.

Let's say Nino decides that he does not want to allow the two colleagues to go home early – at the very least, until he establishes from elsewhere whether the practice is acceptable to the business. His objective, therefore, is to get this message across to the whole team as, believe me, what he decides now will be communicated around. He also has to consider how this situation will establish his credentials with them all. So he may support his refusal with some evidence.

Once he has informed of his decision, he should **step back** and observe the consequences. This applies more to the ongoing effects in terms of team attitude and behaviour, rather than any immediate reaction on the part of the two senior colleagues who made the request. This immediate reaction would likely need to be dealt with in the course of the initial communication.

Depending on the outcome Nino can **sign off** this situation as having been addressed there and then. Bear in mind that any medium to long-term reactions might have to be dealt with – attitudes and behaviours especially, but that becomes a separate situation to be addressed.

Just now I mentioned that Nino must meet the two colleagues and inform them of his decision. Take a little time now to consider the nature of that encounter. What would the **REASON** be?

Exercise:

[Answer the questions]

R   Relationship in this situation would involve what?
E   Explanation of the encounter would include and should take how long?
A   Account – Does Nino have to ask any further questions or get the team to account for themselves? Or is this the part where Nino informs them of his decision?
S   Summary of the key point(s) would be what?
O   Outputs – what does Nino need to be clear about the outputs of this encounter?
N   Next – what will happen next?

Possible response

This is not meant to be a definitive answer, only an illustration of the process. It is fine to disagree and to develop what would be your own response in a similar circumstance. So long as you can demonstrate that you have followed the process through without omitting any of the stages.

The relationship phase would be very short, probably because this is a potential conflict situation and one that involves a potential disciplinary matter.

The choice of words would be his/yours, but the explanation would be relatively short also. Wherever Nino chooses to deliver the message (under the circumstances this would best be in a quiet or private area), he should consider acknowledging without disputing that what they said; their enquiry; and even thank them for asking (at least they didn't leave without doing so). Then he might explain in one or two short sentences, that they were meeting now so he could tell them what his decision is and why, and they could ask questions afterwards.

Nino has already made his decision and it is unlikely he would need to ask any questions in this particular meeting. Note however, that after he has made his enquiries, he might be having another meeting with them in which some questions might well be appropriate. So it would be straight into the information i.e. that there would not be an 'early drift' for anyone this week.

Quoting regulations at this stage might again, be a trigger for some conflict. An option would be to advise them that he wanted to look at staffing levels on the night shift and would incorporate the custom into his consideration and get back to them (within a specified time). At this stage Nino has the option to invite questions, having considered in his planning what they might be (and having some prepared responses).

As it is a short, uncomplicated encounter (in terms of content) it may not be necessary to summarise. Such could be included in a couple of sentences with the outputs phase, which itself need only be that the two need to get back to work, that they will be working on the tasks he has now allocated them, and that he will update them in due course as to the outcome of his review. What will happen next will be that Nino will allocate some time to enquiring and establishing the way forward as regards the policy and then how that is to be communicated to the whole team.

This is also an opportunity. Because Nino knows his **STUFF,** he is aware what this team is capable of and that it is within their role description to do other tasks. The possibility therefore, exists for him to indirectly 'justify' the refusal by allocating them some work around those tasks.

Tip: You should now be able to come up with a plan to 'set out your stall' and also be able to describe the benefits of communicating your standards not only to those you will be supervising, but also your peers and bosses.

End of Chapter Activity 1:

Do you have a plan to manage your transition into the role of a manager (or did you)?

Which elements of the move needed prioritisation and focus on? (If you have been in post for a while) Which did you forget or not have time to do then, but would like to do now?

Determine your solution(s), and select one from the **TOP-DRAWER.**

Plan and assess your plan to see if it's **CRAFT-T** enough

End of Chapter Activity 2:

Take some time out to self assess the extent to which you have established yourself in your role.

Are you consistent in your decision-making? Do your team and other colleagues know and understand your values – what you find acceptable or not? Are these consistent with the organisation's expectations and requirements?

If you are not satisfied with any of your responses how do you propose (if at all) to ADDRESS the issues?

Nietzsche said: *"For a tree to become tall it must grow strong roots among the rocks."* [36]

36   (Nietzcshe n.d.)

21. Working with your team

One of the types of promotion situations I didn't include earlier was that where a new team is created in either your existing, or a new organisation and you have been appointed to head it up. In addition to the activities I listed earlier, no doubt you would then be expected to engage in 'team-building' activity.

You may have observed the 'industry' that has built up around this concept. Many organisations strive to be novel, and to introduce new 'fun' ways to 'build the team'. Indeed you may have been compelled or otherwise encouraged to participate in formal arranged team-building events. These are often off-site and arranged by highly paid external providers. Don't get me wrong. In the past I've enjoyed leading on, and attending as a delegate, some such events. However, I have found that in many cases, whilst these events are a very well received day out from work, the feelings of 'team' and other benefits that they generate can be short-lived.

I always insist that any such event I run is primarily a learning one – targeting specific development needs of individuals – not some sort of 'jolly' that gives participants a free day off work. By introducing appropriate exercises the team-building benefit should then be a welcome additional benefit.

Many client organisations may think they *need* teambuilding. Many supplier organisations that survive by providing such events are more than happy to confirm this *need* and to supply a/their solution. Unfortunately, the buyer very often cannot define what a good team looks like to them. Neither are they very adept at defining what they expect from the event. The supplier therefore, doesn't get an accurate enough brief. So even if it's on target, the buyer has a job measuring the impact that the event has on their organisation's outputs. They cannot evaluate whether it has been money well spent.

Try to be very clear on what your organisation considers to be an effective team and indeed, whether or not it actually cares. Then determine whether or not the team you are moving into actually reflects that. A clue might lie in how they define their expectations of you in respect of the teambuilding competency. If you were putting together a new team you would be looking at what you are going to put in place to achieve what is expected. Bearing in mind that new teams are often created as a result of restructuring exercises, and that some members might not have wanted to be restructured; there could be extremes of resentment or relief (that they've escaped from the clutches of a previously poor manager). Remember: attitude always affects behaviour!

You must then decide whether the work the team will have to do: the roles allocated; how tasks are divided and communications set up; will of its own accord be sufficient to 'build the team', without taking them out on some artificial 'getting muddy'/'crossing gap with plank & rope' day away.

Getting a new team together to get them to contribute to the set up tasks just mentioned, could also be a good way to kick things off. If it's a completely new team of previous strangers and/or a completely new operation, you have a golden opportunity to create the team in your own positive image. As they know nothing else, you can set your own terms and conditions and communicate:

- Your way of working
- What you will accept and what you won't
- What success will look like etc.

I remember opening several brand new pubs/bars for a national company. We were able to use activities during the two-week initial training period – there was a lot to learn – to make learning fun. The teambuilding always seemed to come naturally and never required 'forcing'. Whilst task-learning, staff also learned about each other and what each was capable of. It also served to establish common goals and give them ownership of outcomes.

The key is in the 'Determine Solutions' phase of ADDRESS. What it is you are hoping to achieve? Think about the reaction of your bosses and your team to you trying to introduce something that's alien to the existing culture. Ask yourself: is the solution suitable for your environment? Will it have the desired effect? Don't jump directly to the obvious because it's worked for you before elsewhere.

Recognising Team roles

You should be aware that you will have job-description roles, often clarified by use of a role title, and you will have behavioural or trait team roles that people bring to the team regardless of their job title. Knowing what they are and how they affect team performance will help you manage them and their individual contributions to team goals.

What is it that people do when they are put into a team? You may already be aware – or at least have heard the name 'Belbin' in relation to team roles and personality theory. You may have even taken the related test. Alternatively, you might have heard of Myers Briggs personality types theory. Both are used extensively by organisations that can afford to, to gauge individuals' suitability, affinity, or potential for working in a certain way in certain team situations or setups. Use your search engine to look them up if you want to explore further. However, for now I want to 'keep it real' and register the activities/attitudes that individuals apply in a team over and above what their official reason for being there might be. I count twenty and in the table below they are listed in the form of roughly corresponding opposites.

The team promoter	The self-promoter
The hare	The plodder
The ideas person #1 – the giver	The ideas person #2 – the keeper
The leader	The follower
The risk-taker	The risk-avoider
The achiever	The 'promiser'
The light-seeker/problem-solver	The doom-monger/problem seer
The comedian	The dramatist
The expert	The novice
The talker	The listener

Table 3: **Team Roles**

Before reading my explanations, take a little time to note your own ideas around the attitude and behaviour that the different individuals might use/display.

First, let's be clear. None of these roles are inherently bad, nor better nor worse than the other. Those names I mentioned earlier make it clear that different teams may need some or all of the different roles in different numbers, at different times. One should also be aware that an individual might display more than one of these traits all the time or according to circumstance. The key is understanding who they are, how they influence outcomes, and how you manage them individually AND within the team context.

Secondly, you should understand my roles are based on observation, rather than scientific analysis or psychology. Consequently my views on what they mean are subjective and personal.

Thirdly, I would resist using these classifications to determine without further enquiry the frequency, extent and level of supervision that you afford to individuals. Just because they display a particular dominant trait, they may do so at different extents than a similar colleague.

For me, this is what the classifications mean:

Team promoter vs. Self promoter

Some like working in a team, others are not so keen. This is not about whether one likes being there; it's about how they use their presence. The team promoter contributes to the team, because they can see advantage for all in being successful. They are not blind to the fact that success will bring them some benefit. They recognise that their success comes from their own and others' contributions. So they will put effort into maintaining the team's coherence and focus. The self-promoter on the other hand is likely to focus more on being prominent within the team – possibly to secure for themselves a more advantageous role or better conditions. Additionally they may well be focussing more on how their participation in the team will further their advancement and so other team members' needs come secondary or can even be sacrificed.

Team promoters may need regular if not frequent praise and thanks or recognition for their effort. Whereas self-promoters may need to have their needs recognised, but be managed so their drive is properly channelled and others are not 'put out' by it.

Hare vs. Plodder

The hare is the person who gets everything done quickly. Remember though that speed is not necessarily a good thing. What if they have deviated from the plan? What if the quality of work is not to the required standard? What if they pressured others to work faster to keep up? What if their speed has a knock-on effect to other areas? Instead of encouraging the hare to be fast, maybe we should set realistic deadlines and encourage them to be on time.

The plodder will work at something until it's done. Paying greater attention than may be necessary to detail. They can be depended upon to do a good job – if a little slowly. This can have a detrimental effect on the overall plan as delivery might be delayed, milestones missed and other resources standing idle while waiting for the plodder to finish. We should set this person realistic deadlines and managing – possibly training – them to maintain the level of quality yet be able to meet a challenging deadline.

Idea givers vs. idea keepers

Some individuals are innovative and full of ideas as to how a task might be done, or done better. Some are more willing to come forward with and share those ideas than others – often for fear of others thinking the idea was stupid, or because they have been told (in an autocratic set up) that this is how the job will be done and there's no discussion. There are of course other reasons for people not coming forward with ideas. Some might even be malicious.

Others may spew forth ideas without perhaps thinking them through. Although in some organisations such processes are encouraged and once everything is 'up on the board' it can be thought through afterwards. Still others might have the idea, but by the time it has been properly thought through and packaged the moment has passed.

Managing these people is situation-driven. It may be the situation where there is time and resource to allow for all ideas to be put forward and – importantly – to create the environment in which that can happen. Other times might prevent such discussions and there might have to be a decision from the top that is then followed. There may then be time afterwards to review and see if anyone has ideas as to how things might be better next time.

In either case it would be for the team manager to manage the expectations and environment; and be open about how ideas will be treated at an early stage of the team being established. What we want to avoid are the opportunities for individuals to say, "I wouldn't have done it like that," or "I thought that might happen."

The leader vs. the follower

You don't have to be in a managerial position to be a leader. Some managers find it difficult to lead others and some leaders find it difficult to manage others. Anybody who has previously proven to be good at what they do, or to have some form of specialist knowledge, or to have previously gained the trust of others – the followers – may find themselves in a situation wherein they are looked on as the 'leader' for that particular situation. Similarly some individuals either because of their position all their nature always seem to be following the instructions or guidance of others. Still further – as it is situational – an individual might be a leader for one part of a situation or project, yet to be a follower for others.

I believe we need to move away from the notion that striving to be a leader is an inherently good thing, even when the individual might not be up to it; and that being a follower is an inherently bad thing. Where would the brilliant general be without the right sort of troops in the right numbers and where with those troops be if they didn't have a competent general to lead them?

You may recall me talking about the sources of power in Chapter 4, Section 1. There is often a correlation between the power an individual possesses and where they get it from, and in the extent to which they find themselves leading in situations and the form that leadership takes. There are many combinations. For instance, an individual with considerable 'knowledge power' might lead a situation through application of that knowledge even though they are following others' instructions, because many other aspects of the project are dependent upon the speed and manner in which that knowledge expert carries out their particular tasks.

The risk-taker vs. the risk avoider

Most organisations will take risks of one kind or another. Those that introduce a new product or service can never be 100% sure that it will be a success. However, in preparing for the launch they will do everything they can to mitigate the risk. Organisations known for their innovation understand and accept the risk of investing sometimes huge sums of money to develop a new product, and that at the end of the process they might not be able to produce the perfect solution. In some organisations the risks are obvious. Think about the Armed Forces, the police or the fire service. Most of what they do entails risk on a daily basis. However, one likes to think that they are trained and equipped in such a way as to minimise those risks.

It follows that organisations and teams need individuals who can accept and deal with risks appropriately. Non-risk-takers are unlikely to be suitable in the high-risk situations or those in which innovation are required. Similarly, if the role is one likely to attract a high level of interest or criticism a non-risk-taker is rarely likely to expose themselves to potential hardship. One could say therefore, that the risk avoider is highly likely to be a follower too. So there is a place for them.

We do want some people who are able to, and to feel comfortable with taking risks. We need them to be the sort of individuals who take calculated risks and who are able to foresee the potential consequences of their activity and at the planning stage at least minimise the risks to an acceptable level. It is arguable that someone who takes excessive risks and who ultimately would be the only one to suffer any adverse consequences is acceptable. However, it is very rare for the risks and actions of one person in a team not to have an impact on the remainder of the team and its effectiveness.

Identifying individuals' attitude towards risk is useful when considering which tasks to allocate and the level of control that might need to be applied. An irresponsible risk taker is likely to require more supervision and control than a careful one, or indeed, a risk avoider.

The achiever vs. the 'promiser'

The achievers are the individuals to whom tasks can be allocated in the near certain knowledge that they will be accomplished in the time and to the quality and in the manner expected. The level of supervision they require should be minimal. Although an achiever who is also new to a role, or is facing a new process, piece of equipment, or team may need a slightly higher level of supervision/ support in the early stages. When they promise something you as the manager can feel confident that it will be done. This is in stark contrast to the promiser.

Having coined this new word I will explain what I mean. Quite simply, the promiser is an individual who says they will do something by a certain time, in a certain way, or to a certain standard but fails to do so. I'm not talking of individuals who are prevented from delivering by circumstances that evolve after the promises made. Rather, we are talking of the individuals who promise to do something in the full knowledge that they are unable to fulfil the promise. This could be for a whole host of reasons: perhaps they don't have the required knowledge skill and are trying to cover up the fact. Perhaps they are trying to make themselves look good in the manager's eyes; or perhaps they have an overinflated view of their own capabilities.

When dealing with either achievers or promisers the good manager will seek to test out what is promised in order to establish whether it is deliverable. Appropriate supervision of both types will ensure opportunities to either praise, or take remedial action.

The light-seeker/problem-solver vs. the doom-monger/problem seer

You will find something of the light seeker/ problem solver in leaders and risk-takers. These are the individuals to look for solutions to situations; as opposed to the doom-mongers who will very often see a problem and bring it to your attention, but rarely if at all, do so in a positive way or accompanied by some form of solution. It seems like the latter only ever focus on the negative, which has a detrimental effect on the focus and morale of the remainder of the team.

Very often light seekers will relish a challenge and will be willing to put in additional efforts and resources to find the best solution. The purpose might be for self-betterment or furtherance, or it might be more for the benefit of the team and the organisation as a whole – does it matter? I would argue not really, provided they are properly managed. These people can be vital at the planning stage to identify accurate goals and potential obstacles – allowing appropriate plans to be made. During the project they can help deal with unforeseen crises and therefore to keep a plan on track.

Whilst the problem seers may be viewed negatively – especially if that's the only thing they do – they should not automatically be dismissed. Primarily because the problem they foresee or identify may indeed be real. A common management tactic is to encourage them to come forward with a solution. This can work if you believe a) that they have a solution and b) that it can be coaxed out. But maybe you don't have the time or the resources to do this. Previous experience may lead you to believe that this would be a fruitless exercise. Though who's to say on this occasion it might not work. It may well be that the most effective course of action would be to thank the problem seer for raising the issue, which can then be passed to one or more problem solvers.

The comedian vs. the dramatist

Most of us will have experience of individuals who can or will make light of any situation. Then there are others who will make much of even the most minor situation or setback. The comedians can be very useful – with proper management – for lightening the mood, for maintaining morale, and for maintaining perspective. Care needs to be taken that others will be able to see the funny side and that in fact what the comedian says/does a) remains within the bounds acceptability and legality and b) is generally in tune with what everybody else is feeling or thinking. You also have to consider that humour is an emotion and that too much emotion can have a negative effect on individuals' performance. Too much of a good thing can be just as bad as not enough.

Sometimes but not always, the dramatist will also be a problem seer, in which case action should be taken not so much about the fact that the problem has been raised, but rather the manner in which it is raised.

The expert vs. the novice

In a similar way to us having 'achievers' and 'promisers', we have those who are genuine (proven) experts in their field – or who are at least very competent – and those who 'talk a good job', but who when it comes down to it, are not as competent as their publicity suggests. It should go without saying that we should encourage the former, but if we experience the latter, we need to be managing them appropriately and be prepared to confront underperformance.

Novices can bring fresh ideas and should be keen to develop and contribute what they can. They may have the required knowledge and understanding of, and/or a certain level of skill and ability to apply what is required, but lack experience of doing so.

In a project situation the level of supervision and support they need may initially be greater than can be afforded should the task be urgent or exceptionally important. In an established team, there should be time and resources to properly integrate the novice *and* bring them up to the required levels of competence. On the other hand you should not assume that someone new to the team is a novice at what they do; nor that someone identified as a novice because they do not have a long period of experience is unable to 'hit the ground running'. Remember it's not the duration of the experience, but the quality of it that counts.

The talker vs. the listener

You will find more on this subject in the following chapter, as what you do having identified these types of individual will be influenced by your skills in communication. It may well also determine the frequency and intensity of your communication.

The talker may also be an ideas person who is not afraid to share them. They might also be the problem-seer. They are the individuals who are not afraid to say what they think. Preferably, they also think about what they say, but that's not always the case. In this classification, the talker is someone who focuses on the talking, rather than a balanced mixture of the two. Thus they can override others and/or appear not to be hearing what is said before or after their contribution.

The listener is an individual who noticeably rarely contributes towards team – or even one-on-one discussions. It can sometimes be difficult to gauge whether they have 'got the message' as verbal feedback has to be teased out of them. Thus in my classification being too much of a listener can be as bad as being too much of a talker.

So as their manager, you will need to be prepared and practised at controlling the inputs of both types; perhaps lowering or improving the quality of those of the talker, and encouraging good quality inputs from the listener.

Rather than relying on a Belbin or Myers-Briggs assessment, which is only strictly relevant to the time and day the test was taken in a 'laboratory' environment, the classifications I identify are based on *your* observations, in real time, and in real situations where it should be more difficult for individuals to mask their true selves (for anything other than a short period of time).

Managers – especially new managers – can avoid properly getting to know their team through a reluctance to venture into what they see as 'psycho-babble'. That's easy to understand when one sees volumes thicker than this devoted to the psychology of teams and individuals' roles within them.

My argument is that by applying practical labels, founded on first-hand practical evidence, you will be able to better assess situations and determine better solutions. It will also inform very much the style(s) and approaches you take to individuals.

You may be 'inheriting' an already established team, with or without the opportunity to change the membership. It might be a new team, again you may or may not have a say in its composition. Or you may have been in role and in charge of an established, stable team that changes composition and tasks only occasionally. There is no point in putting effort into establishing the traits and capabilities of your team in any of these situations if you are not going to use the information. So what should you be doing?

You might use allocated operational tasks, or indeed a teambuilding event to test the members of that team in order to establish which of the trait(s) I have illustrated apply to each of them. In that way you should be in a better position to anticipate their needs and reactions when you seek to have them follow instructions and/or perform tasks on their own initiative. The following steps may assist you:

1. Look for existing information. For this you may need to look at previous performance review records. If taking over an existing team strive to question the outgoing manager as much as possible. Ask about *all* the team, not just the stars or problem children. The second line (your) manager may well have information about general team performance and/or those stars and problem children, though this is likely to be less

detailed. If building a new team, you should also consider conversations with the relevant managers of each of the proposed members.

2. Open a book (or file) on each member. This can be as (in)formal as you wish. Depending on the culture of the organisation and the openness of you and the team members, you should consider making this an, 'open book', with reasonable access being afforded to the subject. If this is done the contents should comply with the requirements of **A CHEAT'S** guide. I recommend that the opening page should include notes on the individual's needs, concerns and expectations and agreed objectives in terms of individual performance and team outputs. Subsequent entries should contain notes on occasions that evidence performance relevant to the agreed objectives or any other significant good/poor performance.

3. Exercise control. If you witness or become aware of an issue – positive or negative – ADDRESS it as soon as practicable. Don't simply ignore it and don't just record it in your book. Recognise and praise (appropriately) the positives and confront (appropriately) the negatives.

22. Communicate, communicate, and communicate!

Everybody does it. Most people think they're good at it. So why then are so many failures attributed to a 'breakdown' in communication, otherwise known, as 'You never said'? Normally, textbooks consider the need for effective communication, which in turn requires:

- The right Message(s)
- The right Audience(s)
- The right Location(s)
- The right Time(s)
- The right Method(s)
- The right Feedback

But you can read about those anywhere. I want to focus over the next three chapters on the practicalities of:

- What is communicated, and how – the outgoing
- How we know it's working – the incoming (watch listen and feel in the next chapter)
- How we manage both (managing encounters in the one after that)
- To do so, we consider six questions that you might ask to test the quality of your communication and work towards achieving the effective communication criteria listed above.
- What is/are the message(s) we are sending out? (See language, non verbal and tone later)
- Why are we sending those messages – what is the purpose or objective of the communication?

- Who are we sending to – the audience(s)?
- When are we delivering a particular message? Is it to forewarn or advise before something; to update on progress or completion; or to report on the success or otherwise of a past/recent event?
- Where are we delivering – what locations?
- How are the messages delivered – how do we ensure there is consistency and what methodologies should be employed?

How many times have you heard the phrases: "We're always the last to know!" "Thanks for telling us!"(The sarcastic version) "I told you about this last week!" You might even have used them or something similar yourself. There is a saying, versions of which are attributed to George Bernard Shaw and Wilfred H Whyte –"The single biggest problem in communication is the illusion that it has taken place.[37]" And that beautifully encapsulates the issue. For whatever model of communication you choose to apply, whatever medium and whatever the message; however competent and compelling the theory, they all go to pot if you don't apply them fully and properly.

I support the idea that communication is a principal and over-arching requirement and responsibility of the First-Line manager, indeed of *any* manager.

Communication is a 'life skill' that those of us with a complete set of senses take for granted and which, by the time we have reached working age, we like to think we have mastered. Strangely enough when one speaks, one tends to concentrate more on the content, than how it's coming across. However, we constantly send out unconscious signals, which are registered consciously or otherwise, by the other(s) involved in the communication. When we're writing, we very often try to make sure something is phrased correctly because we're trying to make up for the absence of the visual element of a conversation. It can be that the only time we take notice of how we communicate is when we lose the ability to do so properly because we lose the capacity. For instance, if we lose our sight, the power of speech, or hearing.

At the other end of the scale, communication can be overanalysed to the point where we are concentrating so much on trying to get it right, that we lose spontaneity. Because we focus on one element at a time, the other elements suffer. Then the true intended message gets lost.

37   (Whyte 1950)

How we communicate is a very personal thing. It can be affected and influenced by numerous competing and conflicting factors. In the time and space available it would be very difficult to try and cover off every eventuality. I do not want us to be bogged down in abstract concepts or deep psychological theories, nor repeat what you might find elsewhere. So let us look first at the 'outgoing' element.

You will be prompted to examine your personal use of the raft of communication technology platforms and gadgets that are currently or are likely to be available to you. The final section of the chapter emphasises the importance of using appropriate styles, methods and content to provide a complete, coordinated and effective piece of communication and activity that you can conduct for your own development in your workplace.

As well as day-to-day management, as a First-Line manager you are often at the forefront of change processes. These might include the introduction of a new piece of technology or an organisational re-structuring. The messages you send out are often vital for effective operations.

Good Communication or Effective Communication?

There's a comparison to be made between good communication and that deemed effective. For instance, me coughing loudly and making audible sarcastic comments so that the individuals disturbing me at work overhear and stop, may well have the desired effect – they stop. But is it good in the long term?

The eighteenth century theologian Joseph Priestly reportedly said (though ironically this is difficult to confirm), "The more elaborate our means of communication, the less we communicate." I agree! By trying to cover off every angle, by trying not to 'upset' anyone, or trying to 'spin' the story to make ourselves look good, we lose the core message. Some call communication a science, some an art. Why mystify this most basic of functions?

Very few species get by without communicating: they may do it orally, visually, with scent or taste, or a combination. We may not understand all of it, but we certainly seem able to interpret the bits we need to. Vibrantly coloured beasts are often so adorned so as to advise potential predators they are not too good to eat. Other beasts adopt a stance and posture that leaves one in no doubt they're not happy – think how a cobra displays.

Communication can occur not only between members of the same species, but also between different species, even though the 'language' may be different.

All we need is a message, an audience, the opportunity to convey it, and a language in which to do so. Do we need to know if the message has got across? On balance we probably do.

Parlour/party games such as Chinese whispers and charades expose our deficiencies when important elements are taken away from us short term. Paradoxically the more we concentrate on trying to get it right, the worse it gets. The fact that some who lose a sense – such as sight or hearing – develop heightened capability in their remaining senses, demonstrates that we can indeed continue to communicate. There are also occasions when we subconsciously recognise that what we are saying may be a bit complicated so we try to reinforce it with descriptive hand gestures even when these are fairly useless. The classic example is watching someone using a mobile telephone giving directions to someone on the other end of the call miles away. For some reason the guide seems to think that 'air-drawing' a roundabout, a left turn or something else will give a better idea.

Language, please!

Language is important! We naturally try to reach a point where we are speaking the same language as the person(s) we are engaging with. The less successful attempts involve the 'speaker' raising their voice (often accompanied by over-exaggerated gestures) or going into excessively slow-speak.

Even if the same verbal language is not available we are often able to utilise props or signage to get our message across. Whilst we need to be aware that some gestures mean different things to different cultures or races, we can generally get away with some commonly understood gestures: using fingers to denote walking, drawing a shape in the air, making an exaggerated sniffing gesture, placing a hand to the forehead and over the eyes to signify searching or looking. I'm sure you can think of others. Alternatively, we can help bemused visitors to our city armed with a map of the metro by taking it from them and tracing a finger across the route they must take. Simple isn't it! We do it without thinking. Once we get the language right, we can then work on getting the right proportion or ratio of words, tone and non-verbal to convey the actual message you want to get across.

We are told that we communicate using three broad formats: verbal language, tone, and non-verbal language. I used the word ratio just now because the proportion in that commonly accepted model, are rarely 'balanced'. We also see that the ratio shifts according to environmental, psychological and physiological factors and circumstances.

We have Professor Albert Mehrabian to thank for identifying this model. Others however are to blame for only focussing on his fundamental idea. He identified that 7% of communication is verbal with the remaining 93% being shared 38% to tone or the way things are said and 55% the accompanying body language or facial expression[38].

Unfortunately this was seized upon in a manner that he – I don't believe – intended, and that over simplifies the subject. Those who trim down his work omit the very important caveat that the ratio is dependent on many factors. These might include the ages of the parties involved, the situation and its intensity, their knowledge and understanding, their cultural background. The model is clearly appropriate, but must be viewed in the context of: whom we're dealing with; are they rational? Do they talk the same language? Come from the same background? Feel the same way about the subject as you? Share the same values? And so it goes on.

To compound matters, there are models of 'effective communication', most with common components, that have been misinterpreted to illustrate that they represent an organisation's 'two-way' communication. Many organisations are actually terrible at communicating. They will say by word or deed, that they very much want to hear and understand the workforce, but go on to demonstrate quite the reverse through their reaction when they don't like what they hear. What we end up with is the application of a 'model' that professes to have considered potential barriers and to fit the prevailing circumstances. However, it is so high level that by the time it gets to you, the content might as well be in a different language.

Consider these two points:

- A good discussion will include lots of effective communication, whilst the reverse is not always a requirement
- Two-way communication is not necessarily the same as a discussion

38 (Chapman 2004-12)

Picture if you can the person in charge of a squad of riot police in the middle of a riot. The team must advance to clear a junction of rioters: petrol bombs and rocks raining down, noise, confusion, danger! Is that really a 'Gather-round-and let's-mind-map the alternatives' kind of situation?

What the squad leader needs to do is get their message across – the orders – in a language, with clarity and volume, and at a proper pace to make sure all those in the squad understand. Maybe some questions, but no discussion. The fact they go on to take the junction and do it as required, would be good evidence that the communication was effective.

I argue that two-way communication can often be misinterpreted as, or confused with, discussion. In this instance there was two-way communication as the commander sends, others receive and feedback (in the form of nods, grunts or verbal confirmation) that it was received and understood. There was no chat around alternative ideas or the efficacy of one approach over the other, with everyone chipping in. Now that would be a discussion!

Discussion comes into play when time and circumstances permit. When we examine methods of problem solving and decision making, or when on any other occasion, there is a series of exchanges each of which conforms to a model of communications. Points may be agreed, alternatives offered etc.

Know too, the difference between one-way and two-way communication; also that between 'top-down' and 'bottom-up' communication. 'One way' – whatever the direction – incorporates no consideration of whether there is any understanding and resists feedback. 'Top down' is a version of one-way from those with position and/or knowledge power to those deemed not to have it. 'Bottom up' is communication in whatever format, from those also with position or knowledge power to those usually accepted to hold some form of authority over them.

Then there's what I call 'Car-Crash' communication. This is 'top down' (from you), 'one way', using (often) the wrong medium to the effect that the wrong message(s) – over and above the original content – is/are delivered. It omits seeking or recognising feedback as to whether the intended message has been delivered and understood and only recognises its lack of effectiveness when there's only partial or total non-compliance.

Think about the methods you employ to communicate in your organisation and environment and note them down. Consider, examine and ultimately determine whether the methods you currently use are effective for your needs and if necessary, explore some additions or alternatives.

We tend to go with a limited number of methods for a variety of reasons: It could be organisational structure or culture that constrains your options; it could be that you only feel comfortable or sufficiently proficient with the ones you use out of habit. Alternatively, you might not be aware of the options available. The point is that the methodologies we use the most, or that we find the easiest, may not be the most effective in the short or long term or in particular circumstances. Using the same methods every time – apart from being lazy – can cause problems. So taking some time to either check out that one of your favourite methods is appropriate will mitigate them. Then, if you honestly believe it will work, go ahead. Otherwise seek an alternative.

Your Message – the right message

Consider not only the headline, but also the underlying message that you (intentionally or otherwise) will be sending. For example, in an office block, parking spaces are allocated to named individuals. One day someone parks in the wrong place. The next day notices appear around communal areas stating: "Under no circumstances will anyone park in any space that isn't allocated to them!" OK, one message has certainly been delivered, but what about the underlying messages?

The innocent might ask, "Why am *I* being told off? I never park anywhere I'm not supposed to. This is unfair!" Others read into it that the manager hasn't the courage to deal only and directly with the guilty person. Still others might be the rebellious types who question the fairness of anyone having an allocated space in the first place. So the notices merely serve to reinforce antagonism. If the business is struggling some might question why the bosses aren't focussing real issues rather than something so petty.

Assuming everyone is aware of the rule (though not necessarily in agreement with it), a more appropriate approach would be to confront the person at fault directly to secure future compliance. Only if necessary, raise it with others e.g. at a team meeting. Unless it is a general recurring problem, dealing only with the 'offender' directly, would be sufficient. Why raise it with anyone else?

As few communications carry just one message whether this is overt, subliminal or suggestive; whether we recognise it immediately or a little way down the line; whatever the communication, firstly be clear in your mind as to what *all* the messages are that you will be sending. Once prepared, assess it and see whether all those messages are addressed and catered for.

The purpose of Your Communication

Think about what you are trying to achieve with this piece of communication. Is it part of a larger piece of work and contributory? In which case it needs to be consistent. Knowing the purpose of the communication will inform the methodology, the tone and the timing.

Is it to forewarn or advise of an upcoming event? Consider the difference between notifying of impending compulsory redundancies and a message informing everyone of the Christmas party.

Is it to update on progress during or after an event such as a project, to inform senior management or the project team, does it need to be motivational or simply advising the facts?

Is it to exercise or maintain control by outlining or repeating policy, or to seek the views of others?

Is it on completion of an event to critique and/or circulate lessons learned?

I hope you can see that the purpose of each of these examples is very different. Generally you should be asking, "What am I intending to achieve with this piece of communication and will the way it is constructed and distributed achieve that purpose?"

Communication – Your Audience

Consider your audience: how big is it, where are they, are they emotional or rational – how are they likely to react to the communication, why do they need to get this particular message? Do you need to address the whole team, or specific members as in the car-parking example above? Think of the collateral effect too. Whilst you are communicating directly to one 'audience', which other audience(s) will hear and maybe react to the message? Who else uses the area? Maybe staff from other departments or teams, maybe even customers or clients of the organisation.

In marketing and broadcasting you often hear the phrase 'target audience'. It is a common defence to allegations and complaints of inappropriateness for the broadcaster to make the case that the complainant is not in the target audience. Others can argue that in the case of broadcast media, listeners and viewers do have control via the 'off' button.

The point is, that when 'broad-brush' communication methods are used, it is very difficult to control exactly who – beyond the intended target audience – gets to receive the message(s) too.

Communication Timing

They say, "There is a time and a place for everything". If you can get timing right, your communication stands a much greater chance of success. How many times have you been caught on the hop; just on your way home, off to lunch or another meeting and how much of what was being said to you consequently didn't register? So think about that when it's you doing the communicating. If it's your habit to try and pass on important information to someone who is unlikely to take it in, how effective is that likely to be?

If it's a one-to-one performance matter, it is best to 'strike while the iron is hot' and to address any issue whilst the incident is still fresh in mind (yours and theirs). That advice has to be tempered in so far as you need to afford time to reduce levels of emotion and to gather the facts etc. Can you remember precisely what you were doing this time last week? So if I approached you today and praised, or criticised you for doing something that happened then, you could easily have forgotten it. You might question why I am raising it now, even resent me doing so.

Project-based and other foreseen situations can be the subject of more planned and/or scheduled communications. This could be advisory, in advance of something happening, or of the reporting nature to update others as to progress.

Generally speaking, telling someone about something that will affect them, after it has happened – especially when *you* knew about it in advance – is not well received.

Communication Location

Location can have more of an impact on the quality of communication than you might think. The phrase 'praise in public, criticise in private' gives a clue as to the nature of the location for these particular types of activity. The canteen might be empty and so private for the time being, but is this really the place to be initiating or continuing a difficult conversation? Similarly, a walk-in storage cupboard might be private but again is it suitable? If you're planning a one-hour sit-down meeting, training session or workshop for twelve; a room in which they can just about fit is unlikely to be conducive, especially if it's a mid-summer afternoon. Yet it might be OK for the same number, if they're only going to be there for five minutes and they're all standing.

Consider the length of time and effort it will take the participants to get there. Many large organisations, with regional or head offices still insist in pulling contributors physically to one location even for the shortest or apparently less-than significant of meetings. How many times have you spent a couple of hours getting to and from meetings and afterwards wondered why you had to be there at all? If it's difficult for people to get there, they may turn up late or not at all. If they arrive after much effort, they could well be in a less than receptive state of mind and consequently not contribute/hear as effectively as required. The same is true if they know they've got a long difficult trip ahead of them after the meeting. Communication technologies can save time and money, negating the need for mass travel. I discuss the use of technologies later.

Communication Method

Using the parking example, one method would indeed be to put up reminder notices. You might feel raising the issue at the next team meeting, or the quiet chat to be appropriate. Another would be to ban anyone not having an allocated space from entering the car park at all. All send out a series of different messages – not just the headline. Choosing method is no less important than the content.

Let's remind ourselves of potential delivery methods:

- Face-to-Face – one-on-one, group meetings, presentations, training situations
- Face-to-Face – via media such as video phones, webcams etc.
- Actions, e.g. locking a door to prevent access, voluntarily clearing a backlog
- Telephone – one-on-one, or conference calls or VOIP systems
- Letters – you may have heard of these predecessors of email

- Electronic communications – emails, instant messaging, texts
- Notices – posters or plasma screen versions

You may have some more, or less; however, you may recall that communication is made up of three elements: verbal, non-verbal and tone. Emotions and other potential blocks may affect the quality of any communication. It is possible to identify strengths and weaknesses in different approaches:

- Notices on walls miss out on verbal communication, there is only the visual and the opportunity to get the right tone is limited.
- Telephone rules out the visual though we can generally communicate the desired tone and words.
- Letters and emails suffer from the same problems as notices, though they can generally contain more by way of explanation and scene setting. Texts are even worse!
- By themselves, actions as we recall, 'speak louder than words'. They can indeed convey a strong message, but in the absence of a verbal explanation as to *why* something is done, can be subject to easy misinterpretation. By definition, actions lack tone. Having said that: the manner in which something gets done could be taken to communicate the feelings of the person completing them.

What we're coming round to is the fact that any method that loses one or more of the components should not logically be deemed as effective as one that contains them all. By the same logic, we should look for methods that *do* have all three in order to maximise our chances of effective communication. In my list above this would seem to be either of the face-to-face options. So why do the optimum methods not get used all the time? Some of the excuses – I mean, reasons – could be:

- Lack of time on the part of the sender or the recipient(s)
- Sender's lack of knowledge of alternatives
- Lack of skill and ability on the part of the message sender/receiver(s)
- Organisational culture/custom
- Lack of resources or facilities
- Laziness

I don't think it necessary to elaborate on these and there may well be more. Suffice it to say that you should be working on not allowing any of these negative factors to negatively affect your decision as to which method to use.

The Impact of Communication Technologies

Please examine why and how you use the array of communication technologies that are available to you. It is important to achieve an appropriate balance between technology and human interfaces. Properly used, communication technologies can save time and cost; such as the time spent travelling to meetings, or the cost of distributing materials to a wide or extended audience. I stress 'properly used'! I remain unconvinced that technologies are being used to best effect by a significant number of us.

I worry that they are exterminating some essential and basic individual communication skills, rather than serving as a valuable support. There is a danger that over-reliance on these tools will eventually render some individuals bereft of basic skills and unable to function when the technology breaks down. It's like teaching children mathematics with calculators without the ability to first be able to do basic calculations mentally. If a calculator is not available they cannot do even simple things like adding up your bill or calculating your change.

Peter Drucker the writer and management consultant said "... Internet and email... have practically eliminated the physical costs of communications."[39] I disagree. The proliferation of email in particular (and the self induced necessity and laziness of users) has led to the printing off of more paper than was ever required of the humble letter. How many of you, rather than jotting down a couple of salient points from a long email, will print off the whole thing and then go to work with a highlighter pen? Or how many of us would 'print off' so that we can read it whilst on the move?

Why, if these machines are so brilliant, do we have a hard copy – 'just in case'? Why do office blocks still maintain file box upon file box of 'paperwork'? Can it be that computers and software, saving the rainforests, have actually achieved much the opposite?

'Must have' communication gadgets, supposed to free up so much of our working time and make life easier, are imposed upon us by our employers.

---

39   (Drucker n.d.)

It's not unusual to be just given the box and for it to be assumed that in true flat-pack style, we will be able to fathom out how the thing works, what it can do, and how we can get the best from it. I'm probably not a good example, but I probably use 30%-40% of my Smartphone's capabilities. If it had feelings, I'm sure it would be upset at that. Very few of us use devices to their full potential either because we don't know how to – and can't or won't invest the time to learn – or we don't need to. We are therefore constrained until shown otherwise, by our own limitations, rather than those of the device.

Communication is being dehumanised; yet there is still not a computer in the world that can do all the things a human brain is capable of, but so many pieces of wizard technology profess to come close. We believe the marketing and then spend an age complaining that it doesn't do everything 'they' promised it would. Well, actually, it does. But unless we are competent users, the device's capability is wasted.

I find it quite unnerving to witness the manner in which individuals seem to be shackled to their PDA, Smartphone or other device to the exclusion of everything and everybody around them: inappropriate conversations at inappropriate volumes that disturb other commuters, or banging into others and fixed objects. Walking the streets there is a new breed that does so with its head down reading or tapping away, oblivious as to what's going on around them. A subspecies exists, furiously exercising their thumbs instead of making a call and actually speaking. Commuter trains are fast becoming an extension of the individuals' offices. I wonder a) whether they're getting paid for this work; b) if they do all their work on the train, what they actually do when they get to the office and c) why they think the rest of the train would possibly be interested.

In many countries laws have been passed to stop smartphones and PDAs killing people! I'm not referring to the debate as to whether usage can induce illnesses via the ear into the brain, but to the fact that most people cannot seem to concentrate on more than one thing at once. So they've had to be stopped from using them whilst driving vehicles or indeed, operating machinery. Fatalities, injuries, and much damage and destruction to property are caused by individuals being unable to resist the temptation to use their gizmo when they shouldn't be.

I doubt I'll be around to see it, but what scares me ever so slightly is reaching the doomsday point where the dependency on IT is total.

Every so often someone completes a survey that shows that, in schools and universities, simple mental arithmetic cannot be performed by many of the students. Even some of their tutors have problems! Core skills are being too easily lost, to the point that control and power will be in the hands of an elite group of programmers and fixers.

The point of this apparent ramble is to urge you to have personal resources, skills and understanding that allow you to function and communicate when the technology doesn't permit.

I am now envisioning the 'techies' up in arms saying that I don't understand communications technology how it works, the benefits it can bring. Well, actually, I do – on both counts and I'm all for it. However, those benefits are only realised if the technology works as intended; if there is not an over reliance on it, and if the users maintain skills that they can resort to as and when (not if) the technology breaks down. Rather than make life simple – 'suspicious me' believes these things are engineered to fall over or require excessive amounts of training and technical support for the benefit of those selling such services. Even if it's not by malicious design, does anyone out there know of a piece of software bought off-the-shelf, or made for their organisation that hasn't had bugs, hasn't needed 'patches', or has done exactly what was required of it? I'd be genuinely interested to hear of it. Even American computer scientist Andrew Tanenbaum admits, "*A refund for defective software might be nice, except it would bankrupt the entire software industry in the first year.*"[40] As a customer how many times have you pulled out what little remains of your hair, talking to machines, selecting 'Option 3', or talking to people reliant on machines whose machines are 'down'?

There is a growing catalogue of evidence that social skills are being lost in adolescents. This is the prospective next generation of team members that you might end up managing. There's a significant proportion of their number reliant on gadgetry for work and social interaction. I do not think it is being a Luddite to suggest the technology should be there to facilitate and support you in your tasks, rather than take over and make you redundant. Frank Lloyd Wright made the point that if this keeps up all of man's limbs will waste away through lack of use – except for the finger that pushes the button.

40   (Andrew S Tanenbaum 2002)

Emails can be particularly wasteful: there's the time spent drafting, re-reading and rewriting, and the additional time required to phrase correctly to make sure the right sentiment comes across. Then there's the fact that, once sent, it falls into the competitive morass that is the recipients' in-box to wait for a reply. Emails are increasingly used as a backup, as 'confirmation' or to clarify. Whereas what we are actually saying is, "I don't trust you to do what we agreed so I'm covering my rear end, by creating a record!"

Things can get put into electronic mail (or on voice messages or notice boards) that we would never contemplate saying to someone if they were standing in front of us. Some consider the distance provided by these mediums to be a wall from behind which they can fire off with impunity, or at least take shelter from the anticipated reply.

Another problem arises around the security of sensitive information about projects, bids or colleagues. It used to be that those engaged in snooping or industrial espionage first had to break into or have access to the building, then the office and then the filing cabinet or safe. Nowadays they can do it all from the comfort of their lounge, which incidentally can be the other side of the world!

In spite of the weaknesses of email, they can still be viewed as quicker, more expedient and the best way to reach everyone. We seem to ignore the follow-up time spent answering phone calls from recipients seeking clarification or wading through the replies. Emails also have a habit of containing things wholly or partly that they should not, or not containing the things they should, ending up in the wrong hands, or being lost when "the system crashed".

There seems to be a reluctance to put the time or effort into making the quality and content of a face-to-face meeting as effective as they might be. Hence the need for 'back up', rear end covering, hard copy confirmation. We will write an email because we can't be bothered to rise from our well-padded executive chairs, or move from one part of the shop floor to another (though I accept that this may not always be practicable). Sometimes we don't want the recipient to see us in the state we're in, or because we know it can be much easier to exercise one-way communication. On other occasions we can't be bothered to tailor the message for the different audiences who might need to hear it, or to set up a series of meetings so that everyone in the same group gets the same message and the same opportunity to question.

Some might be genuinely uncomfortable with interactions generally, or those that are likely to occur in a given set of circumstances. We might know deep down that we are on shaky ground, or we might not personally agree with the message. Using remote forms of communication therefore, minimises that discomfort and/or the chance/ opportunity for the recipients to answer or question back. The more opportunities are reduced, the less effective the communication will prove to be.

Many managers have their personal communication strategies back-to-front and upside down. Face-to-face communication may take more effort and time initially, but if done with REASON, it has the greatest potential to be effective short, medium and long-term. Your role, your organisation and working environment have considerable influence on your options. However, when considering the options, I argue that you should always start with the face-to-face option and work down from there. It affords the opportunity to deal instantly with complications, issues or questions. All three elements of effective communication can be there in abundance. You can adapt to changing circumstances, without the need for re-convening at some other time or in some other format.

Using communication technology wisely

Of course technology has a place: to support the real thing and not act as a substitute! You can if you want reduce the size of your inbox – and thus the time spent trying to understand and then deal appropriately with a sub-standard piece of communication. You can also contribute to saving a chunk of the rainforest. 'Heads down typing responses' is time that could be spent talking directly, letting the recipient see just how you're feeling and why, and building relationships and trust. Maybe you could set yourself two occasions a day to deal with incoming mail, don't be tempted to sneak a peek at other times, have your junk settings set correctly, or skim-read to identify the most important items ('important' being judged appropriately). Instead of emailing a reply how about using the phone or even a quick meeting – keep it human! Remember also that what is important and urgent to others, might not be so for you – and vice versa! And, finally, unless someone's life depends on it – when you're not being paid – switch the PDA off.

This extends to meetings and seminars and the like, where it is now common practice for the chair or session leader to ask for mobiles or devices to be switched off or to 'silent'. There are a couple of arguments around this: the first harks back to before we ever had these devices (some of you I know won't remember that). Attendees would tell people where they were going, tell them they were not going to be available, and meetings would go ahead uninterrupted.

The second is around the assurance that if somebody is unnecessarily disturbed during a scheduled meeting, then his or her time management must be comparatively weak. Alternatively: If they cannot make the necessary arrangements so as not to be disturbed; if they lack the confidence that others can deal with situations totally in their absence, or at the very least until they become free; perhaps something is wrong. Even if a device is switched to silence or vibrate, the circumstance of the recipient responding to the vibration and often getting up and walking out – or not – is not only distracting to the rest of the audience, but also leads one to suspect whether they were actually devoting the required amount of concentration to the matter in hand.

Communication – Smartphone dependency

There may be a time or times when a specific situation means you have to be on call – this is especially true of emergency services workers, but for whom it's written into the job. There may be other occasions when key decision-makers or authority holders are anticipating a genuinely crucial contact of great importance or urgency, but all day, every day?

The phenomenon seems to be more prevalent the higher up the food chain you travel. However, if you are lured into this particular vice, think for a moment: what would be the consequences of *not* making or taking routine calls/contacts except at particular times and certainly not during pre-arranged meetings? Make your choice.

I am not so naive as to not recognise the pressure that some organisations put on their managers – explicit or otherwise. However, if it is explicit there is usually proper compensation via the remuneration package. If it is implicit; you need to make a decision as to whether you comply, or develop other skills and behaviours to manage your time effectively; manage your communication structures effectively; and especially, take action to prevent your use of communication technology invading into time properly allocated to other things.

To sum up: the things that can be done with communications technology are fantastic, but your gadget is not there to rule you!

Exercise

Apply the **ADDRESS Model** to your use of communications technology. If you determine that the situation needs some attention identify the kind of personal strategy you intend to adopt and what amendments (if any) this now requires. Generate a **CRAFT-T** plan to implement your strategy.

It's time to move on and look at the impacts of untargeted general communications that reach beyond the intended audience.

Your experiences could be totally different to mine. Whether use of gadgetry is appropriate is very subjective. The next exercise is intended to help.

Exercise:

Consider the questions on the next page, answering as honestly as you wish.

Once you have done so, discuss your responses with a trusted colleague or two to gain a second opinion.

As a result of answering the questions consider what if anything you wish to do about your use of communication technology.

Communication Technology Usage Questionnaire

1. List the communication gadget(s) you use for <u>work</u> (e.g. PDA, smartphone, tablet, notebook)
a) By putting a number alongside each, rank them in order of volume of usage (column 2)
b) By putting a number alongside each, rank them in order of preference of usage (column 3)
c) Under 'Time' indicate when the particular gadget is switched on and off each day then do the maths to provide a length of time that it is on.
d) Explain below the relationship between the different rating criteria. For instance, if your primary gadget is also your preferred gadget – why, if it is not why not?

Gadgets	Rank by Volume used	Rank by preference for use	Time		
			Switched on	Switched off	Duration

2. Now list your gadgets again, this time in order from primary down.
a) Indicate the amount of time you spend referring to a particular gadget (picking up messages/ information/ searching). Tick whether it's on demand (when it beeps), or when you feel like it (impulse), or at set times (controlled), then estimate how much time you spend referring to each one.
b) Indicate the amount of time you spend responding to your gadget and how that is broken down, e.g. do you respond just with that gadget

(same), or do you have to respond with other methods (other). Again indicate the total amount.

c) Provide an explanation below to yourself as to why you allocate time to the gadgets in the way you do, e.g. you feel more comfortable with it, it's easier to use etc.

Gadgets	Reference Time (a)				Responding Time		
	On Demand	Impulse	Set Time	Total Amount	Same	Other	Total Amount

Explanation:

3. Who supplies your gadget(s)? (List them again and then identify)

Gadgets	Supplied by			
	Employer	Me – Paid by Employer	Me – Paid by Me	Other (e.g. sponsor)

4. Please explain to yourself:
a. To what extent are you dependent or reliant on your primary communications gadget to be able to function in your role? Could you do without it – honestly?
b. To what extent would your performance suffer if you reduced your usage of any or all of the gadgets?

5. What do you do with your gadget(s) when you are in meetings? E.g. keep them on, but silent; turn them off; leave them outside.

6 Other than when it's geographically essential, why do you think **others** contact you in the first instance via your primary or some other gadget? (Select one or more of the following):
a. Hit and run – they fear your response/reaction
b. Their bad time management
c. They don't like face-to-face engagement
d. They think that's what you prefer
e. Insecurity – they want some evidence that the communication took place
f. Other reason – specify
7. Other than when it's geographically essential, why do you think **you** contact others in the first instance via your primary or some other gadget? (Select one or more of the reasons listed in Question 6):

8. Does your primary gadget remain on outside of working hours or when you are not on a day off or on holiday? If so why?

What you should now consider is whether the time you spend tied to your gadget(s) is appropriate. Of course it depends on how your organisation is set up; its communication strategies and cultures; or your knowledge, understanding, skills and communications behaviours; but it could well be that alternative methods of communication might be more effective, e.g. a phone call instead of a text or email; a face-to-face chat instead of a phone call.

I want you to consider the methodologies you employ to communicate – not just the gadgets we focussed on earlier. In respect of any 'broad-brush' or blanket approach to communications, the problem is that they are akin to that of aerial bombardment. In World War Two vast numbers of aircraft flew over large areas and dropped a multitude of munitions in the hope that they would hit the target. Post-bombing aerial photography often showed that not to be the case, but vividly illustrated the amount of collateral damage done. Modern day weapons are much more sophisticated, have the capacity to be much better targeted and so much more effective. Yet mistakes are still made. We can't hope to be perfect all of the time. We can at least give it our best shot.

First-Line managers very often find themselves carrying out change. How engaged you are in the process, the commitment you show to it, the manner in which you communicate it, can be key to any change activity being a success. Even in your day-to-day business the effectiveness of your communication drives the engagement, motivation, harmony and effectiveness of your team.

Read the following case study and then complete the exercise that follows.

CASE STUDY: Time for a change

Pearl Electronics has identified that it can save considerable staffing costs in their customer service contact centre. A new telephone system and a greatly enhanced web site will result in only the most complex customer enquiries requiring the attention of a 'live' customer service agent. Spare parts can now be ordered online and service call outs can be completed using 'self-serve' on the phones. In particular there is a reduced need for staff outside of normal office hours. This is a key benefit and one of the drivers for the project.

Chris manages a team of fifteen customer service agents who often work the 'out of hours' shifts and who are used to a shift allowance and regular overtime. Pearl's operations director has determined that there should be regular communication and consultation with all levels throughout the process. Chris is one of a group of managers who have been identified as subject-matter-experts who will have a greater participation in the project. She has attended a briefing with all other shift managers.

One of the actions from that meeting was for all service agents to be briefed and it has been left to shift managers as to how they do it, but the first communication must have been completed within seven days.

Case Study 6: Time for a Change

Exercise

Which elements of **REASON** would apply to what she needs to do and what would they look like?

What might her **CRAFT-T** plan look like?

What **STUFF** would she need to be considering and how might this affect her tone and delivery of the news?

In terms of the qualities of communication, what do you advise Chris to do as the most effective way of delivering this message and why?

Regardless of your views on the organisation's approach, it is the method they chose and Chris was obliged to deal with the task she was given.

Chris's **REASON** needs very little – if any – 'relationship' building. She is organising and leading on the communication, which maintains the existing relationship she has with her team. The explanation phase is her opportunity to outline why she has called the meeting and what she intends to do, e.g. explain the proposed change and how it affects the team and that they will have an opportunity to ask questions. She can explain her aims and objective, i.e. that all the team need to leave the meeting with a clear understanding of the proposed changes and how they affect them.

The account phase should start with an overview or outline, followed by a breakdown of specific points. At this stage it doesn't necessitate Chris doing any questioning (unless later she wants to ask questions of the team to check they have understood the message). She might however, have to deal with questions from the team and if she has done her preparation, will have anticipated what these questions might be and will have answers prepared. She should choose and make clear whether questions are acceptable during or after the account.

Once she and the team are satisfied that they have had the opportunity to ask questions and to have them answered – or an undertaking provided to get them – Chris should summarise the key points of what has been discussed. The outputs should be a) that Chris will have managed to get all the information across and b) all involved understand the content.

The meeting might have produced some questions that Chris didn't anticipate or that can't be addressed there and then. So she and they might also come away from the meeting with some action points and these will be listed in the final stage so that all are clear as to what action she will be taking and what if anything they as a team will be doing.

Using **CRAFT-T** in this exercise illustrates that it can be used for immediate, short situations as well as the more obvious 'grand' plans or projects. Remember this is a test of a plan, not a format for the planning itself.

Before the proposed meeting Chris can spend as much time as she has available to get some **clarity** as to why there is a need for a meeting: in this case it is because there is an important message to get across to more than one individual and holding a group meeting will save the time and inconvenience of trying to speak to everyone individually. It would be very different of course if the information revealed that particular individuals' jobs were known to be lost (when one-on-one talks would be more fitting).

The **reaction** here relates to the plan, not the content of the message. However, given that there is likely to be a financial cost to the team through losing overtime opportunities, the team is likely to be sensitive to the message and as here how it is delivered. So Chris can test whether her planned methodology is appropriate.

Adequacy of Resource in this instance would simply be making sure that she has an appropriate venue in which she can deliver the information and hold a discussion or answer questions. She needs to ensure the space is free at the times required and properly equipped. Chris has to make sure that all the required attendees are free to attend, that cover is available and arranged if necessary; and that arrangements are made for those who cannot get to this particular meeting to be given the same information in the same way. Not having sufficient time or resources would indicate whether the plan is feasible or not. If she couldn't get an appropriate space, or get enough of the team together at one time, she might have to go back to the drawing board.

Does her plan **target** the problem? Yes it's a solution to getting the required message across to the right audience in the right time frame. Chris has to have this done within seven days, remember. So if she couldn't gather the team together within that time, she would have to consider an alternative method of delivery. Notwithstanding this, it will be very easy to measure whether her plan gets the job done within the required time.

In this instance **CRAFT-T** testing need take no longer than five minutes. It serves to sanity check whether what Chris proposes stands a realistic chance of achieving her objectives.

Communication – Providing a complete picture

Effective communication should paint, or at the very least contribute towards, a complete and where necessary, multi-dimensional picture. For instance, a plan appears as a one-dimensional view from above. In order to illustrate where there is more than one level it has to apply a particular set of conventions such as contour lines. A model on the other hand shows things in two dimensions. It allows those being communicated with to see much more and also cuts down on the amount of descriptions or conventions that the communicator must apply. Think how much time is saved trying to describe something fully if we can just say to somebody "take a look at this".

Planners must usually explain more in order to convey what the real thing will actually look like and to help others' picture and understanding of the situation. Even then, like in Chinese whispers, the message intended by the sender is often not what was received.

Very often and where possible, operational military briefings are supported by as much visual intelligence as possible: maps, reconnaissance photographs, and sandbox or blanket models. The latter prove very useful as they can recreate the contours and landscape over which movement is to be made in a much clearer and quicker manner, though we must also factor in the amount of time taken to prepare those models. Still if it means that those facing the task are much clearer about what is before them as a result, I would argue that that is time well spent.

Words alone can be dry and boring. To paint a full picture, you might need a lot of them. So to save preparation and delivery time there is a lot to be said for using pictures, models and diagrams to support either a written or oral description.

A fun way of demonstrating this is when you next get hold of some flat-pack furniture, a gadget that needs self assembly, or something that needs to follow a user set up procedure (preferably one that you get more than one chance to set it up if things go wrong).

Exercise:

Ideally you need two rooms and a way of communicating between them (at a push this can actually be done in the same room). You'll also need a guinea pig or helper to assist.

Your job is to assemble the flat-pack or gadget or complete the set up. Their job is (from the other room, or from a distance away in the same room) to provide you with verbal instructions based on the assembly information that came with the item. They are not allowed to show you, and you are not allowed to peek at the instructions or any diagrams.

If in the same room they are not allowed to draw 'air pictures' either.

See how long it takes before you become frustrated and want to read the instructions or look at the diagrams yourself. Alternatively see if you pick up on any signs or signals from them if they don't think you're 'getting it'. If this doesn't happen you have an excellent helper and you are very good at receiving information.

If it does happen, note what other issues this raises for you maybe around the competence of your helper. Is it going to test the friendship? Then keep that thought in mind when you are giving instructions or messages to your team.

NB: Please don't try this with very expensive items or ones that you would mind losing and this is my disclaimer for any loss or damage caused as a result of trying this. Now that I've said that – how confident are you to proceed with this exercise and what does that tell you about your communication skills?

Communication – 'Dos' and 'Don'ts'

- Don't stay silent on a point when you need to speak up for your own, others' or the organisation's benefit. Assuming others know what you know, believe what you believe or feel as you do can lead to disappointment. Balance this by resisting the urge to throw something in just for the sake of being noticed. The effective use of silence is also a skill. There is a lovely saying that he who asks a question is a fool for five minutes, he who doesn't is a fool for life.
- Don't – or do your best not to – get involved in difficult conversations when emotions are running high. Strong emotion, be it euphoria or anger, will drown out both the words and the meaning of what is said. Sometimes it's unavoidable, but managing a situation such as this requires you to deal with the situation first and then have the conversation when things have calmed down.
- Similarly don't shout – verbally or with the Caps lock on in your emails. As with high emotion it's likely to switch the receiver off.
- Don't say things in white mail, email or over the telephone that you would not be saying if the recipient were standing in front of you.
- Don't put in a call or send an important message when you know the recipient is not around to take or deal with it. Don't reel off a liturgy of woes on voicemail or deliver a bad message that way.
- Don't bury your point or contribution in a fog of technical language or in the middle of a smoke screen. Balance this by putting the salient point across and explaining it if required.
- Don't bury your message deep in something that's only loosely connected. Doing so can lead to misinterpretation and misunderstanding. Keep separate matters just that.
- Don't rely on Chinese whispers. Messages delivered 2nd or 3rd hand can and most often will be diluted, distorted or disjointed, very often quite innocently.

- Do work at matching or balancing the three elements of effective face-to-face communication: words, tone and non-verbal communication in a ratio that takes into account the circumstances. Don't say one thing and mean another.
- And finally: Work at putting your communication into language that your audience(s) will understand and accept

End of Chapter Activity 1:

When next called upon to communicate something to your team, take some time out before the event to test your chosen communication plan against the following criteria i.e. is it:

The right message(s); the right audience(s), the right location(s), the right time(s), the right method(s)

End of Chapter Activity 2:

After you have delivered the communication, take some time out to assess how it went. To what extent do you feel your Exercise 1 assessment was correct?

Were there loads of questions about things they didn't understand? What feedback do you get, e.g. is it being fully and accurately acted upon by the recipients?

If there are discrepancies between what you planned or thought would happen and what actually did, what do you need to do differently next time?

You can repeat this exercise as many times as you wish and until you feel you are hitting the required quality most of the time.

23. Watch, listen, feel

There are two areas in which watching, listening and feeling (or sensing) are important. The first is when perfecting your communication skills and ensuring that your outgoing messages are properly received and understood. You will get evidence for this from the incoming message or feedback element of good communication. The second is about your ability to be aware of what's going on around you on a day-to-day basis. It enables you to identify situations early. It is the way in which you identify situations that enable you to be a proactive manager and one who is able to make sound decisions, based upon facts.

Feedback

There are a number of ways that the recipient(s) of your message(s) will let you know that your messages are received and understood. It's commonly called feedback. It might be that a particular task gets completed fully as directed. It might be that a particular direction to do or cease doing something is complied with fully. It might be that the manner in which you have communicated the headline message leads to a change of approach or even appreciation of your role by them. These are all positive indicators.

The opposite applies too: if a job is not done it should prompt you to examine a) whether the communication was effective or b) whether the communication was as good as it could be. But there are other reasons for non-compliance. Bear in mind that this relates to the main message. If there are some secondary (subtle) messages then the feedback might also be equally subtle and require a keener ear to detect. There is more on this in the next chapter.

We now consider more deeply, the 'incoming' message element. I want to focus on listening as a very particular skill. It includes gathering the information required to properly **ASSESS** situations and formulate a **CRAFT-T** plan.

I spoke earlier of the need for a coherent and credible outgoing message, based on accurate, well founded, and substantial information. We have not yet discussed the practicalities of securing that information, especially when we are in the middle of the situation, or actually engaged in some form of encounter. At the operational level one often has to 'think on your feet' often with intensity driven by emotions or urgency. It is easy to be side tracked or indeed driven to a particular conclusion by not actually hearing what is going on.

The aim is to ensure your actions give success a chance. There's a difference between looking and seeing, listening and hearing. Rather than relying on 'gut feelings' to make decisions, get into the habit of effective listening.

So what's the difference between 'listening' and 'hearing'? Well strictly on dictionary definition: To listen is 'to concentrate on hearing something' or 'to give attention so as to hear'. To hear means: 'to perceive by the ear', 'to listen intently' or 'to listen to attentively'. The latter then is more akin to effective listening.

We recognise the noises of life around us all the time, yet because many have no relevance to us we ignore them. Others we try to shut out because they distract us from what we're trying to concentrate on. So our brains are constantly picking up signals, decoding them, analysing them and determining the ones we need to act upon. How it does so is a mystery to me. How, for instance in a busy railway concourse, do we hear our own names being called above all the others? How in a one-on-one interview situation can we see the other person's lips moving, hear noises come out, but even if they're speaking the same national language, not understand or 'hear' what they're saying? In short it's because we choose to open or close our communication channels largely according to how *we* feel at the time or what *we* want from a situation.

Exercise:

In the following case study, detail what you consider to be the causes of John's situation. Select no more than two causes: one primary, the other secondary.

Apply the first five phases of the **ADDRESS Model** to the primary cause (up to and including 'plan'). You can assume that John acknowledges there is a situation he needs to address.

Apply the **CRAFT-T** test to the plan you would implement

Case study: Out of Stock

John had been a First-Line manager for nine of his eighteen years with his previous organisation. He'd become disillusioned with his job. It seemed that, to get on, your 'face had to fit' more so than being recognised for your skills, abilities, and competencies. In other words: being accepted as company compliant and fitting in was more important. So he decided to start afresh and moved on.

Joining a profit-making company in a highly competitive, highly intense arena required John to apply and utilise all his manager skills, but also required him to gain knowledge and understand a complete new set of technical skills such as accounting, stock control and stock welfare.

After a brief induction period in which John was put to work in a similar environment under the supervision of a very experienced manager, John was dispatched to his own venue having not yet got to know either it, all the staff or indeed, having yet found a permanent place to live.

Three months into the role, as far as he was concerned, John had not been doing too bad a job. The venue was considerably cleaner. Some of the less desirable customers had been dissuaded from coming in. Whilst at the same time income levels have been maintained. However, when the head office stock takers completed a stock take and audit a serious stock deficit was uncovered.

This prompted a less-than-comfortable meeting between John and his then manager during which he was left in no uncertain terms that his career, far from being in its ascendancy, was in fact in serious jeopardy.

Case Study 7: Out of Stock

There are so many permutations and potential causes, that it is not possible to run through them here. I appreciate you probably thought you didn't have enough information to make a definitive response. But that was not the objective. The idea was for you to apply the **ADDRESS** process and apply a **CRAFT-T** test to your plan. Also, because I cannot see your responses, I cannot provide you with an individual critique. You may wish to show the problem to a colleague and discuss your proposed solution with them to get feedback as to its potential.

Consider two primary causes for this situation which for John amounted to something of a crisis: firstly, proper stock controls and security checks were not in place and secondly, one or more of the staff were being free and easy with the stock – stealing – mainly by not registering sales via the tills... It would be easy at this stage to try to add in other 'causes', such as faulty equipment, a lack of training of John, poor supervision and support by John's manager, and a culture that did nothing to discourage pilfering. However, I would suggest that these are contributory factors and therefore secondary. Some might say they are even excuses.

It is important to maintain objectivity – easy for us, as we are not John under threat of the sack! We must hone in on the actual cause(s) or issue(s). 'diagnose' to identify the nature of the situation and 'determine' the causes in order to address them accurately. Arguing over who did what and why ad nausea – especially when time is pressing – is unlikely to resolve the situation. Time is better spent looking forward and arriving at workable solutions.

John's solution revolved around increasing the number of stock checks carried out on the most at risk products to identify the period(s) when the discrepancies were occurring and to narrowing down which staff members were working on the day(s) in question. He would then get assistance from colleagues to make test purchases and seek to get confirmation as to which if any of the individuals was suspected to be at fault.

In terms of resources many were already to hand: computer systems could provide data as to which products were most at risk and accurate records of stock that should be on hand based on the previous day's sales. He considered using friends to make check purchases and also the services of the stock-taker on a more regular basis. Two of the biggest resources John required were knowledge – of how to use the systems properly and what they were capable of – and time.

John implemented his plan with the backing of his manager. Staff noticed the increase in stocktaking activity, which actually had positive effect. However, their lack of knowledge of the capabilities of the technology, along with a feeling of invulnerability meant they carried on with their bad practices. Within a week the losses could be attributed to two members of staff who were subsequently dealt with for gross misconduct.

This is a simplified example of where one plan can be used to address two linked situations: By improving stock control, theft was stopped and prevented in future. This also proved a valuable learning exercise for John who took it as an opportunity to develop his knowledge and its application. So what listening lessons would you consider John learned from this situation, or rather, what are you going to take from his example?

I was taught early in my police service that it is usually better to 'run to a fire and walk to a fight'! That meant you must be aware and then pick the occasions to 'dive in'. Sometimes prompt, drastic action is necessary, whilst at other times it is better to approach slowly and take your time to appraise what's going on. Later I was made aware that in Chinese, the symbol meaning 'to listen' is comprised of the symbols for the eye, the ear and the heart.

Figure 8: Chinese Symbol for 'Listen(ing)'

Watching

How would 'watching' (listening with one's eyes) help? Well for starters, knowing your **STUFF** means you know what to look for. It is one thing to be watching your staff to check how busy they appear to be, it is another to be able to recognise what it is they are busy doing and whether it is what you what them to be doing. How many times has your supervisor passed your desk, popped their head round your door, or watched you from a distance to see you labouring feverishly? At that distance they can't really see what you're doing. Similarly, it is the case that you need to watch not only what is being done and how, but also the outputs of that labour. Team member 'A' might be a slow, methodical worker who always appears calm almost to the point where they are taking it easy and who produces less than most of the other team members, but every output is near perfect; whereas team member 'B' works non-stop, turns out 15% above target numerically, but has 30% of their output rejected by quality control.

Of course this is affected by whether your organisation demands quantity over quality or a perfect blend of the two, whether the targets set are appropriate for the expected quality, and staff capability. How you react and manage the outputs of either team member will be affected by your knowledge of what is expected and how, by observation and evidence they are meeting those expectations.

These observations are primary evidence of performance or of a situation, but it is often the case that what you have seen is open to misinterpretation; that the individual has a legitimate reason for the observed activity; or that someone feeling threatened might seek to challenge you – to disbelieve or contradict your observation. In such circumstances – and even actually in those when you are providing feedback on positive performance, you may wish to have some other evidence. In some operations there are gauges, print outs, screen displays of up-to-date data on outputs.

In call centres for instance it's often the case that screens will display how many calls are waiting, how many have been abandoned, how many agents are engaged on calls etc. Not only can this back up what you observe, it can also give you a first clue for you to do some follow-up and closer inspection of the actual activity. In other organisations, similar output data may be available to you, but it is less immediately so. This may be something like an end of week summary of sales. Alternatively the information is readily available, but you cannot do anything with it until the people it concerns are available.

The points therefore are:

- Know what you are looking for
- Use the information resources that are available to you
- Be ready to question or check out what you think you have seen before 'jumping in'

This latter point is especially true if you feel something inappropriate is going on.

Listen

Someone failing to meet performance requirements may (but not always) have an unconscious air of furtiveness about them. It's like they're always checking over their shoulder to see if they're being watched. If they think they are, there's a perceptible shift in their demeanour and behaviour. However, you don't want to be embarrassing yourself or anyone else by putting – albeit honestly – a false interpretation on something. So this brings in your questioning skills and your ability to investigate and get to the cause of things and the need to listen to what's going on.

Working environments differ greatly, but no matter where it is, there is a level of noise that generally reflects how things are when things are working 'normally'. We very quickly get accustomed to this to the point that we often take it for granted. To newcomers or strangers coming in it is interference. We have learned to live with it – even ignore it. Yet when that hum is disturbed, maybe by a group chat breaking into raucous laughter, something being dropped and smashing on a hard floor, or when a piece of machinery suddenly stops, we notice. We notice sudden changes in content and volume of noise – otherwise emergency vehicle sirens would be pretty useless. But if you were asked to describe the normal 'noise' at your workplace, it can be difficult.

From a management point of view, it is these sudden variations upwards, or downwards, that can provide a clue that there is something happening that requires your attention. Just as with the observation, you might have to check out what you think you have heard; hearing an unusual crash you might choose to pop out of the office and make sure everything is alright; overhearing a heated conversation between two colleagues, you might want to step in and referee, or you might want to make a note of what was being said and check it out with them a little later either to make sure everything was alright, or to deal with something that was wrong. You might be asking questions such as, "Did I hear X correctly?" or, "I heard you say 'Y' and wanted to check out what was being discussed as you weren't quite right about the process".

Have you ever walked into a meeting room and notice the conversation drop off, or cease altogether? Most disconcerting if you have a persecution complex, but rather helpful if you're in charge of the meeting and everyone recognises that now you've arrived they have to shut up and pay attention to you. In this instance it is your window into taking control from the 'off'.

With 'listening' in this context, the key points are:

- React only to the sudden and unexpected noise
- Don't allow yourself to be complacent. Just because there is an absence of anything unusual, don't assume that everything is OK (unless you're totally confident that it is)
- Check out what you've heard to make sure you've decoded it correctly

Feeling

In practice it really does take not just the ears, but also the eyes AND the heart to 'hear'. Look at the words. 100% of 'H-E-A-R' is in H-E-A-R-T. If the minority of communication is usually verbal, it is logical that we must listen with things other than the ears.

You see a smile and 'hear' what it means by associating it with past smiles of the same kind that we have stored in the brain, which then informs our hearts. Beyond that, we seem to sense whether it's a genuine smile; we can tell if the tears are genuine (joy or sadness); and we can tell if a promise is likely to be kept. We can understand why a person might be red in the face or shaking whilst they're talking to us – it could be the temperature, or it could be that they're angry or scared. Even then we need to check it out. Is the athlete collecting their gold medal on the podium crying with joy, or because of the pain of the tendon they tore whilst earning it?

It is only through our experience of communication in the culture(s) and environment(s) in which we operate that we build up a picture. Thus our brains put <u>all</u> the messages together and tell us how to react. This build up of experience can help, or hinder, depending on how you use it and how you choose to let past experience affect what you do now. For instance, is the current situation exactly the same as the one you're drawing on? We can be influenced by our emotions, preconceptions or beliefs. In other words we only hear what we want to. We either ignore or shut out that which doesn't fit nicely into the 'that's what I thought' category.

Top tip one: perfect your listening skills. Top tip two: don't waste those listening skills and the fruits of them by ignoring or dismissing what you have heard. Top tip three: objectively assess the nature of the information, its quality, its reliability and what it relates to, whether it requires some form of response immediately or delayed and if delayed, by how long. Top tip four: be decisive as to what you do with the information.

For instance, In World War Two Operation Market Garden was the Allied attempt to shorten the war with an ambitious plan to use paratroopers to seize bridges ahead of an armoured column that would link up with them in succession. Paratroopers are comparatively lightly armed. They rely on courage, surprise and swiftness to succeed. They encounter severe difficulties when faced – as in Market Garden – with battle tanks (two divisions of them that were being rested nearby). By all accounts the Allied planners secured well in advance, reconnaissance information of the tanks' presence, but took the decision to plough on anyway with disastrous consequences. Of 10,000 who went in, only about 2,000 returned.

That the planners had information is not disputed, but it is questionable whether they listened to it. If they did listen did they hear? There have been suggestions that the generals chose to doubt the quality or reliability of the reconnaissance. Yet it is not known whether they did anything to check out the intelligence. What is clear is that the information didn't reach the operational troops until they were staring down the not inconsiderable barrels of enemy tanks.

Some First-Line managers do indeed have to make decisions in immediate, perilous or life-threatening situations sometimes. However, that only serves to heighten the obligation to make those decisions based on the best information one can muster and at the right time. Listening with ears, eyes and heart is therefore, an essential requirement.

You have to want to 'hear' what you are seeing and listening to and, yes, this can include listening to what your gut instinct is telling you. If you are embarking on a listening process, the clue is in the title – 'listening'. That means shutting up and only interrupting if things are getting out of control, seriously 'off-subject', or you need to get some clarification or explanation of what you are hearing.

Don't waste your own or others' time by asking irrelevant questions; those to which you have the reasonable and sufficient answer already, or those you throw in just so they make you look good. Others won't thank you for it, the questions won't be convincing and others will pick up on the underlying messages you're sending. And finally if you do ask a question don't answer it yourself – "What colour was the car – red?" – And give the respondent time to do just that.

I'll leave this chapter with the thoughts of two wise men: Ernest Hemingway (1899–1961) who said, "I like to listen. I have learned a great deal from listening carefully. Most people never listen." And those of Diogenes Laertius, who said, "We have two ears and only one tongue in order that we may hear more and speak less"

End of Chapter Activity:

The next time you are in a large, busy environment, such as a cafe, canteen, airport lounge or the like with five or ten minutes to spare, pick a pair of 'subjects' who are obviously engaged in a conversation. They will be far enough away to be inaudible and so they won't realise you're 'listening'. Try and work out from body language what they're saying and how they feel.

Then try and eliminate the surrounding noise and see if you can begin to pick up the odd word or the tone of what's being said.

24. Manage every encounter – let's be grown-ups

This is the third chapter to deal with communication issues. The aim is to examine how, beyond using the models illustrated in Section 2, you can manage the different types of situation you face. I want in particular to identify things that impact your ability to manage or control particular situations by recognising and then dealing with some of the psychological or sub-conscious factors that can impact upon a successful outcome. We have to accept that we are unlikely to be perfect adherents to best practice 100% of the time. No level of knowledge of models or theories can guarantee that. However, by the end of this section it is intended that you will be able to:

- Explain and illustrate some of the major impacts upon encounters
- Understand and explain how your attitude and behaviour to and during situations can affect the attitude and behaviour of others
- Identify and manage the level that you and other parties to a situation are operating at
- Understand how to manage encounters and the emotions they can generate
- Relate and explain how your ego can affect the progress and outcome of encounters
- Integrate the above concepts into your considerations when applying the **reason** model or dealing with situations

There are far too many and too great a variety of encounters to provide you with some form of indexed catalogue that would allow you to look up the problem and have a set response laid out for you. It will help if you can recognise what is actually happening and have a store of strategies in your 'bank' to resolve it. We start by examining the types of encounter you may experience. Then the influences on you and others during encounters and in particular those that affect the conduct and therefore, the outcomes of any encounter-type you might face in your role. You will perhaps recognise elements of conflict management or resolution concepts. I have purposely avoided delving too deeply into conflict management per se as the intention is that in the first instance, the models and concepts discussed elsewhere can help you to 'plan out' conflict, and plan to deal with it in the second. Once you have been introduced to the concepts to the depth that time and space here allow you have the opportunity to apply them using a case study.

I include some well-tested theories along with a model framework to help you remember the key features of every encounter. In case you'd forgotten all about it, you will have more opportunity to apply **R-E-A-S-O-N** to deal with them. You may already have studied some of these models before. So feel free to skip them if you wish. Those I have included are:

- The Attitude/Behaviour cycle
- The stages of Escalation
- The Emotional Brain versus Rational Brain
- The Three Levels of behaviour

The nature of your encounters

Most of the time, your role will involve you asking, telling and indeed, being told. Whether it's difficult conversations, collaborative interactions or those aimed at relationship building, your role and position in these dealings will be substantially different to when you were not a manager. You interact with or encounter people you work for, those who work under you, peers, and maybe those from outside your organisation, team and environment.

The 'nature of the beast' is that as a First-Line Manager of people, you spend significantly more of your working day dealing with interactions and people-based issues. This of course is affected by the nature of your business, the numbers your position is responsible for and whether you had a large network, or interaction with large numbers before promotion. Previously you were more likely to have been dealing with issues directly related to your own expected outputs. Now it's those plus the ones that are passed upwards or downwards to you.

It will be rare for you to be in any situation without there being at least one other person involved. So you will invariably be having at least one encounter with them. I work on the idea that there are six distinct categories of encounter:

1. The 'Brief Encounter': A corridor conversation, the quick telephone enquiry or similar.
2. The 'Close Encounter of the Third Kind' (I'm sure you see where I'm going with this?): These involve situations and/or personalities that either we've not encountered before, or they are so rare there's little to reference them to.
3. The 'Go Between' relates to the situations where you provide the channel for either upward or downward communication in either crisis or non-crisis situations. By 'crisis' I mean those of great urgency and/or importance.
4. The 'Groundhog Day' category includes regular meetings such as performance reviews or appraisals fall into. Performance reviews are critical to the maintenance of a good manager-subordinate relationship. We have other regular 'catch-up meetings' too. Often these are inserted to maintain networks and organisational communication. However, they have considerable potential to be 'matter-of-fact', mundane and to lack innovation. Thus they can be boring and unproductive for all involved.
5. The 'A-Teamers' include those situations that may not be unique like a 'Close Encounter', as we've dealt with something similar before. However, they stand out because they are somehow more serious, urgent or difficult (for instance because of a lack of resources). These may call on resources we don't currently have, or require a new and different approach.
6. 'Perfect Storm' encounters are unexpected events; possibly because we were doing the enquiring/investigating part of our role, or maybe they were not on our radar. They may pull together a series of common occurrences which, taken in isolation are relatively simple to address, but when happening together, they turn it into one complex situation. They require your prolonged involvement and more than one subsequent encounter. They fall outside the 'Brief Encounter' category.

You will shortly look at a framework onto which you can apply different circumstances and desired outcomes and through which you can manage encounters. Firstly you need to understand the differences between the categories of encounter labelled above.

Exercise:

In the table that follows please apply a numerical score to each of the listed characteristics of each encounter. All scoring is out of a maximum of 10. Generally, 1 is the lowest or shortest or of low severity/seriousness; 10 is the highest or longest or of high severity/ seriousness.

For Location: 1 is the most public: 10 would be the most private

For Environment: 1 is the most relaxed, 10 would be the most formal

For Future Meetings: 1 is least likely, 10 most likely

In the final column total these figures to provide an overall rating for the encounter type.

Situation Type / Characteristics	Brief Encounters	Close Encounters	Go Between	Groundhog Day	A Teamer	Perfect Storm
Duration						
No. Of Participants						
Risk to Business						
Risk to Participants						
Length of Warning						
Length of Preparation						
Relationship Required						
Complexity						
Importance						
Urgency						
Style						
Location						
Environment						
Frequency of instances for you						
Likelihood of Future Related Meetings						
Total Rating						

In this second exercise you get the chance to articulate or suggest some evidence as to why you scored a particular meeting type as you did. I want you to consider your attitude to encounters as if you recall, or attitude affects your behaviour.

Exercise:

Now complete the table again: insert into the available space one or two words, or a short phrase that comes to mind when considering the characteristic described, e.g. for 'Style' under a Brief Encounter you might put 'relaxed' or for a 'Go Between' environment, you might think this would be 'workplace only'.

Generally speaking, the higher you have scored a particular type of encounter, the more complex and important it is likely to be to you. This can give you an indication of the amount of planning and preparation you should be affording to it. If you found yourself putting quite negative comments about a particular encounter type, it's just possible that when you find yourself in one, you do not apply yourself appropriately and do not therefore maximise the potential benefits. Alternatively, it could be that if you are over-effusive about a particular meeting type you might use it too much, for the wrong purpose/content, or in a complacent manner. Your team could be thinking, *Oh no! Here we go again, another 'informal' chat!* I have a vision of a manager walking down the corridor, colleagues seeing them coming and either turning around, or ducking into the nearest available bolthole.

The framework can give you an indication of the extent to which you need to apply yourself, focus, concentrate and seek to be in control of the encounter. If you scored an encounter type particularly high or low, you should now be considering the amount of effort you should be putting into it; whether it is appropriate; and even whether you should be having fewer, or more of a particular meeting type. For instance, if you find yourself only having the opportunity to discuss important matters with team members in a 'Brief Encounter', you now have the opportunity to question whether that is appropriate. If you think not, then you can begin to plan a way for them to be more 'Ground-hog'.

Situation Type / Characteristics	Brief Encounters	Close Encounters	Go Between	Groundhog Day	A Teamer	Perfect Storm
Duration						
No. Of Participants						
Risk to Business						
Risk to Participants						
Length of Warning						
Length of Preparation						
Relationship Required						
Complexity						
Importance						
Urgency						
Style						
Location						
Environment						
Likelihood of Future Related Meetings						

It may help you in your preparations for each type of encounter to think about them in three distinct phases. As with all my other frameworks, they should not be adhered to rigidly and are intended to take account of varying duration and complexity or encounters. These can be separated simply as 'Ready', 'Set', 'Go'.

The 'Ready' stage is the one in which you might get notice of the impending encounter and in which you would plan your action. The length of notice can vary considerably and so therefore, might the time available to complete planning-related tasks. Acknowledging that practicalities and time are factors that affect whether, or not, and the extent to which they are all completed, 'Ready' can include identifying:

- Participants
- Time (to start and duration)
- Location
- Objectives – what does each party expect to get out of the encounter?
- Content
- Evidence
- Methodology
- Style – e.g. is it appropriate to be confronting, to act as a catalyst for action or to provide the opportunity for a cathartic release?

In the 'Set' stage you would be gathering, collating and analysing the information and resources you need to deal with it. It requires the arranging of the components gathered at the 'Ready' stage (logistics). It is the planning phase of the encounter

In the 'Go' stage you will get on and deal with the encounter. This is the point at which you enact your plan. It may seem that it's taken an age to get here. If you feel that, then it may well be that you have indeed spent too long in the preparation for the situation. However, it may also be the case that you are concentrating on the process, and just like the learner driver, you are moving from conscious incompetence through to conscious competence. In other words you are building up your knowledge, skills and abilities. The intention is that you will over time be able apply a framework within which you will be able to consider more options, more quickly; discount non-starters more easily and come up with an optimum plan. Remember this is equivalent to the Execution phase of the **ADDRESS Model** and you then need to step back, maintain control and ensure the implementation goes as you intend.

In a 'Brief Encounter' ready, set, go – or execution – could all happen in a matter of minutes, with the first two stages being very short. That doesn't mean to say they should be unnecessarily or inappropriately curtailed. In other situations, any part of the process can be extended according to its complexity, urgency or importance. So in an 'A-Teamer' or a 'Perfect Storm', you should consider spending more time in the Ready phase; maybe finding out others' agenda(s) and goals beforehand, working out a couple of potential alternatives, or gathering more supportive evidence for your viewpoint. You may see some similarities with **CRAFT-T** planning and **TOP-DRAWER**. I hope you do. This is an alternative, simpler model should you find either of those too laborious or detailed for your purposes.

What I want you to do now is consider what affects individuals during participation in encounters and consequently the extent to which you, your organisation and your team benefit from those situations.

The Attitude, Behaviour Cycle

This is a simple, model with four stages. It is of particular use when your decisions and plans are met with challenge or resistance. It highlights what to many is obvious, i.e. that my attitude affects my behaviour, which affects your attitude and therefore your behaviour.

For instance, my boss gives me an important task. I decide (because I want to impress) that this job must be done very quickly and urgently. I adopt an attitude that does not encourage questioning or excuses. So will be very prescriptive. This will translate into me being very directive, issuing orders and cutting off discussions. Whilst this may instil a sense of urgency into my team as required, it also risks engendering in them an attitude that they are being treated like 'slaves'. In turn this might lead to malicious compliance. Whilst the job might indeed be completed quickly, who can say what the quality will be like, or what incremental damage has been done to the manager-team working relationship?

Understand that it is your reaction and attitude to situations that starts this chain. Therefore, it is your responsibility to set the scene correctly. Recognise that general attitudes take a long time to change or develop, whereas behaviours are much more immediately actioned. Only an individual can alter or truly change their attitude and subsequent behaviour. Invariably this is as a reaction to some form of stimulus or evidence.

If you view this illustration as a cycle, understand that in any given situation it can go around more than once. For instance, you as the manager might go into a performance-related meeting with one of your team completely open-minded and prepared to listen to what they have to say. You are armed with a number of potential solutions that are right for the circumstances. However, the team member might for whatever reason, be closed to your feedback (maybe because they are not being too 'adult 'about it. They may initially, therefore, display an unreceptive non-caring attitude, resulting in defensive postures and responses. If you're not careful their attitude and behaviour will then impact upon you, adversely impacting upon your attitude. So you become (maybe) frustrated or annoyed and seek then to impose a solution. You begin to say to yourself 'you (team member) are going to do as I say whether you like it or not'. And you move from being open-minded and supportive to being critical and prescriptive. This may indeed secure the compliance you require, but could also lead to them being even more entrenched. This is an example of how a situation might then escalate.

Escalation

Escalation is another concept that relates to your attitude when you feel you are not being believed, understood, or listened to. Alternatively you believe that what you are offering is not being acted upon. Like the attitude and behaviour cycle it is reactionary and involves an element of choice. Choice is influenced by the circumstances of the situation, the environment in which we are working, and the personalities we are working with. We progress through various levels of escalation depending upon whether or not we feel we are being heard. This often includes an appreciation as to whether you are being respected by the other parties involved. There are numerous models of escalation to be found in teaching around conflict, some with nine stages, others with five etc. I use four stages with the rider that 'mediation' or action to prevent escalation can of itself be a stage in any process. In which case it would fall between each of the four I identify.

If things are going okay in an encounter, if there is mutual respect and we are getting what we want from it, it is highly unlikely that we will move into the first stage of escalation, that of 'Frustration'. It is easy to recognise the non-verbal, agitated signs that one displays, and the types of phrases used when people are frustrated. Be aware that in addition to repetition and raised voices some might react by withdrawing from the process if they believe they are not being listened to or acted upon. These signs are ignored at our peril and to the detriment of the situation. To do so inevitably leads to the next stage.

If we believe that in spite of our efforts we are still not being listened to, or even worse we are being ignored, the potential is there for the situation to escalate to the point of 'Anger'. At this point an individual might use an even higher pitched or louder voice, more demonstrable gestures and other non-verbal communication. Even if verbally silent their reddening face, biting of the lip, or gripping of the arms of their chair speak loudly as to their feelings.

Fortunately the next stage is the highest that most of us will ever encounter when dealing with manager-team relationships, though it is certainly not unheard of for things not managed properly to go still further. Similarly, those managers who get called upon to deal with difficult customers might also find themselves going beyond this stage. If the 'angry' person is not managed appropriately and continues in the belief that they are not getting satisfaction, then there is the risk that they will move into 'Aggression'.

By the time we get to here, words are becoming fewer and shorter and are being delivered still more forcefully and loudly. Gestures become more exaggerated, pronounced, and aggressive. Taking us back to caveman days, this is an individual or group sending out warning signs for the other side to back off or suffer some damage. It's a sort of final warning. This is the 'squaring up ', invasion of personal space, shutting off, and 'red mist' phase. As with all the others, if not properly dealt with, there is only one more place to go.

The final stage of escalation is that of 'Violence'. Note that this will not necessarily, nor exclusively require there to be any form of physical contact. It is thankfully rare to get to this stage in workplace situations. Things must have deteriorated considerably for that to happen. For that reason and that reason alone I do not propose to expand on it any further.

Remember that individuals' attitude can be affected by culture, by what they have been taught, by the environments they are in, and by the strength of their beliefs.

Remember too that you could come into a situation where one or more of the parties are already at a particular level in the escalation process and it would be your role and responsibility to try to bring them back down to a manageable level. The higher somebody goes in escalation the more emotional less rational they are likely to be.

Emotional You vs. Rational You

"When dealing with people, remember you are not dealing with creatures of logic, but creatures of emotion."

Dale Carnegie[41]

When being rational, individuals are said to be agreeable to reason, sensible, exercising sound judgement and good sense, calm, sane, and lucid. It is rare to hear of circumstances in which a series of events 'caused' someone to be rational. It seems that we go into situations with a degree of rationality that is then affected by circumstances (recall attitude & behaviour). These cause either a positive or negative fluctuation to our rational norm. We hear how "John was very calm throughout even though Alan was provoking him", while Peter "looked really angry and he began to shout". Both are reactions, but we do not know how John, Alan or Peter started off in those situations.

When we are being emotional, we are said to be in an 'affective' state, during which we are experiencing something that causes us to feel such things as: fear, hate, joy, and love. The feeling(s) may be accompanied by some physiological changes: the racing pulse, heavy breathing, crying, and the shakes.

The more rational we are the less emotional and consequently, the less physiological give-aways there are. People who are exceptionally happy are just as unreceptive to reason – just as unhearing – as those who might be exceptionally upset. Humans are very reactive beasts; reacting to what we see, hear and especially feel in or about a particular situation.

As developed, experienced beings we rely heavily on the tone of communications. It can become difficult therefore, if for psychological, physical or educational reasons we lack the capacity to interpret the tone. We like to see some emotion – some passion – for what is being done. After all if they can't be bothered why should we be?

---

41 (Carnegie 2007)

As the manager, it is your responsibility to control the situation and by implication the emotions of those involved.

If we are 'high' on emotions, whether extremes of joy or sorrow it is very easy to shut off from reality and raise barriers that prevent communication. Our outgoing communications can seem over the top – indeed irrational – whilst our receipt of incoming communication is marred because our receptors are busy elsewhere.

Think of a time when you've been happy, fit to burst. Maybe a few drops of alcohol were involved. You were jumping up and down, on the tables even, and oblivious to the dangers or pleas to calm down. Then there are the opposite occasions when we have been so sad that we haven't really heard the words of comfort or condolence expressed by our friends. In order to manage a situation and so far as is possible ensure that the message gets through, how do we properly deal with emotions?

First things first, an attempt has to be made to bring excessively emotional individuals back onto rational ground. You might be the person to do this, or if there is a personality clash of some kind, you might not. In which case removing yourself from the situation in a controlled manner might be best for effective resolution of the situation and therefore, for all concerned. I recognise of course that this might not always be possible if there is no one else around.

If you *are* the right person for the situation and without wanting to sound clichéd, techniques like (mentally) counting to ten, consciously making efforts to control breathing, or concentrating a little more on listing your options (in your head) may help you to control your emotions.

Emotional effects are reactionary and they can take time to 'kick in'. This is often the case when we temporarily block things out, and don't actually deal with them. It's highly possible when we do this for the reaction to take place after (you think) the situation has been finalised. In other words be prepared for emotions – good or bad – to be on the rise even when you've walked away from the incident. If that does happen, and because the immediacy has gone, you can consider options like taking a walk, jotting down some notes, talking it over with someone, finding a diversion by dealing with something else less important, but which will help you take your mind off things. That's your emotions sorted, but during the event, you also have to consider managing the other party's emotions too.

This can involve a combination of words and placating hand gestures that seek to get the others to calm down. Telling or ordering someone to calm down, rarely has that effect. Telling someone you can see they are angry or upset can invite them to argue that they are neither. So phrases such as, "I can see this is having an effect on you," inform the other that you are registering their emotional signals. Asking them to explain 'how' and 'why' extends this empathy and they begin to register that not only are you registering an emotion, you are prepared and able to address it. Coming at a situation from another angle – whilst maybe a little more time-consuming and difficult – might be more effective. Once you have minimised their emotion, you are then able to deal with the original purpose of the encounter.

Alternatively, you might not be the right person to deal with the situation. Recognising that fact and going on to make alternative arrangements evidences a considerable amount of maturity and control of a situation – even if it doesn't seem so at the time. Many – especially managers or those who are expected to control a situation – are reluctant to lose face by surrendering or being seen to let someone get 'one over' on them. So they remain, they persist, they insist; they start to get frustrated and annoyed and the situation just escalates. If you recognise this to be the case, then the advice is to remove yourself from the situation temporarily or permanently.

You can call a halt to the encounter and you can call someone else in to take over from you. Either way, and even though you think the other side might not be listening to you, it is good practice to tell them what you are doing and why you are doing it. This technique should never be implemented just because you can't be bothered to deal with the situation. However, we have to recognise that: personality clashes do exist; that individuals can for whatever reason, be so entrenched in a particular view or opinion; or we lack the requisite skill, or will to continue with a situation; that it is best to take oneself out of it. You do this as a way of achieving a resolution to the situation that is acceptable to all, or failing that, minimises the potential collateral damage.

Three levels of behaviour

The attitude we adopt is very much influenced by how we might be feeling at a particular time and our behaviour is impacted accordingly. This next concept combines both by examining the level at which we approach and react to situations. This section is based on Transactional Analysis (TA, a theory developed by Dr Eric Berne in the 1950s[42]. It can help us to manage situations by enabling us to recognise the level and consequent attitude and behaviour of the others involved in an encounter. This can go a long way to improving the effectiveness of communication and therefore, the outputs and outcomes of each encounter.

If you are sufficiently aware of your own attitudes and behaviours and how they impact on others, you can manage and control encounters by either adapting or reacting with an appropriate response. TA is not a small subject. Indeed it is possible to gain high-level qualifications in it. It features in degree courses across the world. True to my earlier undertakings though, I do not want to get you too deeply immersed in quite high-level psychology and theory.

You can benefit from thinking about and understanding how you and those with whom you interact at work enter into and react during encounters. So I have done my best to outline the key elements in so far as they relate to the task in hand. If your interest is heightened you can check out 'Transactional Analysis' on the Internet. Here I use TA as a tool that can be applied during specific encounters. I will endeavour to simplify the concept so far as is possible without detracting from its principles of key learning points.

As a foundation, consider the things that parents do. Sometimes they criticise and rebuke; sometimes they take time to comfort and explain, to guide or control. Then there are the things that real life children get up to: they can react to a rebuke with tears or a tantrum, they can be disarmingly honest with how they're feeling and piercingly direct with the questions they ask, and they can go off on their own and revel in getting covered in jam or mud. Finally, I want you to recall an occasion when you've watched two individuals engaged in what you perceive to be an 'adult' conversation and how they are behaving towards each other, what they're saying, and how they're saying it. As well as being physically adult, they are acting in a calm rational manner and dealing with things as they are.

Berne turned these into specific categories – what he termed 'ego states': Parent, Adult, and Child. He further subdivided each state into positive or negative sides. For our purposes I think it is more relevant to identify these as 'levels'. Each level influences an attitude, behaviour and subsequent approach that one can take during a particular 'transaction' or encounter.

42   (Berne n.d.)

I will be referring to these levels and there are exercises you can complete based on them. Firstly by way of illustration let's take the simple example of a child who does something naughty – it doesn't matter what it was.

Some parents might adopt an approach that is critical. The pitch and volume of their voice might go up, there might be some accompanying facial expressions such as a frown, and even something wagging all aimed at getting the message across. They might not consider explaining why something was naughty so long as the message 'don't do it again' is received and understood. Being on the receiving end of this message, and especially the manner in which it is being delivered, the child could well be stunned into silence or even want to shut out badness by crying. It is only by monitoring whether or not the same naughtiness is ever repeated in the future that the parent would know whether or not the message had actually been received and understood.

Some other parents might choose to maintain an outwardly calm, balanced tone. They take time to explain not only that the action was naughty, but also why it was naughty. It is arguable that the response of the child is far less likely to be one of stunned silence or weeping and the parent is likely to have much more confidence, albeit subconsciously, that the message has actually been received.

Now that's a very simple example, but let's bring it into the working environment and think about an occasion that you have been party to, or have witnessed where someone has not fully complied with the instructions of the manager and things have subsequently gone wrong.

What was the approach or level that the manager in charge applied when bringing the error to the attention of those involved? Was it that of the critical, finger-wagging parent? If so, did those on the receiving end react by shutting down, 'letting it all go over their head' or maybe developing it into a blame-based shouting match? How could that manager be confident that the same behaviour would not be repeated in future by accident or even malice?

Alternatively, did the manager take the people involved to one side, maintain a calm approach, explain what the original intention was, why actual performance was not what was required and discuss how not only the current situation would be remedied, but how such situations could be avoided in the future?

This is about how we relate to and the manner in which we communicate with others. In this context it can be used to understand your own and others' attitude; modify behaviours where necessary and thereby, work towards getting the best reaction or result from an encounter. The theory recognises that people – you – can change both your attitude and behaviour in the long and short terms. For example, if you recognise that someone with whom you are dealing with is behaving like an errant child – sulky, emotional, in a tantrum – you can use your skills to bring them out of that state and into one more rational and easy to deal with. Let's take a few moments to establish an understanding of the three levels, how they are divided into positive or negative and potential outcomes of these differing approaches. Remember these are states or attitudes that individuals adopt according to circumstance.

Being a Parent

At this level we think, behave or feel like a parent regardless of whether you actually have offspring. Often we do this in a way that we have learned – consciously or not – from the example of our own parents, and grandparents, or those who have influenced us at home. The old adage 'Like father, like son' reflects this. Behaviours could have been picked up from influences at school or previous places of work.

Parents can be authoritative, controlling, critical, disappointed, judgemental, loving, nurturing, or patronising at various times, or in confusing combination. They can display positive or negative sides of these same two coins: Berne identifies these as 'Nurturing' and 'Controlling'.[43] Whilst the former conjures up positive thoughts and the latter negative, this is not always the case. It very much depends on the situation.

In the workplace, a 'nurturing' parent-type manager might be thought of as very supportive of their team, promoting good behaviour and practices by explanation and consultation, and encouraging their team's development. They take time to explain situations and the reason for them and encourage. This may – I stress, may – secure a mature reaction from that team. However, if this was taken to the point that this manager is overly protective – shielding their team from the realities of a situation – this could have a negative effect when realities hit home.

On the other hand, the perception of a controlling parent-type might be that they are always standing behind the backs of team members to make sure things are done right, cracking the whip so to speak; constantly

43   (Berne n.d.)

critical of their team. This would be seen as negative and is likely to be met with a typically negative childlike reaction. However, exercising control can be done very subtly and positively. Indeed control is a key First-Line manager function. A controlling parent-type acting in a positive way could be providing much-needed structure and objectives to a team that needs building, is new, or who has an urgent deadline to meet.

Being an Adult

Adults are adults no matter what. They are the ones who appear calm, don't get over emotional and can work around, influence and even control others' emotional level and thus their behaviours. Adults tend to deal with present situations and personalities without being influenced by stereotypes or maybe the past behaviours and attitudes of the other parties involved. They are comfortable with dealing in tricky, maybe intimate, situations. The adult will not rush into ill timed, poorly based decisions or responses. They have the skill and will make the time, to gather information – even if that information might be unpalatable. They will do this in preference to making assumptions about either the persons or the situation. Having said that, the 'adult' will not use past negative influences.

They will use past experience and knowledge and previously acquired skills in a positive way by integrating what has worked well in previous similar situations to the current one. The skilful, wise adult will learn from experience and will build a library of knowledge, or a bank of tried and tested solutions that they can bring to bear when meeting new situations.

Being a Child

The child displays feelings, attitudes and behaviours that we resort to or that are replayed from our childhood. When called in to the boss's office, some people automatically acquire 'butterflies' or their stomach starts to churn. Maybe they have a 'guilty conscience' generally, or they could realise they've been found out. Either way, their mind goes back to school and the occasion when they were called in to see the head teacher for repeatedly failing to submit homework. It is important to remember that not everything at the child level is always negative. Children can be kind, thoughtful, disarmingly honest and fun. If we are fortunate enough to have had a warm and loving, supportive childhood; situations, tastes, smells, and what we hear, can bring back great feelings and memories that can provide comfort and support in times of difficulty.

When we watch real parents and children interacting, it is possible to identify physical postures, positions and gestures that are used to reinforce the verbal content. Watch parents as they lean forward to get their point across. Watch the jabbing and finger-wagging gestures. On the other hand, watch children pull back or withdraw. I reiterate that these are only indicators and it is how you assess and interpret the information.

It takes time for a child to be able to interpret the meaning of words; how one word can mean several different things depending on the context in which it is used and how it is said. They then have to learn that the volume or intensity of content has different meanings. Furthermore, they have to learn and understand the types of non-verbal communication or visual communication: what these are normally and the confusions and contradictions that can exist. Maybe not surprisingly then, someone acting or reverting to child level will choose to hear only the verbal content and disregard the rest.

I talked earlier about knowing your **STUFF**. When seeking to know and understand your staff, an ability to recognise the level that the other parties to an encounter are displaying at a particular time can inform your initial and subsequent approach to them. You might observe them in their dealings with others in similar environments and note how they react then. In addition you might also be sufficiently self-aware to be able to recognise the level that the other party engenders in you. For instance, does the fact that this person always behaves like a spoilt child around you cause you to behave like a critical parent every time you have dealings with them?

Consider whether or not you have the time or the inclination to find out enough detail about a person's history or upbringing that would enable you to understand why they behave or react in a particular ego state. If you have: It may assist in managing the level of your encounters. If you have not: you need to be prepared for, and more understanding of the unexpected.

Encounters as transactions

So those are the levels. What about the 'Transaction' part? Any meeting or encounter may involve: some form of give and take, an exchange of information, maybe the provision of a service or product in exchange for a reward. If that is the case then you have a transaction. Just like making a purchase, there will be elements to this kind of transaction along the lines of:

- What each party wants
- Why they want it
- When they want it by
- In what form they want it
- Who's going to provide it
- By when
- How much it's going to cost

How many times have you received something you didn't want, in the form you didn't want it, at a time you didn't want it, or for a price that was different to the one agreed? So clarity and complete understanding by all involved, of each other's expectations and requirements is very important. If you don't have it, it opens up opportunities for more problems later in the process.

Whilst working towards positive outcomes and wanting everyone to be clear on what is wanted, there has to be an element of what we *don't* want too. But in that order! Always start with the positive. It's a bit like your insurance policy – the small print that outlines when they would pay out (the positives) and when they won't (the negatives).

- Have both sides been **specific** about what is expected? Does the look on your colleague's face suggest bewilderment or obstinacy? Have *you* understood what your boss has asked you to do?
- Can any expectation or agreement be **measured**?
- Is what you're asking of your team **achievable** given their current levels of knowledge, understanding, skills, abilities or behaviours? Do they have the time and the inclination?
- Is it **relevant**? Do they see the point? Is it taking them off something, which is actually or perceived to be more important or pressing?
- Is there a specific **time frame** applied? When do you expect completion of the whole or its various components?

Transaction Approaches that work – and those that don't!

By understanding approaches and which are effective, we have a foundation upon which we can build a personal approach to common situations the First-Line manager encounters.

Positive approaches have the greatest chance of producing effective communication with the converse being true. Remembering that our attitude and approach affects others' attitudes and subsequent behaviours. Positive adult approaches will invite or foster a similarly positive response – adult. If we start off being negative, we are at risk of a negative parental or child-like response.

Positive modes mean effective communication, i.e. the whole message is communicated and the intended response is elicited. We can tell this because we get the information we were after, or what we wanted doing gets done. In addition we haven't wrecked an existing relationship, nor jeopardised the start of one. A communication is likely to achieve the intended response or result. Information is received, necessary action(s) follow and good relationships are maintained or developed. We can also say that this was a 'win-win' encounter or at least all sides leave it believing that to be the case. The opposite is true of negative approaches.

How does this affect encounters?

The first thing to do is to recognise the level at which you are operating and how this will affect your attitude and subsequent behaviour. You can do this in advance, thus helping to predict the level, attitude and behaviour of others involved. Alternatively, if you are sufficiently skilled and in control of the situation, you might recognise the attitude and behaviours of the others as the situation unfolds. This will help you to modify or change an approach when you realise the one you adopted at the outset is not proving as effective as you thought it would be. So it is helpful to be able to assess or diagnose which level (ourselves included) is in. In this way you can respond appropriately. So what are we looking for?

Remember, this is about traits that an individual displays. Each approach or ego is comprised of readily identifiable communication characteristics: verbal – words, tone, tempo of speech – and non-verbal expressions, postures, and gestures. In addition, the 'Parent' typically uses value judgments, adults use words that are clear, concise and definable, and which are delivered in an emotionally balanced tone. Just like the real thing, those of more advanced years who are acting in 'Child' mode use words that are direct and spontaneous, or can withdraw silently – going for the comfort blanket. The child is very often reactionary.

When thinking about how levels are chosen and adopted in any given situation, I usually end up making the comparison with magnetism. This is because in magnetism like poles repel, whereas unlike poles attract. Put another way, if this law is followed, the ego adopted by the person initiating the encounter is likely to attract one or more particular egos by way of reaction. Many of these reactions will not lead to the most conducive of situations, nor will they lead to the best possible outcome. However, as usual there is an exception to every rule (unlike magnetism): in this concept we are striving to achieve being an adult, with the desire or intention that this will attract an adult response- anti-magnetism if you will.

Putting It All Together

As I intimated in the previous chapter about communication, it is all too easy to over analyse what we do and how we do it to the point where we lose the 'human' touch. That's the last thing I want to do. However, you may have evidence that leads you to want to improve your skills and manage your encounters more effectively. You want to leave them secure in the knowledge that you have achieved all, or the greater part of your objectives. So you first need to be conscious of some of the theory behind the methodology. Then by practice and – importantly – self-assessment and learning by experience, you should be able to move from conscious competence to unconscious competence. What many call 'expert'!

In the preceding sections you will have seen that there are three states, each of which can be further subdivided. Overlapping that are different levels of emotion and different stages of escalation. Therefore, within encounters there are so many permutations that they prevent us examining each and every one. So we are going to look at just four. The intention is that once you have had the opportunity to practise, you will be able to apply the concepts to the other permutations in your own time.

The scene is an encounter between a manager and a member of their team. You will be asked to identify how it would probably play out if the parties conducted themselves in a particular ego state. Consider the levels of emotion and rationality and the Attitude and Behaviour Cycle, along with the descriptions of transactional analysis previously discussed.

Case Study: The Job's not over 'til the paperwork is done!

Giles manages a team of sales reps who are each allocated a geographical area. They are tasked with maintaining a relationship with existing customers, dealing with their orders, keeping them informed of new products and offers and also generating new custom. It is a target-driven, performance-related bonus environment. The recent economic climate has proven difficult, but most reps have managed to come close to target. One or two have even exceeded. Leon is one of them. Unfortunately, Leon believes that, because he generates so much business, he can forgo some of the niceties such as completing order sheets accurately and on time so that invoices can be issued. As a result, periodic figures submitted to the company international headquarters are often inaccurate.

This situation was tolerated by Leon's previous manager and, up to now, by Giles. Even some of the senior managers accepted it because the year-end figures were always balanced. However, other members of the team (new and old) are now questioning the importance of submitting paperwork that is both accurate and on time.

Giles has determined that this situation must now be resolved and has arranged a meeting with Leon at the regional office.

Case Study 8: The Job's not over 'til the paperwork's done!

Exercise:

There follows four representations, each with a different approach to the transaction between Giles & Leon.

Consider where you feel either party would be in terms of their emotions.

Then provide a very brief description as to what Giles's attitude might be in this situation and how this might be portrayed in their behaviour

Complete a similar pen picture to reflect what Leon's attitude might now be and how this would be translated into behaviours.

Finally, In terms of Transactional Analysis, how would you address the situation at the heart of this encounter? Identify what you feel would be the short and medium term outcome.

Parent to Parent version

In the first variation, let's say that in the scenario Giles is in 'critical parent' mode and Leon reacts as an equally critical parent.

What happens when you put the same poles of two magnets together? They repel, right? If both parents display the same traits it is highly likely to result in a stand off.

Of course, not every parent is the same: they can be grouped according to the attitudes and approaches they apply to raising their children. Very few parents will adopt the same approach 100% of the time, though they might have a predominant style. This could be critical – maybe always focussing on the negative – or it might be nurturing and always seeking the positive. It is possible to be excessive in either direction: being critical when some nurturing was needed, or resort to nurturing when the facts warranted a more direct approach.

Giles elected to approach the situation as a critical parent. So his attitude would be one akin to wanting to blame and in some way exercise control over Leon. He would likely be thinking "I'm the boss here and I'm telling you...' It is likely that his behaviour would therefore be rather prescriptive with Giles not really interested in or willing to listen to Leon's reasons (or excuses) for non-compliance.

Leon has been in post for some time and no doubt considers himself above the requirements. If he acts at a similar level (parent) he is unlikely to be supportive of Giles achieving his own objectives. He may well respond with a 'How dare you!' or two, or 'You shouldn't be doing this'. He may also be critical of the organisation and its processes, perhaps because he sees them as restrictive. It is unlikely that Giles and Leon are going to see eye-to-eye on this matter if Giles persists with the current attitude and Leon reacts in the same way.

'Nurturing parent' Giles might decide to take the time to explain why the process and Leon's compliance with it are important. He might choose to focus on and praise Leon's high sales figures, perhaps to the detriment of securing Leon's compliance. Giles could also emphasise that he is raising the matter in order to protect Leon from potential performance-related processes. However, if Leon were to continue in critical 'parent' mode (which is always a possibility), he is still likely to blame Giles for raising the matter when he didn't really need to. So it is still likely that they will not reach agreement and his views will remain unchanged.

At best Giles is going to get malicious or reluctant compliance from Leon. Even then it may well be that the compliance will be short-lived and only last until Leon believes the dust has settled.

Parent to Child

How do you think the same situation would develop if Giles adopted critical parent and Leon responded as an adaptive child?

Giles adopts the same ego as before, the same attitude and the same behaviours. However, Leon is now reacting as a child might. The situation could go one of two ways: either Leon could be emotional, responding with a to-the-point explanation of his views on the process and just what he thought about it. Alternatively (as suggested in the study) he could play at conforming whilst not really understanding (or wanting to), or agreeing with the need to do so.

The 'adaptive child' is very feelings-driven. So Leon will be unconsciously remembering occasions when someone who acted as a Parent to him chastised him. It was maybe one of his real parents, or someone like his teacher. He will register now the feelings he had then. If he was chastised a lot when he was a real child it is quite possible that he will have developed a particular attitude and reaction. Consequently it is *that* attitude that is likely to bubble to the surface now, along with previously learned behaviours.

As an adaptive child, Leon will be sensitive to his environment and how he perceives he is being treated. In other situations this could well be okay if the feelings and reactions being displayed are acceptable. For example, if Giles had to tell Leon that he had not been successful in achieving a promotion it would be acceptable for him to be disappointed – even upset – but it would not be acceptable for him to throw a tantrum and go off sick for a week.

There is a suggestion that Leon had been treated by his previous manager as something of a child, as his reward for being a 'good boy' and achieving high sales figures was that he didn't have to worry too much about the reporting side of things. Being an adaptive child, Leon quickly got used to this way of working. Adaptive children will also very often look for what is behind what is actually being said. So as well as reacting adversely to what he perceives as a significant change to his working environment, he could also be seeking out Giles's ulterior motive for raising the issue. For instance, is Leon aware of the disquiet amongst his colleagues? If so, will he go on the defensive and counter with an accusation against Giles that he is taking sides, or only raising the issue because of what the other reps have said?

I cannot prescribe exactly how Leon would react, as it's equally possible that if his trained behaviour is to withdraw in the face of challenge (flight), it could well be that his head would go down, there would be a full and frank confession, or his sales figures would drop to a level where he could manage the accompanying paperwork. The number of permutations of displayed behaviour doesn't really matter. The key is to recognise that what is being displayed is the behaviour of an adaptive child.

If Giles does not pick up on Leon's adaptive child (negative) reaction and so continues as a critical parent, it is likely that Leon will resist changing his behaviour and working practices. In the immediacy of the current conversation and possibly for quite a while after it Leon is quite likely to be quite high on the emotion scale, though this might not be outwardly demonstrated or in evidence. He could be seething on the inside, but carry on with what amounts to malicious compliance displaying no outward emotion. In this instance Leon could well be frustrated about the fact that Giles is not taking account of his good performance in other areas. Were Giles to continue to not acknowledge this, there is a chance that Leon would move into 'angry' territory.

Frustrated that Leon is apparently not listening to him or not doing as he is told, Giles's critical parent is likely himself to become ever more frustrated – even angry – and whilst stopping short of putting Leon across his knee and giving him a good spanking, unless he's careful Giles would become even more critical. A possible manifestation of this would be to threaten or even implement sanctions or punishment against Leon were he to fail to comply again.

So Leon's underperformance is unlikely to be resolved as a result of this particular encounter. At best Giles is going to secure short term, malicious compliance. At worst Leon will continue as he always has. After all, his previous manager was fine with that. In any event it is probable that Giles would recognise the need to raise the issue again further down the line. However, because of this experience Giles might even stray away from a further meeting, thinking it pointless and/or go straight into a disciplinary process. Either way it would be quite possible for both parties to remain or become even more deeply entrenched in their original levels.

Maybe now that you're thinking about it, you are beginning to recognise the sort of behaviours in some of your colleagues. Recognise too, the cyclical nature of the process wherein one individual's attitude affects their behaviour, which affects the attitude and subsequent behaviour of the other, and so on?

Adult to Child

Now let's look at the original scenario with Giles deciding to be an adult, but Leon reacting in the mode of a free child

Giles has decided to approach this situation as an Adult because he recognises the situation that existed between Leon and his previous manager. His intention is to try and secure a matching response. This is in no way guaranteed. Remember that each individual makes a choice as to how they react. Leon can choose to react to an Adult approach as a parent – critical or otherwise, as an adult themselves, or as in this case as a child. We shall continue by assuming that Leon reacted as a free child.

Giles will be opening this encounter based upon his recognition and understanding of the facts as they are. He has no need to bring emotion into it and so has every intention of maintaining a well-balanced, rational approach. He is likely to have considered a range of reasons or causes for Leon's lack of compliance. He will have considered a range of solutions that he would discuss with Leon with a view to Leon identifying the most appropriate resolution himself. Giles will not play the 'blame' game as all he is concerned with is pointing out that Leon is not complying with a requirement and that the matter needs to be redressed. Giles would be very rational. Even if he were to be frustrated (something an adult wouldn't really be), he wouldn't show it. In the normal scheme of things this would be much more likely to secure a longer-term solution.

[By way of caution, don't let the dispassionate, rational adult 'you', get so extreme that you end up as some kind of robot.]

That was how Giles went into the encounter. However, Leon chose to react as a 'free child' or 'natural child'. Here is a child that naturally doesn't understand what all the fuss is about, or how they are supposed to feel about the situation. However, the free child will react spontaneously to the 'here and now'. So it is quite possible that Leon's reaction would be unpredictable. Leon might well approach his job as a game. The achievement of more sales is a challenge. The paperwork is something that restricts his opportunities to play. Thus when he is challenged on this, he could well try to make light of it. After all that seems to be the relationship he had with his previous manager. For this reason he is likely to be higher up the emotional scale and could well display elements of frustration if he feels that his opportunities for fun and enjoyment are about to be curtailed.

Giles is approaching this as an adult. So he will deal with the 'here and now'. He is likely to have a solution that can accommodate Leon's inherent desire for fun, to go with the flow, but through explanation and rationalisation can suggest a solution that minimises any injuries to Leon's ego. Similarly if Leon is in what is a reactive state, it is quite possible that he will be open to influence, especially if any agreed solution still permits him to act as a free spirit and get on with the job in a manner that allows him an enjoyment factor.

The adult to free natural child reaction is probably one of the better ones, providing it can be well managed.

Adult to Adult

Finally let's look at how things would develop and how effective the encounter would be if both Giles and Leon adopted the attitude and behaviours of adults.

However, here we have the 'to-be-expected' exception to the rule of like poles repelling. Unlike the potentially very negative 'parent to parent' scenario, it is arguable that if you are to secure a positive outcome to the encounter, you should be entering into it in an adult frame of mind (attitude) and display adult behaviours. Of course nothing in life is guaranteed (except death and taxation). So I cannot promise, and neither should you assume that if you do this, you will always secure an adult response. But of all the starting points you can adopt, being an adult is likely to have the most success. Even if your knowledge of the situation and the previous history of the other person(s) suggests otherwise, you should be working for an adult-adult encounter.

What happens when an adult deals with an adult? Well, both are dealing with 'the here and now' and are not letting past interactions, future ambition, or any form of hidden agenda to affect process and therefore, the encounter. This is by far the most effective form of encounter, but how do we bring someone out of 'parent' or 'child' level? Do we need to? How do you encourage, foster and maintain an adult level in both yourself and those you encounter?

Telling anyone directly that they are behaving like your dad or your five-year-old is unlikely to get a very positive response unless of course they are shamed into correcting their behaviour. But even then they might resent having this highlighted. They could also be the kind of reflective individual who would appreciate you bringing this to their attention and for whom it might be a positive piece of feedback. Ironically if we do it consciously and conspicuously does that not turn us the Adult into a parent or teacher? Remember, an adult deals with the here and now and what they are faced with. Dealing with the emotion might help. One could also argue that it is for the parent or child to recognise the level they are operating at and the inappropriateness of their behaviour and snap out of it.

If both parties were acting at the adult state during the encounter what do you consider would be the nature and outcomes from it?

First off, both parties' emotional thermometers would be registering low towards the rational mark. This has a positive effect on communication because one – if not more of the principal blocks to messages being received and understood are removed. The person initiating the encounter – Giles – will be doing so with a positive outlook; wanting to secure the best possible outcomes; in a collaborative fashion; and with a sound appreciation of the other party's knowledge, understanding, skills, abilities and feelings. Giles would be pointing out the facts: Leon is an excellent salesman – fact: completion of the necessary paperwork is part of his job. Fact: Leon is not completing his paperwork. Fact: this is having a detrimental effect on the business and the team. Fact: Giles may well want to explore the reasoning for this with Leon and in doing so might shift into 'nurturing parent' for a short time, but in establishing why, he is dealing with the factual reasons for the poor performance.

It is probable that if Giles is using **REASON** to control the encounter; he would discuss the implications of Leon's continued non-compliance during the account phase – taking care not to slip into a controlling Parent level for instance this could be an outlining that if he does not comply he is at risk of being disciplined. Giles would sum up all these facts – including Leon's reasons and provide a factual description of what they had agreed in the outcome phase. Giles would be encouraging Leon to a genuine understanding that his contribution will be appreciated and recognised. As a result Leon's attitude is much more likely to be accepting, contributory and complimentary.

This can influence Leon's behaviour to be positive, open, supportive and receptive. He is more likely to recognise and appreciate the style of approach. Of course he still has a choice, but it is actually quite difficult for someone being treated as an adult to react in any other way. They have to be pretty determined to do so. Leon's adult reaction may be evidenced by: him acknowledging that he had had it fairly easy under the previous manager; that his performance was affecting the business and the rest of the team; and providing genuine reasons for the failure. He would go on to give a firm commitment to an action plan to rectify the situation.

All of this heightens the prospect of a positive 'win-win' outcome to the situation. Ah, I hear you say, 'win-win'. I used the phrase earlier without developing it. Conventional wisdom asserts that a successful negotiation encounter is one in which all the parties leave with the idea that they have 'won' something – or at the very least not lost anything. The key word there is 'negotiation', yet some have tried to extend this to all encounter-types with mixed success. In some circumstances the jump is easy: any encounter where you are passing on good news for instance. The difficulty comes when you have to share bad news or enforce something that is to their detriment. About the only 'win' someone who has just been told they have not secured their requested day off can walk away with, is the notion that the message was delivered politely and empathetically and the knowledge that refusal was for good reason.

For the win-win concept to work in other situations, you have to start looking at them more as negotiations than as what they might first appear. Take Giles and Leon's performance-management meeting: after outlining and explaining the current performance, the expected performance and the gap; there might well be some negotiation between the two as to how that gap was going to be bridged. Putting aside for one moment the actual outputs of the meeting, Giles would consider it a 'win' to have left Leon in no uncertain terms of what was required and to have secured (albeit malicious) compliance. He might prefer to have had a good rational discussion with Leon that ended with him outlining his own solution and agreeing to implement it. A win for Leon 'the child' might be walking away having agreed to do something to Giles's face full square in the knowledge that he didn't really mean and it and that he was going to carry on as normal. Adult Leon however, would walk away with a 'win' if he had put forward both a rational explanation and a solution that was workable and that these were acceptable to Giles. This would be the case even though Leon was going to have to amend his ways and do more work.

The most important thing to remember is that we always choose which state we operate in. It is a choice of attitude and consequently of behaviour. By implication therefore, we can choose to move between states several times during encounters (and often do unconsciously anyway). The only way you can hope to have any control over of someone else's attitude and consequent behaviour is to have control of your own.

Some Interaction 'dos' and 'don'ts'

It is appropriate to summarise the key points to be taken forward from this chapter.

- If you treat someone as a child they will more like as not act like one, if you are happy to treat your team as children and they are happy with that too, so be it. However, be aware that this is likely to make your job considerably more arduous than it needs to be. Strive to be an adult yourself and to treat others as adults.
- Your attitude affects others'. It should not be you who initiates an escalation in others' levels of frustration etc. Work at not allowing others' reaction and behaviour to initiate an escalation in you.

- If you have the facts and there is no real reason for withholding them, use them! Be honest with people. What possible legitimate reason might there be for telling a lie? Your honesty and trust will engender the same by return and will also encourage others to behave as adults.
- If you link the idea of encounter-management to that of communication, remember you have more control over what goes on than you might have originally thought. The nature of your position means that it is likely that others will be inclined initially to pay more attention to the messages of that lie behind what you're saying. It is important that you work at not sending out mixed messages. Endeavour to control your messages so that there is no ambiguity as to content. Your verbal and non-verbal communications should match.
- Be consistent and treat individuals as such.
- Encourage discussion and a mature, respectful conversation (when time permits), listen to views, answer them without being dismissive, and act on them as appropriate.
- Never forget to pay heed to the feedback element of communication so that you can assess whether or not the intended message(s) were received and correctly understood. If you are monitoring yourself and the situation accurately, you will be able to identify through the verbal and non-verbal signals you're picking up on, whether your current attitude and behaviours are appropriate for the circumstances and situation. Whichever method you choose, if your attitude and behaviours are not working it is your responsibility to take action. For instance, if you recognise that playing the critical parent is not working because responses come from a group of adaptive sulky children, it would be your responsibility to change tack and move towards a more adult approach.
- Don't patronise
- Don't appear to be taking sides and if you do find yourself in a situation akin to you being a parent separating a pair of squabbling children (in the workplace), work towards doing so at an adult level, rather than at the level of a critical parent

The following activities are for you to try over the next couple of weeks. You don't have to delay moving onto the next chapter until you have done so.

End of Chapter Activity 1:

Select an encounter that you are party to, preferably one that you are not leading on. A good one to choose is a regular team meeting, where the content is important, but not vital or critical and so you can allow yourself to focus on this task.

As the meeting progresses, observe the other participants and identify:

Who is being a parent, who is a child and who is an adult? What is your evidence for that?

Who is being more emotional than might be expected – why do you think that is?

Whose attitude is noticeably affecting their behaviour and how is that manifesting itself, is it in reaction to someone else in the meeting or an agenda item?

Best to keep it to mental note taking, but as soon as possible after the meeting complete the exercise.

End of Chapter Activity 2:

At another similar meeting to that above, complete the same exercise for you.

What state or ego were you portraying, was it different at various stages?

How did your attitude affect your contribution and did it provoke a reaction in others?

Were you rational throughout or did you find yourself reacting to others' behaviour and/or becoming emotional?
To what extent do you feel you evidenced good practice in relation to attitude and behaviour etc., or there is need for some development and what will you do next time?

You can complete this activity as many times as you want to gauge your development

25. Manage your team's performance

Once you know your team and have honed your communication skills, you can use this knowledge and skill to manage their performance– provided of course you understand what that means. Getting it right is one of the most important things you can do. Others will rely on your decisions, evidence and reports when deciding who gets promoted, who gets a bonus – or not, who gets to join a project – or not, who gets a pay rise and how much of one, and, in extreme cases, who keeps their job – or not.

You will probably be tasked with assessing what members of your team do – producing goods or services, and how they do it. At a minimum it is ensuring that they apply the necessary skills, abilities, attitudes and behaviours to achieve the organisation's missions and appreciation of its values. This will necessarily include making sure they know and understand the expectations placed upon them – through their job description (JD) and individual objectives (set formally or otherwise). Then you must deal with any performance that is at variance to those expectations.

Invariably, there will be standards that are applied to everyone and individual targets or objectives. Your task is to ensure these are achieved. So you need to understand the process of determining objectives: what areas of performance are measured, how that is achieved, setting standards, and the gathering of evidence or performance data.

Much of the policy and system will be out of your hands. So I want to focus on how you assess – where you get your evidence from and crucially how you do a good job. I want also to focus on biases that can adversely affect your assessments. These are the activities you need to undertake at an operational and practical level. What you need to be aware of is:

- What is measured
- How it is measured
- The standards required and expected
- Setting and agreeing objectives
- Identifying where performance data is going to come from
- Gathering, recording and analysing data
- Dealing with team and individual performance
- Biases of assessment

Determining what Performance is measured

This means the aspects of individuals´ skills and abilities and their attitudes and behaviours necessary for them to complete effectively what they are paid for. They are often referred to as competencies. In other words WHAT do the members of your team need to do to fulfil the organisation's requirements?

Knowledge and understanding are required, though these are often recruited in, or trained in, and have to be maintained regardless of changes in the organisations day to day operations. They usually form a relatively small proportion of all that is measured on an ongoing basis.

Larger organisations' usually have large numbers of people doing the same or similar roles. So they set common competency requirements, standard levels of expectation for everyone in a particular role and often state what is acceptable, or not. You may manage a team who all do the same job. To some extent this makes life easy as you are working to just one set of criteria (but see biases below). However, larger organisations and very often, smaller ones, will employ individuals to perform specialist roles that are relatively few in number. So you might find yourself assessing against several different sets of competencies. There is very often a set of core competencies that everyone is assessed accompanied by others tailored specifically to an individual's role.

You have little or no say as to the competencies. They are largely set when the job is created. You will have slightly more of a say in setting individual objectives relating to them, but more of that later.

Determining how Performance is measured

This is set by the organisation and is heavily influenced by its outputs, attitude and objectives. Knowing the science or reasoning behind why the organisation uses a particular approach will not necessarily help you to implement it. Rather, you need to understand how it works and what your responsibilities are. You may be measuring in one of the following ways:

- Scoring or rating each member of your team, and then 'rank' him or her first to last.
- Placing each member of the team into one of a set number of categories e.g. very poor, poor, average, good, excellent – or something similar. In some organisations they stipulate that you can only have a set percentage of staff in each category, forcing you to choose.
- A similar system breaks it down further. You might be given a list of competencies, each of which you must rate on a scale of 1–5, or poor to excellent.
- You may be given two choices around a particular skill, trait or behaviour – one positive, the other negative (often labelled X and Y) e.g. around timekeeping X = rarely arrives on time and ready for work; Y = is always punctual. Whilst some organisations only let you answer X or Y, this causes difficulties for the assessor. What if the employee is only late a couple of times? That's why they put in elements of 'tendency towards...' or 'neither'.

Those organisations that performance-manage their staff, tend nowadays to use more behaviourally-based and target – or objective-driven approaches:

- Individuals are set objectives (based on competencies or existing standards) and the extent to which they achieve them is measured and assessed. This is very commonly called management by objectives.
- Organisations define expected behaviours and then provide the assessor with a series of statements that define examples that they consider evidence of excellent, good or poor performance. There are usually five, but there can be more/less, each of which is assigned a score. So somebody could be set the objective of either achieving a particular level standard, or improving from one level to another.

These are a few of the many systems that can be applied. In some cases there may be a combination of two/more of these methods.

I don't want to discuss the efficacy, benefits or drawbacks of any of these methods. The fact is that whichever one exists in your organisation, you are unlikely at this stage to ever be able to change it. You will have to work with it in a way that you feel comfortable with and that also meets the need of that organisation. You are responsible to the organisation to do the job they put you there to do.

Setting Performance Standards

At this stage organisations decide the expectations on its employees. What must they do in order to achieve? You become more involved at this stage as it should be your job to assist employees in identifying and then achieving their own personal objectives. Standards need to be communicated. They are often contained in a JD. However, standards can change over time. Objectives almost certainly will. So in many organisations there is a discussion between the manager and the team member at the start of the year. If not, there should be! At this meeting both parties should be very clear about what is being assessed, what is expected, and how it will be managed.

Setting and Agreeing Objectives

Objectives should be based on the preceding sections. They are separate because individuals may be at different levels, below standard, or achieving the required standard and need for some reason to move to the next level. Standards tend to be more constant, whereas objectives can vary according to the individual and can change over time.

At the risk of sounding overly smart; this is a time when you can use my **CRAFT-T** model, or the more likely to be known 'SMART' process to check that the objectives stand a good chance of being achieved. It's pretty pointless setting them otherwise.

Sources of Performance data

Where do you get your information? You may follow a particular sports team; be a fan of a particular genre of movie; or a keen observer of politics. Think about how you measure their performance – the basis for your discussions in the bar etc. Gathering information on the performance of your work team and the individuals within it is much the same. It's just that in many cases your organisation will determine what data is legitimately used to evidence performance. There are a number of valid sources of data:

Observation

What you and others see or hear. If you were at the match, you saw it for yourself. If not there, couldn't see it on TV or listen on the radio, you may rely on the testimony of one of your friends who did. Let's call these internal sources as they come from our own circle. Likewise in the workplace you may observe (and record) performance, or talk to other managers/colleagues to get their views on individuals' work. Coming from within our organisation they are internal sources.

What if neither you, nor anyone you know heard or saw the game or the film? Then you may rely on post-event critics and/or reports from external sources such as newspapers to decide. Did the team perform well? Is the film worth going to see? The extent to which you base your decisions on these reports depends largely on the level of trust you have in the people making them. In the workplace you might be able to get information from other areas of the business, suppliers or customers.

It is very often the case that an individual player will be interviewed after the match. An actor may be interviewed after the making of a film (and before its launch to plug it). A politician may be able to comment on a particular policy. All of these are forms of self-appraisal. Depending on your organisation and its performance management policy, your subordinates (and you) may be required to complete self-assessments.

Consider here the biases that an individual may have. It depends on the individual's attitude and ability to self-assess well and also the culture of the organisation. Individuals can often have over – or underinflated ideas about their performance, especially if a future promotion or pay rise is determined by that appraisal. So as the manager you need to be able to either confirm or refute the contents of any self-appraisal with your own evidence.

Observation data therefore may come from managers, peers (co-workers), subordinates either within your team/organisation, or from the outside. It may also come from suppliers or customers – again, both inside and outside your team/organisation.

Performance data

Observation is good for specific occasions, but what about individuals' ongoing performance against expectation and the competition? For this you have the league tables, the stats and the information recorded elsewhere and for organisational purposes, that can also be used to highlight individuals' performance – provided they can be proved to have contributed. Care is needed here. In a sports team, for instance, the team may be in the top four of the league, but did player 'A' play in any of the matches that put them there? If they did, for how long, did they score/save points?

You should be able to find data on both team and individual performance in the workplace that is collected for organisational purposes anyway such as sales figures, number of calls taken/abandoned, number of complaints etc.

Take care when dealing with team and general data. You need to be able to link it to the performance of the individual(s) in front of you. What was their contribution?

Performance tests

The fact that in some fields of work, those practising have to qualify and possibly re-qualify regularly allows the manager to (legitimately) use their results to evidence their existing performance and possibly point towards a need for some development. Consider the implications to the organisation if one of their employees needs to be qualified to use a vital piece of machinery and they fail their annual test for instance.

Some organisations arrange refresher training for staff. This may not be vital, but if the organisation thinks it important – then it should be tested at the end. If it's not it should be! Do we really want people working for us who can't be bothered to do the job as required?

In many professions or occupations those practising them are required by law or regulation (of professional bodies) to maintain a level of performance and to prove it by taking tests or examinations at regular intervals: annually, tri-annually, or some other interval. As well as demonstrating their continued competence, these also evidence performance in areas/competencies such as knowledge, motivation, attitude etc.

IT

Modern IT can furnish a raft of performance data. In call centres – calls can be recorded and reviewed by the manager and operator afterwards. In sales environments numbers of sales can be easily produced. IT can allow us to gather data from customers more easily, quickly and cheaply. In many instances it allows data to be collected remotely and without the manager 'standing over the person with a clipboard'. So you are much more likely to get a 'natural' set of data, identifying genuine trends.

Gathering, recording and analysing performance data

It will often be your function to gather and analyse the data and thereafter, determine whether it evidences meeting the requirements or not. Consider biases that might come into play (see below).

Where should it be recorded? Your organisation may well provide both the annual appraisal forms AND the means to record evidence throughout the assessment period. If it does not provide the latter, you should keep a log or diary on each team member. This might be on paper or on your work computer. Either way, be mindful of legal and other restrictions that apply, such as data protection legislation. That shouldn't be a worry if the data is factual, honest and evidenced.

How do you analyse the data you have gathered. Failing to do so properly does a disservice to the process and the individuals under review. You will rarely be told how you analyse the data, so you have some leeway. You may record the evidence under the relevant headings as you go along. This can make it easier at review times to pick out the best evidence. In this method, you might have to record the same evidence under several headings as one incident rarely evidences just one area of competence. Alternatively, you may just note the incident/evidence as it happens. Then at review time you work though it and note which competencies the evidence applies to.

Be objective and look for the best evidence and be prepared to discount some items if you get the feeling you need to 'shoe-horn' them into a category. The absence of evidence can be evidence of performance in itself.

Identify trends that evidence the areas of performance being examined. An instance may evidence performance, but it should never be taken in isolation, i.e. it should be the best example of a trend (good or bad).

Be prepared to ignore a one off incident of particularly good or poor performance unless it is exceptionally significant – in which case it should really be dealt with at the time it occurred.

You should be looking to put together mutually supportive evidence from across sources. Do sales figures confirm or belie an individual's work on communication skills for instance?

Dealing with team and individual performance – using the data

Employees will underachieve, achieve, or exceed against their objectives. Some performance needs to be recognised and addressed on an ongoing basis. Otherwise it will be addressed at review time. The options available to you fall into two broad categories: the development route or the discipline route. Unless it is a drastic piece of evidence or incident, you would normally be looking to deal with any trends. There are some variances between dealing with team performance and that of individuals within it. Let's look at those now.

Firstly: Keep them separate. As per my comments earlier a team might perform well on paper – achieving all its objectives. But does that mean every team member contributed at the same level, to the same extent, with the same enthusiasm etc.? Did they all 'pull their weight'?

Secondly, when providing feedback and/or addressing performance of the team the organisation may only be concerned with headline figures. So the fact that the team as a whole performed as required is enough. The problem is then that the whole team gets the praise and reward regardless of individual contribution. The opposite is usually true when things don't go well. Thus even if the team performs well/poorly, as the manager you need to be prepared to recognise individual performance within it. Remember too that your performance is often assessed on the basis of the performance of your team.

Thirdly, when managing teams, you are likely to be more general in your comments, more focussed (if not careful) on competencies related to the formation, maintenance and motivation of the whole team; and more engaged in group feedback, e.g. at regular team meetings.

Whether team or individual, you must use the gathered data as the basis for your feedback (see earlier), for your assessment of competence, and for subsequent courses of action. At one extreme it can be the basis for a promotion. At the other it can mean an individual is fired. So be mindful of the qualities of good data and also biases that might affect your use of it.

Biases affecting good performance assessment

The ideal manager only ever assesses on an objective basis, according to the facts. However, we are not always ideal and judgement can be clouded by numerous factors. Having identified these as possibilities, you should do your utmost to avoid them. They are called biases and they can affect not just the giving of feedback, but everything that leads up to it, such as the manner in which you gather and analyse your performance data. They are as follows (in no particular order):

- **It's my bad day:** This is allowing the fact that you are having or have had a bad day so far. If so perhaps it would be best to postpone gathering or analysing data as there is potential for you to only see the negative. Consider refraining from a feedback session, as the last thing you might be able to deal with properly is your opinion/feedback being challenged.
- **I can't decide:** 'Sitting on the fence' or 'central tendency' is where you cannot decide whether the data reflects something good or bad. If there are a number of potential ratings, you cannot choose the right one. In both cases you opt for the most neutral indicator. This is often done in the hope that this is the option least likely to get an adverse reaction. Whilst this may apply to an underperformer, someone thinking they deserve better is likely to react accordingly. Very often this is applied by managers who feel it necessary to be non-controversial to maintain (what they see as) a workable relationship with the individual(s) concerned.
- **I'm always negative/positive:** This happens when no matter how good something is, you mark it down, or the opposite may apply. Either way, whilst you might think this would be motivational in some way it is again likely to be counter productive. Think long-term! Always over-grading could lead to people being promoted inappropriately (on the basis of your assessments); they might get an undeserved pay rise; or could be selected for a key role that they are unsuited for. Under grading could result in them losing something they really deserve. These are sometimes called strictness/leniency errors.

- **I always/never like what you do:** This is where you allow the fact that the assessed individual always does good/bad work to influence your judgement of the work under review – no matter how good or bad it is on this occasion. Be aware that someone who always does a good job can have an off day – just like you. The reverse can also be true of course. [You have probably heard of the halo & horns effects.]

- **I'd have done the same:** Here you assess that you would have done something with the same approach and in the same manner as the assessed individual, regardless of whether that was what was required. This error often creeps if the assessor trained the team, or is over familiar with the tasks or people involved. It can also go beyond what people do, to what or who they are. For instance, shared interests, shared love of a particular team, shared attitudes etc. [Sometimes called 'similar to me'.]

- **My short-term memory says:** There maybe something done recently that was a 'standout incident' and which, because you have no recall of anything else, nor any records to contradict it, you use as evidence of their overall performance. This often happens when the manager suddenly realises it's review time and they have to say something. It can lead to inaccurate data used to create inaccurate assessment, leading to poor decisions being made. [This can be called the recency error.]

- **I remember that:** Some instances stick in your memory because it was particularly good or bad. It is similar to, but not necessarily the same as the recency error. That one thing can obscure other evidence evidencing it was a one-off and not truly representative of the individual's general performance for the rest of the review period. [Others may call this the primacy error.]

- **I think others do it better/worse:** This particularly applies in situations where individuals should be assessed against pre-determined criteria or competencies, but instead are assessed against their colleagues. In other words they can look good or bad depending on how much better or worse they perform compared to their colleagues in the same or a similar role. If the individual performs according to the criteria, as they should, they should be assessed as such. It matters not how their colleagues are performing. For example in a sales environment the requirement may be to sell 100 units per month. Jones sells 100 items Smith sells 102. They have both achieved the requirement. It doesn't matter that Smith sold more. [This can be called the error of contrast.]

In Practice

Regardless of the system you will be enforcing. No matter what standards and objectives are set, how they are measured and used, you have to decide:

1. How rigidly you will apply the criteria (bearing in mind the biases and pressures)
2. How you apply those criteria
3. How comprehensively you apply the standards
4. The level of professionalism you apply to gathering, recording, analysing and using evidence of your team members' performance

Have a system of your own that helps/supports implementation of organisational needs, i.e. allocate time in your diary for evidence gathering, one-to-ones etc. Have a system for recording evidence and use it regularly. Remember you are looking for trends. Patterns of behaviour may take weeks or even months to become evident. So either get a brilliant memory or make comprehensive, accurate records.

26. Friend or friendly

To paraphrase the American football coach Vince Lombardi:

> *"The manager can never close the gap between himself [sic] and the group. If he does, he is no longer what he must be. He must walk a tightrope between the consent he must win and the control he must exert."*

It is important to clarify the distinction between being a 'friend' and being 'friendly'. Whether you agree with my definitions, want to add or amend them, or even generate your own, you should understand them and make a decision as to which you will be. There are benefits and pitfalls to each approach, and the way they affect your performance as a First-Line manager.

In addition, we should look at how you negotiate the (sometimes tricky) transition from being 'one of the guys' to being their manager?

Deciding to be friend or friendly is a decision that should be made with some knowledge of how your effectiveness in the manager role can be affected. All too often, managers fall or drift into one camp or the other, which can cause difficulties when a relationship is tested. This chapter therefore, is very much discussion-based and suggestive as to the potential benefits and drawbacks of either approach. When considering the case study later, focus on how your approach would work in that situation. First though, I want to provide a little background.

Dale Carnegie wrote a book called *How to Win Friends and Influence People*. The title phrase is often used sarcastically when someone does something that affects us and which we don't agree with. Based on personal experience, I actually hold back from putting effort into making 'friends' in the workplace. I accept my definition of 'friend' may differ from yours. So long as I don't make enemies by design or accident, I feel my work time is just that. The 'making' of friends at work, often in alien environments with those whom the only thing you have in common is work, suggests to me an element of compulsion. Question: Do I have to be your friend to manage you and/or do my job?

This can in part be traced back to my past wrangle with the question, 'Do I live to work, or do I work to live?' For me it's very much the latter. My circle of friends existed long before I worked anywhere and I believe will be there long after I move on. I do not feel compelled to make more friends, but of course I appreciate that others might. If a work-based friendship does break out, that's great, but I don't actually pursue it. At the risk of sounding contrary, I must point out that I always try to be friendly with those with whom I work and always remain open to the fact that what I call a true friendship could develop.

They say 'You can choose your friends', though it's even nicer when they choose you. It's great when someone else considers you have the characteristics, traits and personality that they value and that they want to align with. Whatever your definition of what being a friend (noun) entails, it is different to being 'friendly' (verb).

Being friendly involves politeness, an assumption that there is no malice in the relationship, regard for the other and allowances being made for not really knowing the other party. Being friendly is transient and is only required for the duration of the relationship or encounter. It can be faked. There is no limit on the time it takes to become friends, but being friendly in social circles and at work is demanded almost immediately. It is assumed that you will be friendly to those with whom you are thrown together.

The choice is yours. Make it on the basis of some informed thinking based on you, your environment and the other personalities involved. Can your work and social environments and circumstances sustain one or more friendships or vice versa? To what extent does your life revolve around work? To what extent do you rely on work to meet and make new friends and for it to be the basis of your social life? Think about how difficult it can be to tell a friend they've upset you. Do you really want to be thinking about that every day at work?

The acid-test is, "Would a third person (at whatever level in your organisation, or outside it) look at a relationship that exists at work and say that the level of 'friendship' was appropriate?" i.e. are you being too friendly with some or not friendly enough with others, or have you got it about right?

In some organisations familiarity is a taboo; there's a strict and formal hierarchy and boundaries are reinforced; being friends (or more) is actively discouraged. In others the reverse is true. What would be the evidence or criteria against which this would be assessed? How would you know? If in the course of your interaction with colleagues you sense that:

a) Others feel uncomfortable that you're getting too close, or
b) The team can never seem to be serious about anything and/or they act in a way they think is fun, but feels like disrespect to you in the presence of your bosses or other managers, or
c) You cannot raise a negative point, or give negative feedback to someone, because either side believes it would damage a friendship, or
d) The team feels they can break the rules with impunity, or
e) It's always difficult to get the team to do something a little bit extra
f) You're never invited to social functions or your birthday goes uncelebrated when everyone else's is.

These are examples and not to be taken as definitive signs. But if you sense the relationship is not appropriate you should be considering what to do about it. If you are not the sort who naturally makes friends or displays friendliness easily – nothing wrong there – trying to make friends or being overly compensating can be just as bad. We are not looking for permanent smiles glued to your face 24/7, nor a reluctant smile that looks more like a grimace. I'm not banning friends altogether! It's perfectly OK to be friendly when it's appropriate and to make friends. When it's workplace based there are other considerations: such as your responsibility to fulfil your duties as a manager.

If a relationship gets tested in a work situation, one could argue that if those involved are true friends, they will firstly understand the relationship between your role and theirs and secondly; they'll respect you and that you have a job to do. They won't seek to take advantage of the relationship and/ or seek favours; and they will work with you to resolve any conflict between you. Now there's an idea: get everyone you work with to be a true friend! The likelihood of that is…?

What happens if you have a fall-out with a friend outside of work and the next time you see that friend is back in work and you're having a one-to-one feedback session?

When considering whether it's right for you to be friends with colleagues or subordinates, a lot will depend on what your role or position expects or explicitly demands of you. For instance, is it a role with a formal control function horizontally, downwards or even upwards? An example of this would be someone like an internal auditor, compliance manager or internal fraud prevention manager.

You also need to assess or discover whether the relevant colleagues view the friendship in the same way as you. That's not to say you should be paranoid every time someone is nice to you, nor that you should go out of your way to be nasty to prevent a friendship building.

Think about the effect on you, your friend and the status of the friendship if you are required by circumstance to do your job and doing so would be to the detriment of your friend. Similarly, if your business relationships with those who report to you exist on the basis of favours you do for them, or allowances you make, what happens when you cannot let something pass? If you allow a friendship to influence the manner in which you deal with a situation or its outcome, what does that say about your responsibility to your employer? They pay you! You need that money to pay the bills. Let's take a look at a particular situation:

Case Study: Dealing with Discipline

Baxter's is one of a number of privately owned restaurants. It is situated in the town centre. Angela has managed the venue on behalf of the owners since it opened four years ago and has acquired a reputation for 'bringing on' members of staff. Several of her protégés have gone on to be promoted into other sites in the company. John joined the business a year later and whilst not officially Angela's assistant, he had been brought across from another site to provide her with some support.

Angela has been on vacation for a week. Before going she agreed with John that he would deputise for her. This would ensure that essential tasks would continue uninterrupted. It was also beneficial for John's continued personal development. He had already made it clear that he wanted to get on in the sector. Angela had a meeting with John before she left in which she brought him up-to-date and also made it clear what was expected of him, the responsibilities and what authority he had.

On her return there was a hand-over meeting in the morning. This was all very 'routine' and John seemed happy. He had had no problems he said. John took the rest of the day off and was not now due back for two days. He said he was going out of town. That evening Angela hosted a social drink for the staff once the restaurant had closed so they could hear about her holiday.

In conversation a team member let slip some of the things John had been doing whilst in charge. A colleague confirmed this. Angela was surprised to hear what had been going on. Responsibility for taking money to the bank was passed to a junior colleague – strictly against policy and rules and, if true, qualified as gross misconduct. John had regularly 'overslept' and on one occasion had opened up and then returned to bed suffering a hangover. John spent a lot of trading hours in the office when he should have been in the operating area. John had also been spending time on social networks.

Case Study 9: Dealing with Discipline

Exercise:

Consider the following questions:

1. What would you be thinking if you found yourself in Angela's position?
2. How do you think you would deal with the situation – if at all?
3. How do you think you would be feeling?
4. There and then at the social event?
5. About the situation with John?
6. Who do you think you would be talking to initially?
7. When do you think you would be doing something about this?
8. How might your feelings affect how you deal with John?

What actually happened? Angela was very disappointed – more at the breach of trust than anything else. She felt shock at first receiving the news. This turned to anger as she quickly established that the information was true. On the night she found herself uncomfortable with remaining at a social event. John had never been a proper 'friend', which for her made the situation a little easier to manage. She recognised and readily acknowledged that her duty and responsibility lay more towards herself and the organisation AND the rest of the team.

Angela made discreet enquiries with suppliers. She examined computer and paper records, all of which seemed to confirm what she had been told. There was a problem when some team members who realised the implications, indicated they would be reluctant to give a more formal statement. However, Angela believed that she did have enough information to take action.

Angela arranged to see John to get his initial response. There could have been some misunderstandings. John stated that he had been feeling unwell for some of the time, but Angela was not satisfied with his evasiveness and reasons. She suspended him, advised the owner and then organised a disciplinary meeting in accordance with the company policy and guidance. At that meeting it was found that John's actions had exposed the business to loss. Indeed some of what he'd done amounted to minor fraud. He was therefore dismissed. He did not appeal.

It can be easier to make the initial 'friend' or 'friendly' decision when you are promoted from outside. Though this might not always be true. If promoted in-house, it depends how you manage the situation, the maturity of relationships you developed before promotion, and to a large extent, the attitudes of those once your peers, who you now have the power and authority to supervise.

Ask yourself, what are the real, perceived or potential benefits of relationships? In some quarters this is referred to as stakeholder management. As with other areas considered by some to be 'common sense', a 'science' has developed. Suffice it to say, at the First-Line level of management there is benefit to be gained from having control over your working relationships.

Have you ever taken the opportunity to examine the different groups that you have relationships with at work, considered the basis upon which they are founded, how they are maintained, and those that expose you to the greatest risk or provide you with the greatest benefits?

You probably have relationships at work with some, or all of the following:

- Your team
- Your peers
- Your seniors
- Knowledge experts such as those in IT
- Functional specialists such as those in HR or a legal department
- Internal suppliers – those upon whom you rely to deliver other elements of a work piece
- External suppliers
- Internal/External customers

At some stage you might also have to initiate or develop new relationships with any of these groups.

In assessing the nature, benefits and need or desirability of maintaining those relationships, I suggest a number of criteria:

- What they are founded on
- Who initiated them and for what purpose
- How they are maintained and by whom
- How critical they are to the performance of your roles and the completion of a given task
- Your dependency upon them and theirs upon you
- Whether they are based or maintained by personality and willingness rather than necessity
- Whether they need to be carefully managed or are robust
- Have and how often they are refreshed

You could always put these two lists into a table format and score the corresponding criteria out of (say) 10. This could identify those relationships that you could or should apply greater significance to and therefore devote more time to maintaining. If you are already friendly with someone, it could be that on reflection it is a bit too much, or even not enough and you're now thinking 'cripes how do I sort that one?' If you assess and have some evidence that you're being overly friendly, remember your perception may be different to others. Try:

- Declining the odd social event (do they want 'the boss' round all the time especially when everyone always starts talking about work

- Maintaining the current level, but do nothing more to maintain it. This might have the effect of cooling off what's there already.
- Starting to deal with incidents slightly more robustly and as the manager *you* are
- Take actions and provide explanations that demonstrate recognition of your role and are not overly or unduly influenced by the relationship.

If you think you need to start being friendlier consider:

- Making an effort to attend some important or significant social events
- Deal with incidents a little less as the 'company man/woman' and evidence greater consideration of the team
- Share an appropriate joke
- Show an interest in what team members do outside of work

Don't do anything suddenly! Sudden character changes and/or behaviour are generally treated with surprise or suspicion. We've all at some stage wondered why X is being nice – they must want something, or thought Y must have gotten out of the wrong side of the bed today. If you're not careful, your efforts to get things to balance and at an appropriate level could be misinterpreted. You need to show consistency and that 'this is the way it's going to be from now on'. Otherwise, the next time you try, they'll think it's just another 'flash-in-the-pan'.

I reiterate that it is very much for you to determine the approach that is best for you, in the environment you work in, and to maintain control of your relationships according to what makes you and those around you comfortable. Consider the words of Friedrich Nietzsche: "The man of knowledge must be able not only to love his enemies but also to hate his friends." [44]

The essence of Nietzsche is that as a First-Line manager you need to be able to work with those whom you don't necessarily get on with or may even dislike, whilst at the same time you must be able to deal with your friends when they transgress. You might also have to deal with the disappointment that accompanies the latter.

---

[44] (Nietzsche 2005)

End of Chapter Activity:

Get hold of a large sheet of paper, pen and some different coloured highlighters.

Make a list of those with whom you interact at work. You can categorise them if you wish using headings such as bosses, peers, subordinates, my team, clients, suppliers, customers etc.

Highlight those you consider are 'friends'. In a different colour, highlight those with whom you are friendly. Leave blank any of those with whom you interact, whom you consider to be neither and only interact with when you have to and on a 'business' footing.

Leave your list to one side for a while.

Return to it and mark the names of those with whom you wish to be friends, another with whom you would like to be friendlier, and a different identifying those who you would prefer to put a bit more of professional distance between you.

Finally pick one or two for whom you may want to change the relationship and create a **CRAFT-T** plan for doing so.

27. How's your trust meter?

What – I hear you ask – is a 'Trust meter'? Quite simply it's a gauge you can use to determine the levels of trust that exist between you and those with whom you work. It's used to measure existing trust levels and the effects of any action you take. Here, we consider also the benefits of building and maintaining appropriate levels of trust.

Using the trust meter idea you can:

- Identify the levels of trust that exist between you, your manager, your team and your peers
- Identify and explain the implications of having those particular levels of trust
- Identify whether and in which areas you might develop better levels of trust

In Section 1 of the book you were asked to note your views around the question of trust and I want to expand on those now. For instance, is trust something you acquire or earn? Is it something you consciously work on, or a bi-product of the way in which you go about your everyday role and responsibilities?

Measuring trust

Ernest Hemmingway asserted that the best way to find out if you can trust somebody is to trust them. It is impossible to do everything yourself so at some stage you will find yourself allocating tasks to others. If your style is that which doesn't involve you standing behind and watching them do it, you will be leaving them to it. That means you will have to trust them (to varying degrees).

Definitions of trust don't vary too widely. It's a firm reliance on the integrity, ability, or character of others – or oneself, or the condition and resulting obligation of having confidence placed in one. Key words seem to be reliance, depend and obligation.

It is not uncommon for there to be an assumption that in the absence of any evidence not to do so, we should trust. So we enter new situations at a pitch or level that gives others the benefit of the doubt. After all, how many of us have started a new job and walked in on 'day one' consciously wondering whether or not we'll be able to trust our colleagues?

Exercise:

Think for a moment about how you trust – what does it take for **you** to trust someone or something?

What kind of person do you trust at all and/or trust most?

How did they earn that trust or was it automatic?

Trust can be something we take for granted. When it's there do we recognise or reward it? Or do we only take some action when it's damaged or destroyed? There are many questions that can be asked: Is trust important to you? Do you need to trust your team? What if you don't or can't? For instance, they might be a very new team; they may lack some of the necessary skills or attitude to take on a new role or project; or you may have had a past experience that has dented your ability to trust now. Another question is whether you need to like someone to trust them. As you begin to trust someone more, does that necessarily mean that you begin to like him or her more?

On the flip side, does your team need to trust you? What if they don't? How is that going to affect your performance in your role? I suppose that comes back down to your style.

There's no way I can answer those questions for you, as the answers are very personal. All I can do is venture some suggestions as to the effects of having high levels or no trust and leave you to make up your mind.

If one side doesn't trust the other, there are a number of potential effects:

- You may not seek or get the whole story. You or they might hold something back out of spite or to maintain some power or control
- You or they don't fully describe or act on true feelings
- You don't give, share or undertake tasks, delegate or get delegated to
- You have to exercise greater supervision, direction and control
- There's a greater likelihood that you will have to performance-manage, though doing so on a regular basis with small issues may be less dramatic than when a previously strong trust relationship is broken
- It's more difficult to communicate effectively as the lack of trust is a psychological barrier. Perhaps they think you're trying to 'screw them over'.

Just as the opposites of actions to build trust can break it, so the negatives of not establishing and maintaining trust can be turned into positives by doing so.

Ironically, if you are consciously, deliberately and openly working on building or re-building trust it evidences that it doesn't exist now, or maybe has never existed. In itself this could send out a negative message. So if you are going to do so some care is required.

Exercise:

Think of activities that build trust and then of activities that break it

If you're like me, you came up with a second list that represented doing the opposite of that contained in the first. In terms of building trust its activity such as:

- Doing what you promised to do or not doing what you promised you wouldn't
- Keeping a confidentiality
- Following the rules as required
- Not playing one side off against another for personal advantage
- Being consistently honest
- Being consistent
- What you're aiming for is a position high to the right on a scale something like the one below.

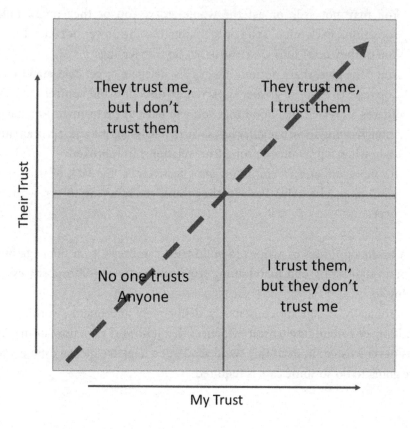

Figure 9: The Trust Meter

Building Trust

What can or should you be doing to build trust? The answer to that very much depends on whether you want to or not. If you do, I liken it to trust being like a snowball you roll up a hill that grows the further you go. But at the top of the hill there's a cliff. We spend time trying to build it as big as we can, but then trying to stop it from crashing off the edge. If you are to build trust you need to be consciously applying the traits that you identified are required in the exercise earlier and avoid their opposites.

Applying models appropriately, consistently, those you've studied previously here, or any you find suitable from elsewhere is a good start. If you demonstrate that you **ADDRESS** situations consistently, search for **TOP-DRAWER** solutions, can plan accurately and **CRAFT-Tly** and effectively, know your **STUFF** and manage encounters, then you will stand a good chance of building trust.

Similarly, when you allocate tasks to others you should monitor their performance. If they do a good job – tell them. If their performance could be improved, don't necessarily 'write them off'. Provide feedback and support them in their development. The investment you make will not only enable you to begin to trust them, it will also increase their trust in you.

My old friend, Chinese philosopher Lao Tzu, reminds us, "He, who does not trust enough, will not be trusted." This reminds us that trust is very much a two-way commodity. What you need to remember is that it is something you initiate. Your actions will promote others' trust in you and your actions (by providing opportunities for them) will allow others to earn your trust. It is a leap of faith to trust someone you've never met or don't know at all well. But how do you know you can trust unless you do? Trust is important, but hardly something you can or should try and build directly. Like confidence, it is one of those intangibles that grow nicely on the back of other positive activities.

Summary

You have been prompted to examine the degree to which you require and enjoy the trust of those with whom you work. Also, what if anything you need or can do about developing it. If you find yourself unable to trust anyone at all or enough, the only solution would be for you to do everything yourself. You will find that the day just isn't long enough; your working relationships will be difficult and, just as an aside, you'll probably drive yourself rapidly towards a mental breakdown.

Just remember the words of Dr Frank Crane, an early twentieth Century columnist, "You may be deceived if you trust too much, but you will live in torment if you do not trust enough."[45]

---

45   (Crane 1935)

End of Chapter Activity:

What are you going to do to build and maintain the levels of trust – where are you now on the 'Trust meter'?

Answer the following questions

1. Does your team get on with the job with minimum fuss and supervision?
2. Does your team have the confidence and feel comfortable with asking appropriate challenging questions?
3. Does your team come to you with sensitive or difficult issues?
4. How would you describe the quality of your communication with your team?
5. If you are not comfortable with your responses or the levels of trust you currently enjoy (in either direction):
6. Is a higher level of trust required?
7. What are you going to do to **ADDRESS** the situation?

28. It's OK to be selfish

How do you/will you look after yourself throughout the process of becoming and continuing to be a manager? What options exist for you to manage your commitments and ensure you don't end up doing others' work for them? In part this is about the amount and nature of work you are ready and willing and able to accept. It is also about how you self monitor and assess, how you step back and take a look at all the demands on you – not just in the workplace, though that is the focus here.

While reading this section, make a list of your responsibilities and the things over which you have control. Think about the limits of what you are prepared to do or not to do. I will explain what I mean by 'selfish' shortly and will illustrate a technique for managing your responsibilities. I will also talk about what you can do to limit the prospect of 'overload'.

Not looking after oneself, not enough self-awareness, insufficient self-monitoring, and not taking action can all be detrimental. This is primarily to you as an individual and as a consequence, to your performance in the role. I have to say the former being the most important. This chapter challenges the notion that being selfish is necessarily a bad thing.

In first-aid training one of the golden rules is that before going into rescue, you must make sure it's safe to do so. It's no good to the victim if you the rescuer end up being incapacitated too. As a manager it's so easy to take on others' problems as your own – often because others want you to, or will let you. They are quite happy to pass you the problem. They may not be aware of it, but this is a form of selfishness on their part. As a First-Line manager the complexity and volume of problems can easily become overwhelming. The result is that you can cease to function properly. Indeed if the problems are 'welfare' matters, it is easy to lose sight of your core responsibilities and functions.

Over the last few decades there has been a considerable and some might say improper overlap of work and home life. We now talk about the need to maintain the correct work-life balance. One argument says you cannot divorce the two, another says you must. On the one hand you're supposed to maintain a 'happy' workforce, by enquiring and taking an interest in their home life. On the other you must refrain from, or take great care in 'using' anything you know to make business decisions, which could then be interpreted as discriminatory. On occasions you are expected to sort out your colleagues' home life before you can get them to do what they are paid to.

Then there's the employee-driven encroachment of home life into work: How much time (especially in open-plan environments) is lost to useless/pointless social chit-chat that does nothing for productivity, but that makes the staff 'feel good'?

If you socialise with colleagues after work or on a day off is it work? No? Well what if you were to do or say something that infringed a company rule, or upset one or more of your colleagues?

Ironically, we seem to reward those who cause us the most problems, and the greatest lack of sleep. We devote to them the greatest proportion of our time and effort. Not only is this unfair to the remainder of our team who get on with their day-to-day tasks with minimum supervision and minimum complaints, it is unfair to us. While we are dealing with their problems, we do not have the time to deal with our own.

Modern managers are constantly urged, prompted, and instructed on what they should do with or for others in the workplace in order for those others to benefit. We are told that we *must* invest time to understand others' motivation, we *must* build the team, and we *must* follow this or that rule. Less frequently asked or answered is the question, what do we do for ourselves? One argument is that, if the manager is in charge, why must *they* do what their workforce say or require? It can seem sometimes that the manager cannot tell or ask someone to do something and for it to be done without unnecessary questioning or selfish resistance?

On the same side of the same coin it can be argued that if a team member or subordinate doesn't like being told or directed to perform in their current role, or they do not like the organisation they work for, it is incumbent upon them to do something about it; not by trying to change the organisation, but by trying to change themselves. If not, move on to a different organisation where their attitude and approach might be better accommodated. In other words, it is their responsibility and choice. Whilst it may be your responsibility to support them and facilitate, that will always be the case.

I think that an argument applied to those seeking promotion is just as applicable to those who report to you. That is, you enter into a working relationship with an organisation or employer, knowing the job description, what is required of you, how you will be rewarded, and what may happen if you underperform. If you do not know any of these things at the outset, it is certainly true that you should get to know them as soon as possible. Is it right or fair for any of us to rail against our employer, or try to change the organisation just because it is asking one to do something one doesn't particularly like doing or want to do at that time?

Home doesn't only encroach into work, the reverse can occur. Sitting on the one-hour commute into the Capital on still-dark winter mornings, I have to admit to being perplexed at those who, almost before they have sat down, have whipped out the notebook/laptop, and/or the hand-held mobile device. Unless they are really bad at time-management – or spend their time in work doing things they shouldn't – why spend their own time writing reports, writing emails, disturbing my stupor with protracted power calls of interest only to them? And... relax!

I'm not saying you should stay away from any and all situations that may present a physical or psychological danger. After all courage is about recognising that these might exist and carrying on to face and overcome them. My version of 'selfish' is about self-preservation in the general sense. It's about having amongst your guiding principles, one to ensure you don't let others cause you unnecessary grief.

By suggesting it's OK to be selfish, I would at first sight, seem to be flying in the face of a good many philanthropists, philosophers and social commentators. Most dictionaries would define being selfish as being concerned chiefly or solely with oneself, to the exclusion of others. I agree that to adopt this trait as *the* one you display all the time would be inappropriate and would probably make you not a very nice person. However, that's not what I'm encouraging you to do!

To rely on others to take on the responsibility of your welfare exclusively, or to ensure everything in your particular garden is rosy, is rather naive and will probably result in you being disappointed as well as disadvantaged. In the same way that you cannot and should not seek to take on the woes and ills of all your team, neither should you expect them or your managers to take on yours. Yes they can help, but ultimately you have a responsibility to yourself to be in control of your own life and what you do with it – even in the workplace!

My version of selfish acts as a safety net. It is about self-management and being self-sufficient. I am suggesting you make time for yourself in the same way you would do so for others. There are two strands to this. Firstly there's the short-term selfish break. This is different from a lunch break or some other break away from work. Those *should* be breaks from work, whereas the selfish break is one you use expressly to deal with work in so far as it relates to you, what you want or need. You may need time to take stock of all the jobs you are currently responsible for, to take stock of changes in circumstance or priorities. Some people put fifteen minutes a day in their diaries; others fifteen minutes a week; some others will just realise that they need a break in order to take stock of what's going on around them

The second strand is more of a psychological break than a physical one. You should ensure that when you **ADDRESS** situations, when you are formulating your **REASON** for a meeting or encounter, your planning and solutions take into consideration 'you'! This is more than the obvious 'what's in it for you'. It includes being aware of the implications any solution will have for your physical and psychological wellbeing. Importantly, factor in a plan to exclude, minimise, or moderate foreseen negatives. Look for a positive opportunity to use the situation to your long-term advantage in achieving personal goals. For instance, it could be an opportunity for you to try out a new piece of equipment, or a new piece of knowledge. It could be an opportunity to build a positive reputation or relationship. It might be an opportunity for you to take on something new and learn.

Whether you like it or not, you do have what are by definition some selfish needs; Abraham Maslow[46] put these into five categories in an ascending order that ranges from the basic needs of air, food and water, through the need to feel safe, the need for love and belonging, a need for esteem or to be respected, to ultimately what he calls 'self-actualisation', which is about wanting to be and ultimately achieving all that you can and are.

Wanting to be the best manager you can be is a personal, selfish need. Achieving that subjective goal – if that's what you really want – may well

46   (A. H. Maslow 1943)

do wonders for your esteem. If it's what you're meant to be, it might also result in you reaching Maslow's pinnacle of self-actualisation. You might need help in achieving that, but if that's what is motivating you, then it's a very personal and selfish goal. You're largely doing it for your benefit, not that of others. I accept that others may benefit from 'you' – the best manager ever – as their boss, but that's not what drives you!

Look at this form of selfishness as a 'positive' and consider how you might use it and how it might manifest itself? Let's look at a case study:

Case Study: I need a break

Dave worked as a first-line manager in one of the emergency services. Not only was he responsible for the day-to-day management (and therefore the wellbeing) of his team, he was responsible for their direction at more serious events and situations. He was a source of information, an arbiter, and a final decision maker. Dave was known not to shy away from difficult operational situations and to lead from the front. He was perceived as someone who knew and understood, or rather had not forgotten what it was like at the 'sharp end' when he got promoted.

It was a disciplined environment and one where the need for camaraderie often excused the odd 'politically incorrect' comment or activity. Institutionally, the organisation had not yet quite got its head around the concept of equality of opportunity and treatment for all, which ran somewhat contrary to its public façade. And that's where the problem lay – or at least in Dave's mind it did.

Dave had a private life. Totally within the law, but not in line with the white, Anglo-Saxon culture that still pervaded the organisation. He was of the view he could not be fully open and honest. Over the sixteen years he'd worked for the organisation, he'd perfected (or so he thought) the deception of leading a double life. By this stage he was not lying, but neither was he telling the whole truth about everyday things such as how he'd spent his weekend, who if anyone he was 'seeing'. This duplicity extended to his home life too as he felt he could not share with his family either.

In that kind of high pressure and stressful working life it's difficult to be in control of one life, let alone two. Gradually and like some sort of creeping weed, Dave began to realise that he wasn't functioning as well as before; he was constantly tired, occasionally slipping up with a cover story, getting irritable with friends and colleagues alike. And, yes, there were the thoughts of escaping.

Case Study 10: I Need a Break

This is not an exercise about 'what would you do if you recognised someone in your team was acting, or you became aware was experiencing something similar to Dave?' The questions I want you to consider here are about you putting yourself in Dave's shoes! They are:

- Was it OK or right for Dave to be selfish in this situation and if so how?
- Are you able to put yourself in Dave's shoes and think what you might have done in his situation?
- How do you think you might deal with finding yourself in a situation maybe not as dramatic as Dave's, but one in which you have competing influences, competing demands and harmful conflict going on in the workplace?

Dave was certainly looking after number one here. Fortunately, the organisations in which anyone would have to go through what he did, are becoming fewer, though we must be aware that a few such bastions still exist. But even if the issue(s) were not so sensitive, nor so complex – just an accumulation of too many issues to be dealt with at the same time – would anyone argue against his right to be selfish – to look after his own well-being?

In actual fact, one of Dave's major concerns was that as a result of the situation he found himself in, he would make some wrong decisions, decisions that could lead to a damaged reputation for his organisation (later recognised to be somewhat misplaced loyalty), harm to himself, or even worse, harm to his colleagues. But he also recognised the situation was doing him no good at all. There was no let-up from the pressure of the day job, and no let up from the psychological environment he had got himself into. Fortunately, he was still in control and he (selfishly) decided that his wellbeing was *the* most important thing. He sought and was given assistance and support without the need to disclose all the reasoning. Basically he took some time out.

This wasn't just a 'get away from it all' moment in the hope that things would get better all by themselves. This was a structured, supported and planned period away from 'normal' work. It allowed Dave a very valuable opportunity: the chance to put things into perspective and crucially, to decide what was best for him in the long term. Those two weeks weren't the 'cure all', but it was certainly the start of the cure.

Selfish or self-sufficient

Being (positively) selfish is not to be confused with being self-sufficient. Many schools of thought suggest that the closer we move to the latter, the better. Whether it's nations being self-sufficient in resources; organisations having control and access to all the resources they need to produce their outputs; or individuals being self-sufficient in terms of being able to live without dependency on others. In the working environment it is very difficult not to be dependent on others in some way. If you're self-employed offering a product or service, you are dependent on customers buying and possibly your suppliers of raw materials. If you are an employing business, you rely on those plus those you employ to produce as required. You need to be in sufficient control of those dependencies and you can only be that if you are in control of yourself and self-sufficient.

Managers rely on their team for support: doing what is required, as required, when required, possibly for friends and friendship, for not providing you with too many problem situations. They rely on their manager or organisation to provide output-related goals, objectives, tasks, rules, guidelines and support to deal with the problem situations generated by your team or tasks. You may rely on peers – to make sure they treat their teams in a manner consistent to how you treat yours. You may be dependent on internal or external suppliers of components or services in order to achieve what's expected of you. Let's not forget the dependency that exists with those outside the workplace who are affected by how you work within it: your friends and family, who may have to cope with your absence, listen to the complaints or frustrations you can't pour out at work, deal with your emotions, your tiredness and so on.

Very few of us are completely selfish – we can't afford to be! However, there are very few of us who achieve total self-sufficiency either. How we manage those dependencies and the relationships they create or require is for another piece. For now consider the areas in which you can be selfish; are prepared and willing to be selfish; and how you'll manage that.

Determine what your parameters or boundaries will be. What sacrifices are you willing to make for the benefit of your organisation (ultimately), your team and other colleagues, and those that your organisation serves. Are you totally ready, willing and able to sacrifice social time, family time, or money? Are you OK with risking that, ultimately, there will be a considerable benefit to you for doing so? What things are 'sacred' to you that you are totally unwilling to give up? Firmly stating your goals now allows you to create for yourself a set of principles and 'permissions' through which you can monitor and measure the benefits over costs.

Exercise:

Commit to paper your response to the above paragraph's questions. This can be broken down into lists, or you could write a paragraph of what you want, need or intend you and your life to look like.

Be realistic. It is one thing to have a goal and aspirations, something else to go off on a 'flight of fancy' when deep down you know you are not willing to sacrifice some things, that you are not likely to ever have the necessary combination of knowledge, understanding, skills, abilities, attitude or behaviour, or do not have the requisite control over your current or future environment.

Will 'selfish' work?

Finally, I want to examine whether your need to be selfish will lead to a conflict of interest with those in your team and your organisation. How does the list of areas you thought of above balance with the needs and expectations of those for whom you work, or who work for you?

Let's not forget those interdependencies. If you work for someone who pays you a wage, it's fair for them to have some expectations, one of them being that you actually look after the interests of the organisation as well as your own. Whether that's a 50-50, 60-40, or 70-30 split is up for discussion. I do not want to let organisations off the hook altogether either. They have a responsibility to properly recognise the contribution you (and other individuals) make to their existence, function and success. What is it that *you* want from the role, with the organisation you are in or want to be in? How much of that is selfish and how much will benefit both? Narrowing it down to day-to-day operations, under what circumstances will it be OK to occasionally put up a 'Do Not Disturb' sign or say 'No'?

Determine how much you *can* take on. Amongst other things this might be subject to your time in the role; your knowledge, understanding and skills; the levels and nature of support you enjoy; the role-description, e.g. are you expected to do production tasks as well as supervising others? Consider the size of your team, how long you're actually at work, the nature of interdependencies, etc.

Determine how much you are *prepared* to take on. You might have the capability and capacity to do all of the above, but do you really want to? Do you have to (in fear of losing the job)? What are the benefits to you of doing so? For example, a particular task or responsibility might be good for your esteem or self-actualisation. It might serve your future promotion prospects well. You might be happy staying at this level and so putting in more than is actually required might not be right. [Note: you should always be doing what you get paid to do.]

Determine how and to what extent your (selfish) expectations and goals can be matched and mutually supportive of those of your organisation. If there is a significant disparity, maybe you're not in the right role. If you're in the right role, maybe it's not the right organisation. But if neither is the case, there is room for negotiation. Mostly, the more 'you' grow and develop your skills as an individual and manager, the greater the benefit to your organisation. Many organisations see this. Therefore, they are prepared to make an investment in you, albeit with varying degrees of commitment support and success. Just because your organisation may be weak in support, you are not prevented from choosing to get the most possible from the role, or to find another one, in another organisation, where goals are more readily achievable.

Determine a plan for managing expectations. Are your expectations **CRAFT-T**? Specifically are they reasonably achievable and (currently) relevant when you take into account your organisation's structure, culture, processes, strategy and objectives, business and those you manage?

Determine a plan for what to do when your (selfish) expectations and goals are not being realised. I once acquired the impression (or illusion) that my skills and potential were not being adequately recognised by my employers. I believed there to be nothing wrong with the quality or quantity of my work. Indeed if anything, I was acknowledged to be above average (cool my swelling head), but after my first rejection for promotion I was faced with a choice around what I then thought my options were:

- Change my (selfish) goals and expectations and start anew
- Keep the same goals, approach and attitude and risk rejection the next time too – the equivalent to blaming the organisation for their incompetence in not recognising my undoubted potential
- Change or make my goals more 'realistic' or
- Keep the goals and change my approach

I chose the latter and was fortunately secured promotion at the next attempt. I have shortened the story considerably and omitted the 'how' as it's not really relevant to the point, which is that you have the choice. If one plan isn't working, you have to be honest and accurate in your reflection as to why.

Determine what to do when you need your 'selfish' time. This is the specific point of what to do when you realise things are getting too much. Is the solution an outside support network, internal help from your manager, can/should you be delegating more? The longer you leave it untreated, the worse it will become and the harder it will be to remedy. Think back to Dave and what might have happened had he not had the awareness, the presence of mind and the will to take some positive – selfish – action to remedy his personal situation.

Summary

Being selfish can work, providing you approach it correctly and not to the avoidable detriment of those around you. Working 'smarter' is invariably more effective than working longer. Motivational speaker Earl Nightingale says, *"The biggest mistake that you can make is to believe that you are working for somebody else. Job security is gone. The driving force of a career must come from the individual. Remember: Jobs are owned by the company, you own your career!"*

End of Chapter Activity:

Consider your normal week (Monday to Sunday) and the activities that go to make it up.

What proportion of your time is devoted to activities that benefit you, your organisation and those you work with? Who benefits the most, most of the time?

What proportion of your time is devoted to activities that benefit you and your family, friends and social circle? Who benefits most of the time?

What proportion of your time is devoted purely to you and the fulfilment of your personal goals?

To what extent are you satisfied with these ratios? What would you prefer the balance to be?

What if anything is preventing you from doing something about that?

Make a plan now to do something over the next week that is significantly more for your benefit than anyone else's (though doing something that benefits others is totally allowed).

NB: By 'Benefit' we are talking self-esteem or self-actualisation.

29. Persevere

Trying new techniques such as those I have introduced here involves an element of (calculated) risk. So let's face it, unless you're perfect, you're going to make mistakes. The danger is that you repeat those same mistakes time and again. The leeway you're given by your bosses and your team will diminish in proportion to the number of times you are seen to be repeating a particular failed strategy or methodology. You might think that people learn from their mistakes without the need for any form of structured practice. Put your hand into a flame, you get burned. So you're unlikely to repeat the practice. What about less obvious or dramatic situations? What about learning from positive situations, rather than the negative (as often seems to be the case)?

This chapter encourages a structured approach to reflecting on significant situations and learning from them. This aims to minimise future repetition, or if a similar event does occur, it is less severe. Even better, it aims to ensure that you highlight good practice and successful approaches that can be carried forward into regular use.

You may have noticed that I like to use the odd quote to reinforce a particular practice, or as a prompt to remember a specific point. However, I have held back from using 'motivational' quotes that state categorically or implicitly that 'anything' and 'everything' is possible. That's because it's not! You can't get younger, you can't recover your virginity (naturally), and you certainly can't get a burger from a fast-food outlet that looks anything like the one in the picture! Having started on a false premise, they continue by implying that everyone can do everything. It's the equivalent of your newspaper's horoscope where the same thing is supposed to apply to every Sagittarian across the globe. Quite clearly we have different abilities to those around us. Alternatively we may have the same abilities but, to different degrees of competence. My cynicism does not mean that you shouldn't push at boundaries to explore just how good you can be. Neither does it mean that when something doesn't go right first time, or second, or third that you should just throw the towel in.

When the going gets tough, or indeed when things go well, just remember why you are in the role, or why you put yourself forward for it in the first place. Many forget, because they're rarely given the chance to remember. There is usually some degree of good to be taken from even the most comprehensive hash-up. Furthermore, trying to be all things to all people can be a recipe for madness. So it's better to work at being true to oneself. The philosopher Plutarch asserted that, "Perseverance is more prevailing [SIC] than violence; and many things which cannot be overcome when they are together, yield themselves [SIC] up when taken little by little."

Appropriate self-monitoring and self-assessment will remind yourself of the good things about the role and your motivation for wanting to do it. It's so easy to lose sight of this. If we don't remind ourselves, it is all too easy to focus on the negatives, to be disheartened, and to quickly develop a sense of regret.

There is no magic formula, or unique technique to apply to this process. What you can do though is a) identify when and how it's appropriate to remind yourself of your motivation; and b) apply a structure, a self-assessment cycle, to the process.

A First-Line manger can go untested for a while, in which case it may be necessary to deliberately refresh your skills; take some time out to review how things are going and not leave it to any formal opportunities you may have (such as a formal mid-or-end-of-year reviews). If you're not being tested you're probably not pushing your boundaries either. So your opportunities to develop will be limited. I'm not suggesting you go out and cause a ruckus just so you can test you conflict management skills. Neither should you be seeking to fix something that isn't in need of it.

Other than a Native American bullet, what do you think was going through Colonel Custer's mind at the battle of the Little Bighorn? 'It's the wife's birthday tomorrow', 'Where is Mr. Gatling (the machine gun chap) when you need him?'(He was offered some!), 'I must save Comanche (ironically the name of his horse)', 'Wish I'd listened to old Mitch' (his scout), or 'Remind me why I split my force...'

Flippancy aside, as the commander he was probably devoting all his thoughts to trying to extricate himself from the mess he and his command were in. I doubt there was time for niceties, but I wonder if at any point he tried to remember just why he was an officer in the US Cavalry. Why they were there? Whether it was a sense of duty and bravery displayed by soldiers many times before and since, that maintained him to the last?

For military First-Line managers and sometimes those in emergency services, life or death decisions could well be a management issue. Thankfully for most outside of those areas they're not. This should help to put into perspective the fact that whatever your troubles, they are unlikely to be life and death. It's rare for any situation to be so hopeless that it cannot be recovered, nor for one that cannot be recovered, to be fatal. So what *do* I mean?

Honest self assessment is about listening and valuing any feedback you get before, during and after an event. It's about that awful word 'criticism'. It's also about encouraging you to practise analysing accurately your performance in what you do, extracting the positives, learning by experience, not making (exactly) the same mistake again, and remembering what your primary motivation is.

There will be critics: some good, some bad; some accurate and honest, some not; some well intentioned, others not; some who can and have dealt with similar things, others who haven't and are unwilling to put themselves up for it. If you are lucky you'll get criticism that bears **A CHEAT'S** qualities (if not in that format). Theodore Roosevelt once said, "It behoves every man to remember that the work of the critic is of altogether secondary importance, and that, in the end, progress is accomplished by the man who does things." I'm sure he meant women too. But I'm sure you get the idea. So how should you go about learning?

The Experiential Learning Cycle

I have seen many versions of experiential learning cycles. Some are influenced by learning 'styles', others not. Some reduce it down to 'Do', 'Review', 'Plan'. I prefer a simple and process-driven model; one over which any personal style can be laid. I'm not saying what follows is *the* cycle to use, but I have found it useful for myself and when used by those I have supported through experiential learning and training. You will see that it is not dissimilar to those of the Debriefing and Feedback Cycles illustrated earlier. This helps for consistency.

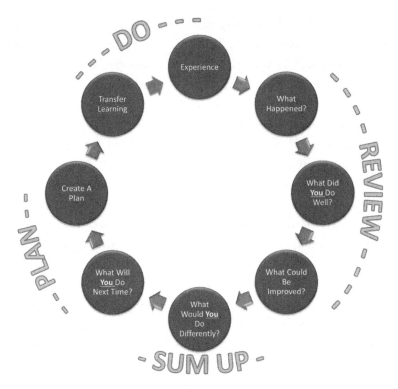

Figure 10: An Experiential Learning Cycle

Though it is a self-assessment tool, it can also be applied to others when guiding them through their development. What does each of these elements mean, require and entail when you apply them to yourself?

The experience might be a minor situation, or one of great significance. Whatever it is, it is one that you recognise (and *acknowledge*) has some learning to it.

'What happened?' This means conducting a dispassionate, non-judgemental appraisal of what actually took place, a blow-by-blow account outlining the facts. One way of doing this is to think how sports commentators inform their audience what is going on. They don't have the time for too many flowery descriptions. So it's: Player 'A' crosses to player 'B'; 'X' hits a long shot into the rough etc. Get into the habit of listing just what happened chronologically. Do it as if you were commentating, not participating.

The 'What did you do well?' needs to be equally dispassionate and very honest. We are often reluctant to 'blow our own trumpets'. Once the event is over, you can identify the aspects of the things you did that evidence good performance and especially those where work on something you were trying to improve has paid off. This includes examples such as, I held my temper even though 'G' was provoking me, I organised the team and briefed them properly so everyone knew what they had to do and when. This is an opportunity to be positive, to recognise success, and to celebrate. Focus on how you used your knowledge, what skills and competencies you displayed, what attitudes you approached with and maintained during the event, and the behaviours you evidenced.

'What did you do that could be improved?' is not an exercise in beating yourself up and again needs to be dispassionate. It too needs to be honest and realistic. If for instance the circumstances were such that no one could have done it better, don't beat yourself up. Otherwise if you believe you could have done things more skilfully or with better content, note it down. One simple technique for doing this is to score yourself out of 10 for each element, with half an eye to improving that score each time. Anything less than a ten suggests you could (if it's important and possible) do something more next time. You might like to assess whether the solution you applied was **TOP-DRAWER**. You must be committed to trying to do something differently next time. Otherwise what's the point of completing this process?

The next section allows you to indicate what you *will* do next time, considering possible *solutions*. It is the stage when the pros and cons of alternatives can be discussed. Try listing the options that you now think would have been available to you in the situation, assess each against the **TOP-DRAWER** criteria.

Either you assess that the solution you actually used was from the **TOP-DRAWER**, or as a result of the latest stage, you think there's a better one. Whichever you think is best, in the 'What *will* you do next time?' section you decide which one it will be and set yourself some performance objectives and goals.

You then move on to *execute* that solution by planning what you will do the next time during or in advance of a similar situation. Remember that it may be some time before a similar situation presents itself, or the skills under examination are required to be used. Remember too that just like any other plan, this one needs **CRAFT-T** qualities.

The 'Transfer of Learning' is the ultimate element of execution and requires conscious application of your plan.

Simply knowing and being able to apply the cycle is not quite enough. Get into the habit of applying it every time there is some learning to be taken from an experience – no matter how small. When only small steps are being made, or when it's difficult, you will need the trait of 'perseverance' too.

There are a host of reasons why something may not work first time, or indeed second or third times. The old cliché about "if at first you don't succeed… " is often quoted in these circumstances. Cynics append an alternative ending – "Give up!"

The key to perseverance is accurate self-assessment and learning by experience, with some courage and determination thrown in. There has to be a desire to achieve a goal, coupled with a methodology for searching for a solution, and a responsible attitude to failure. Do you think inventors get it right first time every time, or do they analyse, revise and move on? Entrepreneurs and inventors celebrate failure as they've actually discovered another way of not doing something.

If something was not as successful as intended, you have choices: to self assess and evaluate, or not; to look for another way of doing it, or not; to implement something new, or not, or you can indeed give up. Yes! Giving up can be a legitimate choice. However, only after a realistic appraisal of the situation, the environment, and one's capability. If there is a goal you really want to achieve, it may be that you have to give up on it for the time being; go away and do something different; but return to it when circumstances are more favourable and (perhaps) you are more competent and ready to take it on.

What if you know exactly how to do something, have proved you can do it, but want to do it better? An athlete may win most of their races, but want a world record. Do they need better technique, or do they look where else they might need to develop? Maybe they need to build up muscles; maybe they need to cope better with the pressure of competition, or the presence of large crowds; maybe, there needs to be realisation that they need to shift their goals as they are just not built to compete against the current record holder. Either way, progress is usually made in increments. You progress by perfecting each of the required elements, including the art of bringing all the elements together at exactly the right time.

Summary

There are three key principals to remember:
1. Reflect and self-assess honestly and accurately. Not doing so adversely impacts on all that follows. You will be investing time and effort on solving the wrong issue(s).
2. As difficult as things may seem, you invariably have the resources to make a decision based on the inherent desire for self-preservation, balanced with the ability and desire to win through.
3. How does doing what you're doing fit with your reason for being or wanting to be a manager?

End of Chapter Activity:

Pick an activity you feel you could be better at, be it work, a hobby, sport or other activity.

After you next complete that activity take some time out and complete a self-assessment.

Ask someone to observe you during the instance and then provide feedback (optional)

Create an action-plan for your next go at the same activity.

30. Get a punch bag!

A real one! Or at least an activity or two that takes you away from work and contributes towards maintaining good health, social life and wellbeing. For many it's the gym. There you not only train the body, but chat and laugh about different things. You can focus on anything or nothing. Most importantly, a little bit of controlled pain and a lot of sweaty effort readily shifts the mind away from whatever went on during the working day. That said, any activity that is completely different to work will suffice.

If you think about it, paid average working time takes up less than a quarter of your week. Some forget they have a life outside of work. Others readily blame 'work' for giving up on decent pastimes. Not having an adequate release from the day job is generally agreed to be unhealthy. Continuing the theme of using models taught earlier, you can apply **ADDRESS** to solve situations of 'stress'. You can learn a suitable methodology for ensuring that you can 'switch off' from work. You can override anything preventing you from enjoying a life outside of work. If you know that's happening you can adopt a course of action to take to give you separation.

We need to separate incidents often referred to as 'stress', but that should in many cases actually be referred to something else. You need to be able to identify why you get 'stressed' what the triggers are, and the effects. Once that is done, you can start to apply appropriate remedies.

The punch bag is a metaphor for any activity you adopt to eliminate or minimise stress. Learning how and when to say 'No' for instance.

Think about what you can be like around others when you're over-tired, over-worked, upset, trying to juggle too many situations all at once. Are you nice to be around? Whether you are, or not, we've seen it's your attitude at such times that affects your consequent behaviour. If you are (albeit understandably) negative, your behaviour will be too. This will potentially infect others with negativity, or a corresponding level of stress. Alternatively, other people may not have the time or the desire to try to understand why it is you are behaving in the way you are. So they choose to react adversely to you.

Stress is commonly described as 'a natural reaction to perceived danger', whether it is some form of physical presence, or a mental build-up. The word 'danger' puts us on our guard. This may dissuade some from confronting even a minor issue that they are more than capable of dealing with. That said; remember that a build-up of too many minor issues all at once can have a negative effect on anyone. This is all relative. Some people – perhaps those with a greater knowledge of the tasks in hand, or of methods for dealing with multiple tasks effectively – may well be able to deal with more than somebody lacking those skills. So I avoid using the word 'stress'. It gets too freely used. It can be misunderstood and misdiagnosed by those claiming to be a sufferer. It is used too readily as an excuse. Consequently overuse belittles the phenomenon to the point where those genuinely experiencing it can be viewed with suspicion and distrust. I prefer to refer to circumstances when the individual has taken on too much at the time given their particular circumstances, skills abilities and current capacity, as 'overload'.

Think of the children's game 'Buckaroo' where players take it in turns to load items of equipment onto a mule – anywhere on the mule, not just its back – until there's too much for it to take and it 'bucks', throwing the lot off. The bucking is quite a violent process and even though the players can guess that it is coming, because of the amount of kit they're placing on, it still comes as a shock. It is even known for the pesky mule to buck with very little on its back. The game wouldn't work if the players knew just which item, or where an item was placed would cause the mule to buck. Neither would it work if the mule bore all the weight and imbalance – refusing point-blank to buck.

Transfer this idea to the workplace. You are the mule. The players are those with whom you interact: bosses, team-members, suppliers, and customers. As time passes each will, if given the chance, load things onto you. For the most part the items are all legitimate and the players do so by the rules. But because they're not cheating and you're not bucking early, you can easily reach the point where you just have to offload.

The players at work might see how much you've got on your plate, but because you're not bucking, they'll give you some more. Even when they see the signs of an impending buck, some choose to ignore them and seek to add more. The Buckaroo reaction causes shock – people lose. They might be unfortunate. They might be totally innocent and well meaning. They just didn't realise or recognise the signs, or if they did, didn't know how to deal with them. Alternatively the losers might be those totally unconnected with the straw that broke your back, but who now suffer the fallout.

What would be 'cheating' in Buckaroo – removing some items before loading others on, is key to how you manage your workload. An early buck might help. More often than not, things – and you – will function a lot better if you don't allow the build up in the first place!

Equally as negative for our wellbeing can be a lack of stimulation. How many of us have woken reluctant to get out of bed and turn up for work? Not because we are fearful of what awaits us, but because we know it will be the same routine that we have been completing day after day, for some time, without any form of recognition or development. Whilst our job is not particularly arduous, the amount of time we spend doing it could easily lead to 'burnout'. I refer you back to my observations on those who seem unable to resist the temptation to whip out the PDA, laptop, or raft of paperwork the second they get onto the train and not put them away until journey's end. These individuals are adding a couple of hours of – no doubt – unpaid work per day to their working week. That's an additional 10 hours! Due payment aside, this does nothing to help them distinguish work from pleasure, nor to leave any workplace worries behind them when they should.

Coincidentally whilst I was researching for this book, reports were appearing of research by Dr Jesus Montero-Marmn for the University of Zaragoza to the effect that people who spend more than forty hours per week working are six times more likely to suffer burnout. My advice to you if you are one of these individuals, is to consider whether what you are doing is appropriate or healthy for you and to **ADDRESS** this, as a situation that warrants your attention.

It's not necessary for my purposes to debate whether particular types of organisation or activity are more susceptible to individuals suffering overload. The phenomenon is a very personal thing. People in what we perceive to be 'easy' jobs, can suffer just as much as those in what are generally acknowledged as high-intensity, life-critical occupations. In poor economic climates, organisations are not unnaturally seeking to get more and more out of their workforces for as little cost as possible. This could result in managers feeling pressure to produce more and more outputs for fear of being considered ineffective and therefore, surplus to requirements. How often do we see that when economies are being sought, the first areas to be reduced are those of management?

My argument would therefore be that rather than working more, you need to consider being more effective within the paid-for time frame. Doing what you can to stop being the Buckaroo is bound to have both short and long-term benefits; not only to you, but also for your organisation and those who report to you.

In 2009/10 of the 3,621,000 days lost to illness generally by managers, as many as 1,608,000 were attributed to stress, anxiety or depression. That's over 44%.[47] Putting the human cost aside only briefly, at an average the cost of employing managers for a day of £100 or $100 plus the cost of providing replacement cover, the financial cost to organisations is huge. It could also be you that's losing out financially too. I've used the upper figures (as opposed to the mean) because the statistics only refer to those who self-reported their illness. What about those who 'take it on the chin' and never report?

Recognition prompting action

Why, if most people are now aware of and refer to the phenomenon (with varying degrees of accuracy and sincerity), it persists and indeed grows in terms of incidence. How it has grown is well documented, and methods for addressing it – including the one I will promote shortly – are equally well publicised and relatively easily implemented; yet still some of us seem reluctant to do anything about overload. Why is that? I suspect that some:

- Are so wrapped up in what they are doing they don't recognise the signs or symptoms;
- Might recognise the signs and symptoms – something changing in their attitude and feelings – but not know the cause
- Might fall in the category above, they however realise the cause(s), but do not know their options, nor where to look
- Recognise the signs, know what they mean, know that help is out there and/or what they could/should be doing about it, but don't

47 UK Health & Safety Executive. Self-reported work-related illness (SWI) and workplace injuries: Results from the Labour Force Survey (LFS) 2009/10 published on www.hse.gov.uk

It is not at all uncommon for individuals not to report or seek help to deal with their overload because they believe that in their organisation doing so will be seen as a sign of weakness and will adversely affect their future prospects. They fail to realise that not doing something is likely to be even more detrimental. They and some others may also not want, nor want to be seen to be, admitting 'defeat' and throwing in the towel. Fortunately more and more organisations are recognising overload, though many seem incapable of actually doing something about the causes via their policies and procedures and working culture.

Doing something positive about overload is much less likely to reflect badly on you – well much less than if you were to 'lose it' one day, go 'Buckaroo' on us and drive your car into that of your boss – repeatedly and only stopping when your poor vehicle is incapable of doing any more damage!

Why do we not apply ourselves to the overload situation in the same manner that we would apply ourselves to any other? You can use **ADDRESS** as a practical tool. It requires two things:

- The first is for you to be accurately self-aware, to realistically self-assess and to recognise your limits and when they are being unhealthily stretched – what is the straw that's likely to break this particular camel's back?
- The second is some form of diversion into which you can escape.

Firstly then you have to recognises and acknowledge that you are approaching or actually in an overload situation. Try this exercise:

Exercise:

Explain how you recognise when someone around you at work is overloaded. What are the signs?

What do you do about it? E.g. do you avoid them or do you make an approach?

How do you tell if you have taken too much on?

How do others treat you on such occasions?

What do you do about it?

We are not all made from the same mould. Not only do we look different, we behave and react differently to given stimuli. Generally there is a band of acceptability within which our social conditioning causes us to operate. For instance, when we are pleased to see somebody, it is socially acceptable to either shake hands, embrace, or give a kiss on either cheek. We do whatever is acceptable within the society we are currently operating in. We understand that what is acceptable in one culture or nation, might not be in another.

Acknowledging the situation

Even though we recognise that some individuals can suffer from overload, it can sometimes seem that we are more reluctant to recognise and acknowledge the signs, to address the symptoms, or remove sources. This can be as true of us recognising those signs and symptoms within ourselves as it is in our doing so with our colleagues at work.

Someone suffering a bad case of overload might be seen to be more moody, irritable, agitated or short tempered than usual. Conversely they might withdraw from situations, or even put on an obviously false brave face. It has been known for them to communicate explicitly or implicitly a personal feeling that they are lonely, depressed or that the world is against them. You might find a sufferer having difficulty remembering simple instructions, tasks or appointments. They might not be able to concentrate sufficiently on the task in hand. They could fail to exercise good judgement in decision-making or even when handling machinery. Some seek solace in alcohol, excessive smoking or other drugs. Others resort to what may be perceived as unhealthy activities: from eating more, to putting themselves physically in harm's way.

There are also physical symptoms: other ailments or injuries such as aches and pains; susceptibility to frequent colds; or irritable bowel syndrome. More extreme are ulcers and even heart attacks. None of this is very pleasant. Yet even when we recognise the signs and symptoms within ourselves, there is a common tendency to dismiss them as being temporary, ignore them altogether, or to carry on in the (false) belief that we can handle it. One must – if it exists – acknowledge the situation.

If this is resonating with you now, I suggest it is time for you to have a realistic appraisal of what you are doing and what it is that may be causing any one or more of these symptoms. I sincerely hope that's not the case.

Having acknowledged an overload situation, we can move on to a diagnosis of the causes. Very often these are broken down into simplified categories: too many hours, a heavy workload, or 'personal problems'. However, if you are going to come up with a well-targeted solution, you need to be very specific when identifying the cause. It could be combination of one or more of this (non-exhaustive) list.

- Too much volume or complexity of tasks at a particular time, over a given period, or even not enough work. It could be that that the volume is normal, but the amount of time you have is suddenly reduced.
- Too much of a specific type of work that stretches your capabilities (at that time or generally) too far. It could be that you have a certain level of proficiency, but have not had the chance to grow into more complex versions of the task and/or there is a lack of acknowledgement or support from the allocators of the task of that fact.
- A lack of knowledge, understanding, skills and abilities not only for the task(s) in hand, but also of methodologies for prioritising and coping. It could be that because you are good at one thing it is assumed that you will automatically be good at another. Alternatively, it might be assumed that because of the post you hold, you woke up the morning after getting it with every bit of knowledge that you need.
- Not balancing perception of need, aspiration and intention with capability – in other words: taking on too much because you think it's necessary to please or impress. This is you thinking or second-guessing what you feel the boss wants, or what you have to do in order to get on in the organisation – if only because that's what everyone else does.
- Inappropriate decision-making when considering taking on additional work. This can extend from not being able to say 'No' to not using available resources to share the workload. It takes some courage to say 'No', but this has to be about looking after you first (see it's OK to be selfish).
- You might add the poor practices of those around you who, recognising the situation you're in, persist in giving you more, or fail to take some

away. This extends to those above you, to the side *and* below you in the structure. Sometimes you cannot really blame them if they don't know of your predicament – if they are ignorant. But if they should realise, but don't, maybe they need a prompt.

These are broad areas and it would be for you to fill in the particular signs and symptoms according to the category under which they fall. Once you have done so it is time to move on to determining an appropriate solution.

Do something

As indicated I want to promote getting a punch-bag, or at least a diversionary activity. I am not so naive – and neither should you be – so as to think that if you do take up diversionary activity, everything would be rosy in your garden. The root causes will have to be **ADDRESS**ed too. No amount of exercise for instance, will cause issues to go away.

Prevention is better than cure! Professor Cary Cooper, an occupational health expert at the University of Lancaster asserts that: "To deal with stress effectively, you need to feel robust and you need to feel strong mentally. Exercise does that," and that, "Exercise won't make your stress disappear, but it will reduce some of the emotional intensity you're feeling, clearing your thoughts and enabling you to deal with your problems more calmly."[48] The US Department of Health & Human Services via their website is equally as supportive of the advice to 'get active'[49]. So who am I – or you – to argue?

You should seek medical advice before participating in anything very energetic if you have pre-existing conditions, or if you haven't done anything that drew a sweat for quite some time. It appears a physical activity will give the most benefit. This is because as well as dealing with the mental issues, there are the spin-off physical benefits. Physical activity is recognised as providing physical benefits such as:

- Decreasing blood pressure, reducing cholesterol, and making the heart stronger -reducing risk of heart attacks!
- Raising your metabolism so you burn more calories – possibility of slimming!

48   (Cooper 2011)

49   See www.healthfinder.gov

- Building muscle tone so reducing fatigue – possibility of looking good on the beach!

To this you can add the psychological benefits (not just the feeling of looking good on the beach – though that's not to be discounted). It is very well documented that physical activity triggers the brain to release chemicals such as endorphins and serotonin that help to reduce any feelings of anxiety, depression or 'overload'. It even helps to strengthen your immune system leading you less susceptible to those nasty little bugs and days of sickness. On top of all that a reduction in the waistline can improve one's self-esteem and self-confidence, your levels of alertness, and your ability to listen effectively. If you don't choose to believe me on this one, check out evidence provided in the British Medical Journal or the advice published by United States Department of Health as far back as 2008.

You don't have to take out expensive gym memberships, but you do need to participate more than once every time there's a 'y' in the month. Two to two-and-a half hours per week, with at least 10 minutes of getting the heart rate up, seems to be the accepted advice (of both UK and US governments). You don't have to buy expensive gear (so long as you have the right gear for the particular activity you're doing – safety first). It's all about balance and doing something you enjoy – even though it might be testing, but in a different way to work challenges.

However, a more sedentary hobby such as a craft – carpentry, needlework, philately etc. will be just as good for taking your mind off things. If you do choose a physical activity, choose one that stretches you and gives you a challenge. Maybe one in which you can achieve recognised levels of proficiency as your skill develops.

What I'm going to do now is to assume that I've prompted in you the thought that just maybe, you will go and search the basement, the garage, the attic, or under the stairs for your old gym shoes (though if you have to search for them they might be best replaced anyway). I may have stirred in you memories of the fun you used to have playing any sport or pastime and a harking back to the days when life didn't seem all that bad. What I have to do now is push you a little closer to the starting line and to do that I have to overcome those barriers that you are going to put in the way. These very often fall into the 'resources' category.

You are going to be tempted to say, "I don't have the kit any more" and/or, "I can't afford replacements". But I wouldn't mind betting your biggest excuse is going to be, "I don't have the time".

Firstly, you can very usually find a club you can join (even on a trial basis) that will lend you equipment for a fraction of the cost of you buying it all yourself. So what if your personal outfit isn't quite up-to-date – so long as it works – and is clean to start with!

Secondly, time! The simple fact is that if you really want to do this, because you really can see the benefits and really do not want to suffer forever from overload, you will make the time.

If you're thinking of using a lack of time as an excuse remember the words of Lao Tzu: "Time is a created thing. To say 'I don't have time' is to say 'I don't want to.'" And those of Sir John Lubbock: "In truth, people can generally make time for what they choose to do; it is not really the time but the will that is lacking."

Third, family 'commitments'! Why not get them interested and involved too? Don't blame work – it is – or should be about 23% of your week. Your 2.5 hours is not even 1.5%. You could even combine your physical activity. How about walking all or part of the distance to work or to the shops and giving your arms some exercise by carrying things back?

In his book, *The Rough Guide to Happiness*[50], Dr Nick Bayliss eloquently explains the reasons, or excuses that we put forward for giving up the things that make us happy including time, or the lack of it; work – the fact that there's too much of it; or even the family – the fact that you've relocated, or have grown out of it.

Once you have decided that you do need a diversion and something to allow you to let off steam or forget the office, you might be struggling for ideas. So he suggests that you look in the following locations:

- Childhood or teenage interests
- Subjects that never fail to grab your attention
- Whatever you daydream about for the sheer joy of it
- Experiencing first hand... activities we might have prematurely presumed are not for us.

50 (Bayliss 2009)

Excuses are often accompanied by the assumption that "it will never happen to me – I can cope" and so consequently "I'll be fine." It has to be said that hospital wards, psychiatrists' and counsellors' couches and yes – cemeteries – are littered with people who thought just like that. You have the resources if you choose to gather and apply them.

Do Something

Remember there are three sections to this phase: planning, logistics and execution itself. I'm not going to do this for you, because if I do, it won't be your plan and you'll be tempted not to apply yourself to it as much. Similarly, you might well blame me the first time you lapse. So you need to complete the following exercise:

Exercise:

Choose your activity – maybe one you reluctantly gave up when you started work – or took on the role of manager?

Plan how you are going to take up that activity: What are your goals (apart from relieving the potential for overload at work)? How are you going to do it (on your own or as part of a group/club)? When are you going to start etc.? Apply the **CRAFT-T** test to your plan and revise it until it's right and achievable to you.

Discuss and get it agreed by affected parties.

Gather your resources. Principally allocate yourself the time to complete the activity and – where necessary the time to get to and from the activity's location.

If you've come this far, there's little or no excuse for actually getting on with it is there? Is there! You will recall that 'Step back' actually requires you to control and monitor the success of your solution. In this instance that will be an assessment of the extent to which you no longer feel you are suffering from the symptoms of overload, or have reduced the risk of ever doing so.

At appropriate intervals then (not every week – more like every couple of months) you may apply the same test(s) that you applied when first diagnosing the original situation. It might be subjective or objective. You could, for instance, have a series of scaling questions where you assess on a scale of 1–10 how you feel about things, such as the amount of work you have, the time you have to do it in, the relationships with your colleagues, or the level of control you have over your work.

They key is to use the same test questions and criteria throughout. Either of the websites mentioned earlier have (free) support tools for this. The testing can be repeated until you get to the point where you can, with evidence, say, "You know what, I don't need to test anymore because I feel great!" At this point you would normally move into the 'Sign Off' phase.

But in this particular situation I would hope that you carry on with the practice, or if you get bored with that one, then do something else. Remember we are talking about prevention, building your resilience and helping you to meet challenges appropriately as much as we are dealing with an immediate potentially crisis situation.

You have the choice as to whether or not you follow the advice. Even if you choose not to get a punch bag – real or metaphoric – your happiness might be improved by just saying 'No'.

Saying 'No'

I have promoted activity and exercise as a sound support solution. Now I encourage another preventative measure. It's one supported by health professionals and those involved in advising on stress management. This approach requires you to acquire the ability and confidence, having completed an accurate self-assessment of your current capacity, to be able to say 'No'!

That message needs to be delivered appropriately and be accompanied by a genuine, evidenced reason. I would rather someone to whom I was considering giving a task told me at the outset that either: they couldn't do a task at any time, they couldn't do it right now (and give me an idea of when they could do it), or they could do it now if they had some additional resources. This is infinitely preferable to them assuring me that it could be done (out of some sort of obligation or the belief that that is what I wanted to hear), but then failing to do it.

It is all well and good having a 'yes we can', positive approach to situations, for our boundaries to be stretched and for us to try things that may not have been tried before or very successfully. Indeed in the right environment this is positively beneficial and is to be encouraged, especially if we are seeking to maximise the personal benefits we are seeking to derive from our current role. However, this needs to be balanced and all parties concerned need to set realistic expectations and goals.

We have come a long way mercifully from the total lack of understanding or ignorance such as that displayed when armies took to shooting as cowards those who we now know were suffering from extreme trauma. The sentiment of 'pull yourself together!' might in certain circumstances and communicated more supportively, be appropriate. But it has to be backed up by methodologies and resources to help the individual concerned to do so.

If on realistic and appropriate assessment of a situation, you can justifiably argue that the particular request or demand being made of you is not appropriate, or cannot be met, you must be prepared, willing and able to say 'No'. Whether this is a qualified 'no' such as "I can't now, but can in a week's time", or "If you can let me have another couple of team-members I can do that for you," is up to you, but these ways of saying no are generally much better received than a blunt unqualified version, or one in which you agree verbally but go off and do something entirely different.

End of Chapter Activity (If you didn't complete the exercise in the chapter):

What have you always wanted to do that you've always found an excuse for not doing?

What activities did you used to do, but have allowed to lapse due to the pressure of work and/or 'home' life? Make a list – I love the 'Bucket List' film – and pick something.

Go do it.

When you've done it tell yourself and others how you feel!

Conclusion

This book had two clear objectives: firstly, to help you determine whether the role of manager is right for you and you for it, and, having determined that to be the case, the second objective was to provide you with some models, tools and techniques to support your development in the role.

Striving to get it right from the start, by having sound foundations and by focussing on your ultimate goal, you have greater control over your career and the degree of satisfaction you get from it. Be clear on why are you, do you want to be, or do you wish to continue being a First-Line manager; what being a First-Line Manager involves; your feeling about and approach to challenge; what kind of manager you want to be; and what you have in your arsenal or tool box.

Following models fully and completely can benefit your performance. You now have alternatives to those you might already know, or discover on your future journey. The **ADDRESS Model** is the parent format that helps you approach any and every situation. From **ADDRESS** comes the advice to test your solutions to ensure they come from the **TOP-DRAWER** and that your plans are **CRAFT-T**. Neither these, nor the other models are intended to be compulsory, nor so rigidly applied as to prevent your personal interpretation or application. Indeed it would be great if you can take them and make them better. So long as what you do works for you and those around you.

The intention was to be a little provocative (of thought), helpful and interesting, challenging. Maybe after Section 1 you decide the role is not for you. This is a good thing! It saves you, your organisation and anyone potentially working under you, future problems. Above all I want you to be comfortable in the role and to achieve happiness.

If you are encouraged to go forward, there is no need to be unnecessarily apprehensive of taking on or continuing in the role. Dale Carnegie said,

"You can conquer almost any fear if you will only make up your mind to do so. For remember, fear doesn't exist anywhere except in the mind."

There's a poem by Rudyard Kipling – 'If'. If you haven't read it, please do. For me it sums up the traits of a good manager quite perfectly. You'll find it online.

At the outset I excused myself for using quotes throughout the book. Please forgive me for leaving you with one of my own:

"Learning is something precious, kept in a darkened room behind a locked door. If you really want to learn; not only do you have to unlock the door, you have to open it; you have to walk bravely into the dark; find the switch and turn on the light. Then feast your eyes."

Rob Burlace (2011)

End of Book Activity 1:

Go give the models and methods a try. You never know they might just work!

If they don't, be realistic, was it the model or the way you applied it?

If the former, please feel free to try something else.

If the latter, don't be discouraged or blame the model, give it another try after accurately assessing why things happened as they did and choosing to do it differently next time

End of Book Activity 2:

Above all things and whatever you choose to do within your role as a manager... Enjoy it!

That is the end. There are no more suggestions to make in this volume. If you have, thank you for staying with it. I sincerely hope that I've achieved at least one of my objectives for you personally. I wish you every success in your endeavours and would love to hear your success stories.

Bibliography

Army, US. "US Army Field Manual FM 3–0." 2011.

Bayliss, Nick. *The Rough Guide to Happiness.* London: Rough Guides, 2009.

Bennis, Warren G. *On Becoming a Leader.* Reading, MA: Addison-Wesley Pub. Co., 1989.

Berne, Eric. *Eric Berne MD.* http://www.ericberne.com/transactional-analysis/ (accessed Jan 08, 2016).

Blanchard, Ken. *BrainyQuote.* http://www.brainyquote.com/quotes/quotes/k/ kenblancha204474.html Read more at http://www.brainyquote.com/citation/ quotes/quotes/k/kenblancha204474.html#ZkiQYj3mKkx7cQcb.99 (accessed Jan 07, 2016).

Bonaparte, Napolean. "Unsourced."

Boswell, James. *Life of Samuel Johnson.* Vol. II. London, 1791.

Buffet, Warren.

Carnegie, Dale. *How to Win Friends and Influence People.* London: Vermilion, 2007.

Chapman, Alan. "Mehrabian's Communication Research: Professor Albert Mehrabian's communications model." *Business Balls.* Alan Chapman. 2004-12. http://www.businessballs.com/mehrabiancommunications.htm (accessed Jan 08, 2016).

Cooper, Prof Carey. "Top 10 Stress Busters." *www.nhs.gov.uk* . 2011. http://www.nhs. uk/conditions/stress-anxiety-depression/pages/reduce-stress.aspx (accessed 2015).

Crane, Frank. *Business Education World,* 15 (1935).

Disraeli, Benjamin. *Endiymion.* London: Longmans & Green, 1880.

Drucker, Peter Ferdinand.

Emmanuel, Rahm Israel, interview by New York Times. *Untitled Article* New York, (17 March 2009).

Flack, Frederick F. *Choices: Coping Creatively with Personal Change.* New York : Bantham Books, 1979.

Flom, Edward L. "Speech." 06 May 1987.

Gini, Al. 'Moral leadership and Business Ethics' in J. Ciulla (ed.), *Ethics: The heart of leadership.* Westport, CT: Praeger Publishers, 2004.

Heron, John. *Helping the Client – a Creative, Practical Guide* (5th Edition). London: SAGE, 2001.

Hoffer, Eric. *The Passionate State of Mind: And Other Aphorisms.* Titusville, NJ: Hopewell Publications, 2006.

Honey, Peter Alan Mumford. *Learning Styles.* www.peterhoney.com.

Hull, Raymond.

Jnr, Martin Luther King. *Strength to Love.* 1963.

Jonas Ridderstråle, Mark Wilcox. *Re-energizing the Corporation: How Leaders Make Change Happen.* Chichester, W. Sussex: Jossey Bass, 2008.

Jung, Carl. *Memories, Dreams, Reflections.* Edited by Aniela Jaffe. Translated by Richard and Clara Winston. New York, NY: Pantheon Books, 1963.

Kübler-Ross, Elisabeth. *On Death & Dying.* New York, NY: Scribner, 2014.

Keller, Helen Adams. *Helen Keller's Journal (1936-1937).* New York, NY: oubleday, Doran & company, inc., 1938.

Longfellow, Henry Wadsworth. *Table-Talk: Driftwood.* 1857.

Maslow, Abraham. *A Theory of Human Motivation.* Princetown University, 1943.

Maslow, Abraham Harold. "Abraham Maslow: A Theory of Human Motivation." *Psychological Review* 50(4) (1943): 370-96.

Mintzberg, Henry. *Mintzberg on Management: Inside Our Strange World of Organizations.* New York, NY: Simon & Schuster, 1989.

Nietzcshe, Frederick. "Unsourced."

Nietzsche, Friedrich. *Ecce Homo.* Translated by R. J. Hollingdale. London: Penguin Classics, 2005.

Nixon, Richard. "Six Crises." 1962.

Shinn, Florence Scovil. "Unsourced."

Sorkin, Aaron. *A Few Good Men.* Directed by Rob Reiner. Produced by David Brown. Performed by Tom Cruise. Castle Rock Entertainment, Columbia Pictures, 1992.

Tanenbaum, Andrew S. *Computer Networks.* 4th. Upper Saddle River, NJ: Prentice Hall, 2002.

Thomas, Kenneth W Ralph H Kilmann. *Thomas-Kilmann Conflict Mode Instrument.* Mountain View, CA: XICOM, 1974.

Thoreau, Henry David. *Walden.* 1854.

Twain, Mark. *Pudd'nhead Wilson.* Charles L. Webster & Company, 189

Index

A

A CHEAT'S guide, 87, 175, 176, 178, 184, 210, 322

Ability, 5, 8, 17, 20, 46, 72, 97, 111, 141, 167, 177, 190, 208, 212, 221, 239, 245, 249, 267, 287, 304, 332, 335, 338

Acceptability, 14, 34, 129,130, 145, 188, 207

Account Phase, 159, 163, 168, 173, 182, 233, 278

Accountability, 35, 157

Accurate, 19, 20, 67, 80, 88, 92, 132

Action plan, 28, 73, 76 , 79, 182, 278, 326

Actionable, 176, 177, 178

Acknowledge, 5, 25, 89, 90, 97

ADDRESS Model, 66, 67, 68, 69, 81, 87, 88, 89, 102, 109, 115, 134, 137, 139, 153, 228, 241, 256, 340

Ambition, 7, 8, 15, 19, 21, 25, 55, 56, 277

Aspirations, 3, 41, 43, 316

Attitude, 4, 22, 25, 34, 41, 52, 53,71, 80, 83, 110, 120, 167, 181, 192, 196, 200, 205, 249, 250, 254, 262, 266, 269, 284, 287, 292, 304, 318, 324, 330

Attitude, Behaviour Cycle, 250, 257

Audience, 21, 118, 157, 176, 211, 214, 218, 222, 227, 235

Authority, 3, 10, 19, 21, 97, 112, 192, 216, 227, 298, 299

Autonomy, 14, 27, 31

Awareness, 29, 30, 76, 131, 309, 318

B

Behaviour
three levels of, 250, 262

Behaviours, 4, 20, 22, 25, 71, 73, 115, 120, 182, 196, 227, 231, 257, 263, 265, 269, 283, 285, 324

Benefits, 3, 6, 15, 16, 22, 43, 90, 107, 114, 119, 123, 129, 138, 140, 157, 162, 171, 180, 188, 199, 224, 254, 285, 294, 299, 303, 316, 330, 336

Bias, 108, 143, 283, 287, 289, 291

BRIEF, 149, 151

C

Capabilities
existing, 8

Capability, 19, 107, 110, 214, 223, 244, 317, 325, 333

Capacity, 6, 10, 12, 22, 26, 44, 47, 56, 79, 81, 97, 100, 104, 117, 135, 212, 232, 260, 317, 328, 338

Catalytic, 58, 59, 180, 183

Cathartic, 58, 59, 180, 183, 256

Challenge, 3, 7, 8, 12, 22, 45, 47, 48, 50, 54, 57, 61, 68, 71, 76, 91, 127, 129, 138, 169, 206, 244, 257, 274, 291, 309, 335, 340

Clarity, 10, 93, 137, 143, 147, 216, 234, 268

Communication, 6, 17, 30, 31, 35, 58, 100, 104, 127, 135, 138, 148, 165, 175, 196, 200, 208, 211, 213, 215, 223, 232, 239, 246, 249, 251, 259,

267, 270, 277, 283
audience, 21, 118, 150, 211, 214
dod and don'ts, 237
effective, 119, 148, 211, 213, 215, 221, 226, 235, 269
Email, 135, 179, 220, 225, 231, 237
good, 148, 213, 239
location, 219
method, 219, 220, 232
method, selecting, 172
non-verbal, 104, 165, 166, 215, 221, 238, 259, 262, 280
questionaire, 229
smartphone, 223, 227
technologies, impact of, 220, 222
technology, usage questionnaire, 229
Timing, 219
Competence, 73, 77, 92, 164, 208, 256, 270, 288, 321
conscious, 74, 77, 256, 270
unconscious, 74, 77, 164, 270
Competencies, 19, 30, 72, 83, 126, 241, 284, 288, 292, 324
Confronting, 5, 14, 58, 256, 328
Constraints, 27, 39, 126
Constructive, 80, 176, 177, 180, 183
Contract, 12, 103
Contractor, 99, 101
Contrast, 62, 206, 292
CONTROL model, 87, 96, 153, 156
Control, 8, 10, 12, 20, 22, 27, 29, 31, 41, 51, 62, 81, 88, 90, 104, 135, 141, 153, 161, 168, 181, 191, 205, 210, 218, 246, 249, 254, 261, 269, 278, 294, 299, 309, 312, 315, 337, 340
CRAFT-T model, 39, 71, 72, 76, 79, 87, 94, 116, 128, 137, 143, 147, 191, 234, 240, 257, 286, 306, 317, 340
Crisis, 92, 98, 101, 105, 125, 157, 172,

192, 242, 251, 338
Culture, 4, 17, 18, 22, 41, 43, 105, 146, 190, 201, 210, 217, 221, 231, 242, 259, 287, 313, 317, 331
Customs, 107, 108, 113, 123, 127, 129, 148, 190, 194
understandings , 108, 112
Cycle, 71, 325
attitude/behaviour, 250, 257, 258, 271
debriefing, 99, 172, 181
development planning, 71, 76
experiential learning, 322
feedback, 183
life, 41, 43
problem solving, 88
self-assessment, 321

D
Debriefing cycle, 99, 181
Decision, 6, 13, 23, 40, 42, 55, 58, 60, 66, 90, 97, 105, 115, 132, 163, 172, 195, 203, 222, 239, 247, 257, 283, 287, 292, 294, 310, 322
Decision making, 27, 30, 35, 37, 90, 127, 137, 216, 227, 332
Democracy, 11, 14
Denial, 79, 80
Destiny, 19, 22
Determine, 8, 16, 30, 52, 73, 92, 98, 101, 117, 136, 154, 156, 167, 192, 195, 200, 208, 216, 242, 287, 301, 303, 316, 317, 340
Development
personal, 7, 29, 69, 99, 297
Diagnose, 91, 115, 156, 242, 269
Diagnosing, 110, 194, 338
Drawbacks, 23, 157, 285, 294
Drivers, 232

E

Economical, 125, 129, 130

Effort, 7, 13, 39, 50, 60, 65, 80, 83, 92, 96, 127, 135, 166, 170, 177, 183, 202, 209, 220, 225, 254, 261, 294, 301, 310, 327

Emotion(s), 57, 103, 118, 123, 136, 158, 167, 190, 207, 218, 237, 240, 249, 260, 270, 315, 334

Emotional profit, 15, 19, 20, 28

Encounter(s), 35, 66, 80, 92, 103, 113, 140, 149, 156, 171, 175, 240, 249, 251, 256, 262, 267, 269, 270, 278

manage, 187, 211, 307

as transactions, 267

nature of, 250

Environment, 8, 14, 22, 29, 35, 41, 61, 103, 111, 112, 123, 129, 133, 146, 157, 172, 182, 209, 215, 226, 247, 250, 258, 264, 289, 295, 301, 310, 315, 325

Escalation, 103, 250, 258, 270, 279

Evidence(d), 4, 20, 37, 41, 76, 79, 90, 96, 101, 107, 118, 176, 177, 182, 189, 209, 224, 239, 244, 256, 270, 283, 288, 289, 296, 324, 338

Example

leading by, 56

Execution, 94, 96, 98, 101, 130, 137, 145, 151, 156, 179, 257, 324, 337

Expectation(s), 21, 25, 26, 28, 35, 44, 47, 59, 68, 95, 105, 113, 131, 147, 156, 161, 188, 192, 200, 244, 268, 283, 316, 339

Experiential learning, 322

Expert(ise), 11, 12, 58, 61, 71, 102, 110, 115, 157, 165, 201, 207, 233, 270, 300, 334

Explanation Phase, 159, 161, 179, 233

F

Fear, 11, 12, 33, 39, 48, 52, 60, 65, 104, 189, 203, 231, 260, 317, 330, 341

Feasible, 72, 84, 130, 137, 146, 235

Feedback, 24, 50, 56, 67, 73, 79, 87, 97, 99, 135, 153, 171, 176, 179, 183, 208, 211, 216, 239, 242, 258, 280, 290, 296, 307, 322

A CHEAT'S Guide to, 87, 176

Cycle, 183, 322

Focus, 16, 19, 27, 45, 59, 65, 80, 116, 141, 146, 168, 202, 206, 211, 240, 254, 283, 309, 321, 327

Framework, 56, 71, 74, 81, 87, 95, 125, 140, 164, 170, 250,

Friendship, 3, 33, 236, 295, 315

G

Goal(s), 3, 16, 18, 22, 29, 48, 51, 61, 71, 88, 116, 127, 136, 143, 151, 190, 200, 206, 257, 312, 315, 324, 339, 340

GUIDE, 151

H

Honest, 65, 69, 98, 101, 176, 177, 189, 263, 266, 280, 289, 313, 322

I

Idea

givers, 203

keepers, 203

IIMAC, 149, 150

Incompetence

conscious, 74

Informative, 58, 183

Interaction, 156, 224, 226, 250, 277, 296

dos and don'ts, 279

Intervention(s), 57, 58, 64, 71

K

Knowledge, 5, 8, 11, 13, 17, 20, 25, 30, 34, 38, 40, 47, 51, 58, 65, 71, 81, 89, 93, 103, 107, 110, 115, 117, 119, 127, 136, 141, 145, 157, 160, 172, 180, 190, 204, 221, 231, 244, 249, 256, 266, 270, 274, 277, 283, 288, 294, 300, 317, 324, 333

KUSAB, 3, 29, 71, 73

L

Language, 17, 67, 129, 140, 166, 172, 214, 237

Leader, 26, 27, 42, 57, 163, 201, 204, 216, 227

Leadership, 10, 26, 62, 119, 189, 206

Learning Cycle, 322

Leniency, 291

Life cycle
    organisation, 41, 43

Listen, 21, 51, 167, 169, 211, 219, 239, 240, 243, 245, 248, 258, 272, 280, 287, 315, 335

Logistics, 94, 95, 256, 337

M

Manager
    first-line, 3, 4, 6, 8, 10, 15, 16, 23, 25, 29, 35, 41, 45, 47, 57, 65, 71, 76, 79, 83, 87, 96, 106, 111, 131, 137, 140, 156, 172, 190, 212, 232, 250, 294, 301, 322, 340
    passive, 61
    popular, 60
    practical, 60
    prescriptive, 61
    proactive, 62
    proficient, 62
    progressive, 63

Message, 28, 59, 67, 115, 159, 163, 171, 176, 182, 188, 195, 197, 208, 211, 217, 220, 225, 233, 239, 247, 261, 269, 277, 305, 338

N

Next Phase, 94, 161, 171, 182

No
saying, 339

Novice, 69, 166, 201, 207

O

Objective(s), 11, 14, 16, 41, 49, 51, 56, 77, 81, 84, 88, 94, 103, 117, 123, 140, 157, 163, 170, 171, 181, 190, 211, 256, 266, 270, 283, 286, 290, 293, 315
    aim(s) and, 9, 41, 66, 96, 98, 111, 141, 144, 147, 149, 151, 162, 233, 340
    CRAFT-T, 72
    management by, 285
    performance, 324
    seting and agreeing, 284, 286

Observation(s), 60, 115, 202, 209, 244, 287, 288, 329

Opportunities, 22, 42, 43, 49, 62, 88, 105, 127, 204, 226, 268, 307, 321

Opportunity, 8, 10, 16, 38, 40, 45, 51, 55, 62, 65, 92, 98, 103, 117, 125, 126, 132, 141, 146, 153, 169, 171, 175, 189, 200, 254, 299, 312

Organisation,
    the, 4, 5, 11, 18, 20, 31, 33, 38, 42, 44, 62, 66, 82, 93, 110, 113, 132, 156, 176, 190, 195, 206, 218, 237, 272, 283, 286, 290, 299, 310, 316, 333

Outputs Phase, 171, 197

P

Performance, 5, 20, 25, 34, 56, 76, 83, 87, 98, 117, 126, 145, 154, 157, 170, 176,

179, 181, 183, 231, 245, 284, 289, 291, 294, 300, 304, 309, 322, 340
biases affecting review, 283
data, 283, 288, 289, 291
data, gathering, 213
data, sources of, 286
effective, 65, 175
evidence of, 244, 289
data, 214, 283, 284, 286, 288
how measured, 73, 283, 284
individual, 284, 288, 290
issue, 75, 100
managing others', 187
review, 157, 163, 209, 251
standards, setting, 286
team, 59, 108, 170, 201, 209, 283, 290, 293
tests, 288
what is measured, 209
Persevere, 104, 320
Plan
Communicating the, 148
Planning, 30, 35, 39, 71, 87, 94, 95, 116, 137, 139, 141, 148, 149, 157, 163, 175, 192, 206, 234, 254, 257, 324, 337
good, 87, 140
why, 139
Politically acceptable, 125, 127
Potential, 8, 15, 19, 26, 77, 136
Power, 3, 13, 15, 22, 27, 28, 29, 58, 60, 67, 97, 127, 157, 204, 216, 299, 305, 311
coercive, 12, 13, 14, 16
expert, 11, 18, 58
information, 13
into practice, 16
legitimate, 11
referent, 12, 20, 21, 33, 60
reward, 13, 18

Sources of, 13, 15, 204
The desire for, 10
Primacy, 292
Proactive, 8, 41, 60, 62, 239
Problem-solver, 22, 201, 206
Problem solving, 30, 35, 61, 66, 72, 88, 216
Proficient, 12, 37, 60, 62, 73, 135, 191, 217
Profit
financial, 15, 17, 33
psychological, 15, 17, 18, 22
Progressive, 60, 63
Promotion, 10, 15, 17, 20, 24, 45, 190, 192, 199, 250, 274, 287, 299, 311, 317

Q
Questioning, 80, 108, 163, 165, 183, 233, 245, 310

R
Rational, 215, 218, 250, 260, 261, 263, 265, 275, 279
Ready', 'Set', 'Go', 257
REASON model, 100, 101, 149, 156, 158, 178, 226, 312
applying, 172, 196
for every encounter, 156, 173
Relationship Phase, 158, 159, 161, 168, 197
Reluctance
overcoming, 336
Reputation(s), 189, 312, 314
Resource(s), 8, 13, 39, 51, 83, 90, 93, 94, 95, 101, 107, 125, 128, 130, 137, 140, 156, 192, 203, 221, 245, 315, 326, 333, 339
Resourced, 97, 139
Adequately, 137, 145, 234

Responsibilities, 25, 30, 32, 107, 110, 135, 153, 188, 285, 298, 303, 309
    Task, 108, 111
Reversible, 125, 131, 132
Reward, 6, 12, 13, 18, 29, 119, 154, 268, 290, 304, 310
Risk(s), 14, 44, 52, 75, 82, 91, 103, 115, 118, 159, 164, 169, 182, 190, 201, 204, 242, 259, 299, 320, 334
    avoider, 201, 204, 205
    risk-taker, 201, 204, 206
Role
    Establish yourself in, 188
Rules, 33, 45, 60, 102, 110, 113, 123, 141, 159, 161, 190, 315, 328

S

Self-actualisation, 18, 20, 22, 64, 312, 317
Self-esteem', 15, 18, 20, 31, 180, 335
Selfish, 18, 19, 187, 309, 311, 315, 316, 318, 333
Self-sufficient, 315
Sign Off, 98, 101, 134, 181, 338
Situations, 5, 6, 14, 17, 22, 35, 43, 48, 50, 54, 56, 58, 61, 62, 76, 80, 87, 90, 98, 110, 117, 125, 138, 172, 175, 188, 199, 204, 219, 239, 249, 257, 260, 306, 311, 320, 327, 339
Sources of, 103, 105
Skills, 4, 7, 17, 20, 27, 39, 47, 51, 62, 71, 81, 88, 105, 117, 172, 191, 224, 227, 241, 256, 265, 268, 270, 277, 284, 304, 317, 321, 328, 333
    and abilities, 8, 11, 26
    communication, 222, 231, 239, 283, 290
    decision making, 90, 91, 127
    interpersonal, 44
    latent, 43, 111

    listening, 247
    questioning, 245
    soft, 37
    tactical, 35
    technical, 241
Spanners, Unforeseen, 147
Staff, 5, 25, 41, 91, 107, 108, 110, 114, 129, 200, 244, 267, 285, 288, 310
    engagement, 135
    resistance, 133
Step Back, 45, 96, 134, 196, 257, 309, 337
Strictness, 291,
STUFF model 87, 102, 105, 107, 108, 111, 116, 125, 130, 141, 146, 160, 177, 180, 244, 267, 307
Style, 37, 42, 47, 51, 53, 55, 59, 80, 129, 136, 163, 180, 209, 213, 256, 272, 303
    conflict, 48
    intervention, 57
    learning, 61, 322
    management, 48, 49, 50, 55
    personal, 34 , 188, 322
    tactical, 35
Success, 16, 28, 41, 50, 55, 74, 95, 98, 122, 139, 141, 151, 161, 181, 200, 219, 232, 277, 324, 337
Summary Phase, 170, 171
Supportive, 58, 59, 108, 122, 176, 178, 180, 257, 265, 290, 317

T

Targeted, 29, 72, 137, 147, 232, 333
Team, 4, 11, 14, 25, 31, 39, 41, 48, 59, 82, 87, 93, 103, 107, 110, 120, 125, 129, 130, 137, 153, 175, 188, 191, 199, 202, 205, 216, 250, 259, 279, 283, 286, 290, 293, 299, 303, 315, 317, 320
    building, 30, 35, 36 , 199, 200, 209

engagement, 119 , 120

managing, 56, 67, 108

roles, recognising, 201, 209

Time, 11, 13, 16, 23, 35, 37, 40, 51, 53, 55, 58, 62, 73, 83, 90, 93, 96, 98, 103, 107, 115, 120, 125, 133, 135, 138, 139, 152, 153, 156, 161, 177, 192, 211, 216, 220, 226, 231, 235, 242, 248, 249, 256, 285, 300, 306, 312, 318, 323, 325, 327, 336

bound, 72, 125, 126, 132, 135, 137, 147, 181

cost, 5, 130

management, 30, 35, 36, 311

timely, 176, 178, 188

TOP DRAWER model, 87, 93, 94, 117, 125, 131, 133, 137, 145, 154, 191, 257, 306, 324, 340

Traits, leadership, 27

Trust, 9, 11, 27, 50, 62, 65, 74, 119, 135, 187, 204, 226, 280, 287, 298, 303

buidling, 305, 306

measuring, 303

W

Watching, 187, 214, 239, 244

Wellbeing, 5, 15, 21, 44, 91, 312, 327, 329

Workable, 61, 125, 130, 242, 279, 291